Financing State and
Local Governments

Studies of Government Finance

TITLES PUBLISHED

Financing State and

Local Governments

JAMES A. MAXWELL

Studies of Government Finance

THE BROOKINGS INSTITUTION

WASHINGTON, D.C.

THE BROOKINGS INSTITUTION is an independent organization devoted to nonpartisan research, education, and publication in economics, government, foreign policy, and the social sciences generally. Its principal purposes are to aid in the development of sound public policies and to promote public understanding of issues of national importance.

The Institution was founded December 8, 1927, to merge the activities of the Institute for Government Research, founded in 1916, the Institute of Economics, founded in 1922, and the Robert Brookings Graduate School of Economics and Government, founded in 1924.

The general administration of the Institution is the responsibility of a self-perpetuating Board of Trustees. The trustees are likewise charged with maintaining the independence of the staff and fostering the most favorable conditions for creative research and education. The immediate direction of the policies, program, and staff of the Institution is vested in the President, assisted by the division directors and an advisory council, chosen from the professional staff of the Institution.

In publishing a study, the Institution presents it as a competent treatment of a subject worthy of public consideration. The interpretations and conclusions in such publications are those of the author or authors and do not purport to represent the views of the other staff members, officers, or trustees of the Brookings Institution.

BOARD OF TRUSTEES

Foreword

DURING THE POSTWAR YEARS, state and local expenditure has grown much more rapidly than federal expenditure for civil purposes. As a result, the public responsibilities of state and local governments seem far greater than the revenue resources at their disposal.

The purpose of this volume is to present a nontechnical discussion that will help the interested citizen understand the fiscal problems of his own state and community. The author, James A. Maxwell of Clark University, is an authority on state-local finance and has written widely on the subject. His most recent volume, *Tax Credits and Intergovernmental Fiscal Relations,* was published by the Brookings Institution in 1962.

This volume is part of the Brookings series of Studies of Government Finance, a special program of research and education in taxation and government expenditures sponsored by the National Committee on Government Finance. It is one of two publications in the series which are primarily educational. The other volume, *Federal Budget Policy,* by David and Attiat Ott, deals with major fiscal policy issues at the federal level. The National Committee on Government Finance was established in 1960 by the trustees of the Brookings Institution and its program is supported with funds provided by the Ford Foundation.

The author has had the benefit of criticism and suggestions from a reading committee consisting of Frederick L. Bird, Jesse Burkhead, Dixie Drake, Harold M. Groves, Dick Netzer, and Alice M. Rivlin. L. Laszlo Ecker-Racz was helpful in the composition of

Chapters VI and X as well as in the organization of the manuscript. Miss Annette Pinckney provided valuable research assistance throughout the project. The section on earmarking in Chapter IX was mainly written by her. The manuscript was edited by Phyllis Myers, and the index was prepared by Helen B. Eisenhart. The study was made under the direction of Joseph A. Pechman, Director of Economic Studies.

The views expressed in this volume are those of the author and do not purport to represent the views of the Ford Foundation, the National Committee on Government Finance, or the staff members, officers, or trustees of the Brookings Institution.

Robert D. Calkins
President

June 1965
Washington, D.C.

Studies of Government Finance

Studies of Government Finance is a special program of research and education in taxation and government expenditures at the federal, state, and local levels. These studies are under the supervision of the National Committee on Government Finance appointed by the Trustees of the Brookings Institution, and are supported by a special grant from the Ford Foundation.

Contents

Charts

Text Tables

Appendix Tables

Introduction

STATE AND LOCAL GOVERNMENTS together spend more than twice as much as the federal government to provide civilian services for citizens. Education, roads, welfare, public health, hospitals, police, sanitation—these are state and local responsibilities, and their cost falls mainly on state and local sources of revenue. An upsurge of state and local activity which began after World War II has not yet lost its force. Rates of state and local taxes have been raised, new taxes have been added, and the bases of old taxes have been enlarged.

Most of the expansion of state and local spending has been for old and well established governmental functions, rather than for new functions. The most powerful expansion has been for education, a function in the public sector for over a century. The reasons for the sharp growth in this expenditure are plain. Children are a larger segment of the population, a greater percentage of children goes to school and for a longer period, what is taught is more complex, and to teach it requires more plant and equipment and trained personnel.

Public welfare is another traditional function for which state and local spending has grown, especially services for the aged. The aged, as well as the young, are a larger proportion of the population; a change in *mores* has pushed more of them out of the family; a revolution in medicine has lengthened their lives and enlarged the range of their ailments which can be treated

Roads are another old function for which public spending has soared. In our affluent society, there are more passenger cars than families; the efficiency of transportation by truck has shifted more and more of the carriage of goods upon the public highways;

deficiencies in construction of urban roads and interstate highways
—the expensive kind—have had to be made up.

Traditional functions have not merely grown in size; a vast
change has taken place in their content. A state's public health expenditure is now very different from that of thirty years ago; the
curriculum of a new regional high school is quite unlike that of the
small high schools it replaced; a city throughway bears only a functional resemblance to an ordinary city street. Changes of this sort
may be evidence of increased productivity of government in performing its functions. But any such increase has been absorbed by
changes in quality; it does not bring decreases in government costs.
And when the content of the old functions is stable—the services of
city clerks, police, tax administrators, custodians, for example—little increase in productivity is discernible. As in the private sector,
provision of services often eludes technological progress.

What governmental duties, and what means of finance, belong
at the state-local, rather than the federal level? Broad lines of division are constitutionally provided, but history has blurred the lines.
Moreover, the boundaries of a locality and of a state are porous,
and the effects of state and local financial decisions are not tightly
circumscribed within a geographic area. When are these "spillovers" of national concern? Do the states have too many functions?
Have they the sources of revenue appropriate to their functions?
Perhaps no neat division of functions is possible or desirable, because some government functions should be handled by joint action, through federal-state cooperation. Such intergovernmental
cooperation, discussed in *Chapter I*, provides structural flexibility in
a federal system.

Interstate Comparisons

Chapter II provides quantitative background for interstate fiscal
comparisons. The essential feature which emerges is diversity, both
in overall expenditures and expenditures on particular functions.

Comparisons of state government expenditures are treacherous.
In State A the government may perform functions that in State B
are left to localities. Accordingly, a better basis for interstate comparison is the per capita amount spent (and raised) by both state

and local governments. State expenditures figured on this basis diverge greatly: the highest per capita expenditures are twice as large as the lowest.

What are the reasons? Most obviously, a "rich" state (one in which the residents, on the average, have large incomes) will spend more than a "poor" state, although some states spend considerably more and some considerably less per capita than might be expected. Other reasons—density of population, urbanization, and so on— have less discernible effects. Much of the divergence in per capita expenditure, state by state, can be explained by historical and political differences. When relative expenditure on *particular functions* is examined, once again diversity rather than uniformity is the rule.

A reasonable basis for comparing financial "effort," state by state, is the sum of state and local revenues obtained from their own sources, expressed per $1,000 of personal income. Rich states, on the average, do not have to make as great an effort as poor states to raise the revenue to finance an average level of per capita expenditure. The variety of patterns of taxes levied by state governments is as notable as the lack of variety in those levied by local governments. Even when a similar tax is imposed in many states, it is not necessarily utilized in the same way.

Grants-in-Aid

For decades neither state nor local governments have depended wholly on their own sources of revenue. *Chapter III* examines the grants (intergovernmental transfers) made by the federal government to state and local governments, and those made by state governments to local governments.

Federal grants to *local* governments, still modest in amount, are growing. The special issue they raise is whether or not the state governments should be bypassed. Federal grants to state governments are, in dollars, much more important, and thirty-seven new programs have been added since World War II.

All federal grants are "specific," that is, for particular and limited purposes; their main aim is to stimulate provision of programs in which a strong federal interest exists. Does this distort the size of these programs compared to that of unaided programs? Should experiments be made with "block" grants, that is, grants for a broadly defined function, leaving to each state the allocation of expenditure within the function?

Federal grants redistribute income among the states. The money provided by grants is raised through a progressive tax system, with the result that more is collected in rich than in poor states. Some grants are allocated by formulas which provide more for poor than for rich states. For what grants is such distribution appropriate? What is the desirable amount of redistribution?

State grants and shared taxes provide nearly 30 percent of local general revenue. In 1963 education received the bulk (59 percent) of such aid, with public welfare second (16 percent) and highways third (12 percent). Beyond doubt most states have permitted, and even facilitated, the proliferation of too many local units (over 90,000 existed in 1962); through grants they have perpetuated the existence of inefficient units. The grants themselves have been fragmented in amounts, purposes, and formulas. In many states consolidation would be a clear gain. Moreover, grants should be used as an instrument to speed reorganization of local units.

State Taxes

Chapters IV and *V* examine the taxes used by state governments. The states pioneered the introduction of income taxation in the United States, but two World Wars and the depression of the 1930's led the federal government to the strong use of this source of revenue. At present the high rates, steep progression, and low personal exemption of the federal tax leave only modest scope for state income taxes. Moreover, with some honorable exceptions, state achievement in taxation of individual income has not been impressive. Diverse definitions of income have bred inequities and magnified the costs of collection and compliance.

Congressional rejection of the general sales tax as a federal revenue source during the 1930's and World War II encouraged state entry, just as strong federal use of income taxation slackened its adoption by the states. Twenty states adopted a retail sales tax during the years 1933-35, and eight more during 1947-51. State legislatures were irresistibly attracted by the revenue productivity, and the gradual, somewhat concealed method of payment. The defect of regressivity was sometimes alleviated through exemption from the tax base of purchases of food, clothing, and medicine. Thirty-seven states now employ the tax compared to thirty-three that tax individual income. Twenty-three states employ both, and this number is growing. In the states with both, the sales tax is usually dominant, with income taxation viewed as a supplementary source of revenue.

State taxation of business income has been even less satisfactory than taxation of individual income. In their attempts to enlarge the tax base, states have reached outside their boundaries. As a result, indefensible jurisdictional jostling takes place, made tolerable chiefly by weak administration. State formulas for determining the taxable share of the net earnings of a multistate business create obstacles to interstate trade. State use taxes, levied upon commodities purchased outside a state for use within the state, similarly impede interstate trade. Except for conspicuous commodities (automobiles that have to be registered in the taxing state), application of the tax to users is difficult. More and more the states have ordered out-of-state *sellers* to collect the use tax for them. Should this obligation be limited, through congressional intervention, to sellers who have some definable business connection with the taxing state?

Is there a future in state taxation of income, both individual and corporate? If federal taxes are reduced, might the states move in? Are there devices, such as tax credits, by which such a move might be facilitated? Can state taxation of income be satisfactory in the long run without uniformity in definition of income, steps to limit tax conflict, and alleviation of complexities in compliance? The uncompensated drag upon the efficient operation of the economic system through multiple definitions of taxable income is likely to become less and less tolerable. Economic integration of the nation proceeds apace; it enjoins a parallel improvement in assessment and administration of taxes.

Death taxes—mostly inheritance taxes—were levied by states long before the federal government, in 1916, enacted an estate tax (on the entire net estate left by a decedent). In the 1920's, mostly for the purpose of checkmating the effects of repeal of inheritance taxes by Florida and Nevada, Congress provided an 80 percent credit against the federal tax liability for death taxes paid to the states. Since then increases in the federal tax, with no enlargement of the credit, have reduced the importance of the credit. The Advisory Commission on Intergovernmental Relations has recommended enlarging the federal credit both to increase state revenues and, through the imposition of federal conditions, to spur the states toward simplification and coordination of their taxes. So far Congress has not responded.

Local Taxes

In the last four decades the general property tax, once a major source of state revenue, has become primarily a local tax. In 1963 it produced 88 percent of local tax revenue. Its postwar yield has shown a surprising expansibility and, as a result, the tenor of discussion has turned from a search for substitutes to the possibility of reform.

As indicated in *Chapter VI,* the most serious fault of the property tax is inaccurate assessment. The inequity of unequal valuations to taxpayers residing in the same area is obvious. But unequal aggregate assessed valuations from locality to locality also have serious faults: state governments have used these valuations to set ceilings on local debt and property tax rates, and to determine local shares of state grants and county taxes.

A reform movement has been launched which assumes that state governments will be the prime movers in rehabilitating the property tax through the reorganization of assessment districts, professionalization of assessment officers, strong supervision of local assessment practices, and halting state erosion of the local base. While these steps are feasible, the question is whether state leadership will be effective.

In the 1930's, driven by desperate financial needs, a few large cities enacted nonproperty taxes—New York a retail sales tax, Philadelphia an earnings tax. These examples, which have been imitated by other cities in a limited number of states, are examined in *Chapter VII.* While such taxes have many faults, the persuasive argument in their favor is that no alternatives of greater merit are visible.

Nontax Revenues

State and local governments raise nontax revenue from (a) public service enterprises (for example, water, electric power, gas, and public transit), and (b) user charges for noncommercial services. The former, except for public transit, are usually self-supporting, although much debate goes on concerning what sums in lieu of taxes a public enterprise should include as costs. Public transit systems incur substantial deficits; users are subsidized in kind by taxpayers. Services provided by hospitals, housing, education, sanitation, and so on, are regarded as partly collective or welfare in content, although measurable benefits accrue to individual consumers. Pursuit of welfare objectives through low user charges may be excessive; state and local governments might secure needed revenue from higher charges.

Borrowing

In the postwar years, as *Chapter VIII* demonstrates, most state and local governments have borrowed heavily to finance capital expenditures for highways, buildings, sewerage, and so on. An important and distinctive characteristic of state and local debt is that its interest is exempt from federal income tax.

Most of the states impose statutory or constitutional limitations on their power, and on the power of their local governments, to borrow. The limitations have held down aggregate borrowing, but they have stimulated a mushroom-like development of ingenious devices to escape the limitations. The most important device has been the nonguaranteed bond (as distinct from a bond secured for its interest and principal by the full faith and credit of a state or local government). Nonguaranteed bonds now make up more than half of state, and one-third of local, debt; they have been issued for purposes that are not self-financing. By obscuring what state and local governments are doing, they stimulate imprudent borrowing; they impose interest charges on state and local budgets higher by 0.5-0.6 percent than those on full faith and credit bonds.

Budgeting

As explained in *Chapter IX,* the job of budgeting at the state-local level is one of efficient allocation of limited resources to meet public needs. In forty-four states and a growing number of cities preparation of the budget falls upon the executive, although this desirable practice is often frustrated by the exemption of important agencies from executive control. The next step, examination and appraisal of the budget, falls upon the legislative branch. Implementation of the budget follows, with the executive responsible for seeing that funds flow to the designated purposes, in the correct amounts, and at the proper time.

The comprehensiveness of state and local budgets is often impaired by earmarking, that is, channeling a revenue by statutory or constitutional provision to some particular program. In this way the program is removed from the budgetary process. Such a step may be justifiable for government enterprises, and also when a linkage exists between the benefits secured by particular users of services and the payments collected from them. But most state budgets earmark far beyond these guidelines; twenty-four earmark over half of their tax revenue. The extent of earmarking illustrates the widespread mistrust with which voters appraise the wisdom and integrity of their legislatures.

Some kinds of state-local expenditures raise special difficulties in budgeting, notably those that are large, irregular, and that yield services stretching into the future. Simply as a matter of procedure, these should be bundled together into a *capital* budget (which will be a section of the total budget). Should the items in a capital budget be financed by borrowing? Should the rule be pay-as-you-use or pay-as-you-go? A practicable and effective compromise would be for state and local governments (a) to appraise with severity the capital items for which borrowing is approved; and (b) to vary the volume of capital items provided by borrowing, raising it in years of recession and lowering it in boom years. Such a policy would serve to avoid excessive debt charges on the budget, and would promote countercyclical financing.

Future Trends

Trends in state-local finance are examined in *Chapter X*. Most projections of state-local spending indicate that the postwar rate of increase will not soon slacken. How is this to be financed? Revenue projections indicate that the growth in the state-local tax base will not keep pace with expenditures and that, as a result, tax rates will have to be increased. If, in the years ahead, federal taxes were lowered—either directly or by tax credits—the state-local position would be eased. Other alternatives serving a similar purpose would be an increase in federal grants for specific purposes or the addition of a new unconditional grant.

State governments have critical, unfulfilled responsibilities to their local governments. Local functions often are out of balance with local revenues. Redress is indicated by a shift of functions to the state level, by a larger distribution of state grants, and by rehabilitation of the property tax. Most states hamper the financial effectiveness of their local governments by unrealistic debt and tax limitations. In order to be effective, state supervision of local finance should be flexible both in coverage and administration.

CHAPTER I

Development of the Federal System

"Many considerations . . . seem to place it beyond doubt that the first and most natural attachment of the people will be to the governments of their respective States." James Madison, *Federalist Papers*, No. 46.

"What is past is prologue." *The Tempest*, Act II, scene 1.

THE UNITED STATES is a federal union, governed by a Constitution that splits the functions of government between a sovereign central government and sovereign states. The powers of the national government are enumerated in Article I, Section 8 of the Constitution; the Tenth Amendment reserves to the states all powers neither delegated to the national government nor prohibited to the states. Nowhere mentioned in the Constitution are many of the vital citizen needs that today dominate the domestic scene: education, relief, public health, highways, and so forth. These functions are neither granted to the national government nor specifically prohibited to the states. The assumption is that these are residual state powers.

In addition to the national government and the state governments, a great number (91,185 in 1962) and variety of local governments abound in the United States. Unlike the federal-state relationship, the state-local relationship is not one between sovereign governments. The states are by law the complete masters of these local governments; that is, the relationship is unitary. This concept is known as "Dillon's Rule," after Justice Dillon of the Supreme Court of Iowa who declared:

> Municipal corporations owe their origin to, and derive their powers and rights wholly from, the [state] legislature. It breathes into them the breath of life, without which they cannot exist. As it creates, so it may destroy. If it may destroy, it may abridge and control.[1]

The relations that now prevail, federal-state and state-local, may not seem to conform to these neat legal divisions. Every citizen knows that the practical power of states to alter and control local government is limited, and that the federal government spends money on functions that might seem to belong to the states. In view of the great overlap in the performance of most governmental functions, it is not absurd to ask: What has become of the Tenth Amendment?

The Historical Balance of Federal, State, and Local Power

In the 180 years since the nation was formed, national-state and state-local relations have not remained static. The power of the states vis-à-vis the federal government has waxed and waned as the federal structure adjusted to changes in social philosophy and environment. In this century, and particularly in the 1930's, major shifts in both absolute and relative terms have occurred in the functions, expenditures, and revenues of all levels of government. In the 1930's, many observers predicted the obsolescence of federalism; in postwar years, however, a new intergovernmental equilibrium has emerged in which state and local vitality is manifest.

These developments are reviewed in the following section, which focuses in particular on the relative contributions during this century of federal and state-local governments to overall expenditures for civil purposes, and relates these to periods of significant change in the evolution of American federalism.

[1] *City of Clinton and Cedar Rapids v. Missouri River RR. Co.* (24 Iowa 475, 1868).

The First Century of Federalism

In the years of the Confederation, 1781-88, the states were so strong that they threatened the survival of a national government. Congress had no real power to administer, and especially to finance, its limited functions. Expenses of the national government were allocated to the states; each state was supposed to raise its allotment through its own officers. The results were nearly disastrous, and yet attempts to strengthen the financial powers of Congress by amending the Articles of Confederation failed because of the requirement of state unanimity. The feeling grew that the Articles provided the wrong *kind* of government. A strong nation would emerge only with a government that could levy taxes for its own use through its own officers.

Federal powers were greatly increased in the new Constitution of 1788. Congress received the power "to levy and collect taxes, duties, imposts and excises, to pay the debts and provide for the common defense and general welfare of the United States."[2] This meant that, in addition to exclusive control over customs, it was to have concurrent jurisdiction with the states in practically all fields of taxation. In the first decade of its existence, the national government exercised—and even extended—its financial powers. The debts both of the Confederation and of the states were successfully refunded, customs duties were assessed by national officers, a system of federal excises was established, and a Bank of the United States was created.

Despite these vigorous steps, the divisive forces latent in the new federalism revived. During the next sixty years the state governments gained such strength that, once again, they threatened the existence of the national government. Geographic expansion brought into the Union new states with diverse sectional interests, and, in addition, the old cleavage between North and South was deepened by the spread of cotton and slavery. Most statesmen, obsessed with the perplexities of federalism, came to believe that national functions should be held to a minimum in order to preserve the Union.

---

[2] Subject to the qualification that "all duties, imposts and excises shall be uniform throughout the United States."

The deference paid to the states did not succeed. Instead, the sectional rift deepened until the nation drifted into the Civil War, which settled the issue of national supremacy by force. The Union was *not* a compact among the states; the national government was entitled to enforce its constitutional decisions in the face of state objections.

The effect of the Civil War and of events subsequent to it— such as carpetbag government in the South—was to diminish the prestige of the states. When in the last two decades of the nineteenth century, many southern states remade their constitutions, extensive and crippling restrictions upon legislatures and executives were imposed. Scholars, observing these trends, had forebodings about the future of the states. They foresaw a continuing gravitation of power toward the national government.[3]

What was federal performance at this time? James Bryce, although aware of many defects, was favorably impressed, and certainly this judgment is correct if comparison is made with performance before the Civil War. But the scope and range of federal activity were very modest, as the next section will indicate.

Revival of the States

Around the turn of the new century, the state governments began to stir. A look at overall governmental expenditures in 1902

---

[3] Several examples will suffice. John W. Burgess, Professor of Political Science at Columbia University, observed in 1886 that legislative and judicial powers were "gravitating toward the national government," and that police powers were "passing over to the municipalities." This was not, in his opinion, a "pendulum-swing"; rather did he forecast that "in the twentieth century, the commonwealth will occupy a much lower place in our political system, the Nation a much higher, and the municipalities a much more distinct and independent sphere" ("The American Commonwealth, Changes in its Relation to the Nation," *Political Science Quarterly,* 1886, pp. 32-34.) In 1890 Simon N. Patten, Professor of Economics at the University of Pennsylvania, found an economic explanation for the decline of the states. This was the absoluteness of the boundary lines—"the unchangeableness of the territorial extent of our states." The remedy would be to create "natural boundaries for each state" and thereby restore vitality. ("The Decay of State and Local Governments," *Annals of the American Academy,* July 1890, pp. 39-40.) In the opinion of other contemporary observers, the inert performance of the state governments was not compensated for by vigor at the local level. James Bryce, in 1888, critical as he was of the states, declared that "the government of cities is the one conspicuous failure of the United States." (*The American Commonwealth,* Vol. II [1899], p. 281.)

will provide a base from which change may be judged. Table 1-1 shows that federal expenditure on civil functions was about one-fifth of the total, and local governments spent appreciably more than both federal and state governments together. The relative importance of local governments is, perhaps, the striking feature of governmental expenditure at this time.

Only federal expenditures for civil functions are considered in Table 1-1, since, in these pages, a major issue will be the intergovernmental balance of power. A decision to spend more or less for defense is, beyond dispute, a federal function; no question is raised of encroachment on, or withdrawal from, the state-local sphere. Attention should therefore be focused on spending for civil purposes. In 1902 this totaled $1,243 million; federal spending amounted to $230 million, and state and local spending to $1,013 million.

Table 1-1 hides a decision concerning the classification of *intergovernmental payments,* that is, payments by the federal government in the form of grants and shared taxes to state and local governments, and similar payments by the states to local governments. Against which level of government should these sums be charged? A choice must be made in order to avoid double-counting. The alternatives are: (A) to charge them to the level of govern-

TABLE 1-1. General Expenditure[a] for Civil Functions[b] by Federal, State, and Local Governments, 1902[c]

(Money amounts in millions of dollars)

Level of Government	Amount	Percentage of Civil Expenditure
Federal	$ 230	18.5
State	134	10.5
Local	879	71.0
All levels	$1,243	100.0

Source: U.S. Census Bureau, *Historical Statistics of the United States: Colonial Times to 1957* (1960), pp. 722–30. (Cited hereinafter as *Historical Statistics.* Reference is to these pages unless otherwise noted.)
[a] General expenditure excludes amounts expended on utilities, liquor stores, and insurance trusts. These are approximately offset by receipts.
[b] The federal expenditure for civil functions has been calculated by deducting from *total* federal expenditures ($565 million) the amounts spent on national defense, international relations, veterans (not elsewhere classified), and interest on the federal debt ($335 million). All state and local expenditures are regarded as civil.
[c] In all tables and charts years are fiscal unless otherwise noted.

ment that makes the *final disbursement,* so that a federal grant for highways is counted as an expenditure made by the state governments, or (B) to charge them to the *originating level* of government, so that a federal grant is counted as an expenditure made by the federal government. If alternative (A) is used, the total expenditure of the final disbursing level of government (the level that *receives* the grant) is larger, while that of the originating level of government (the level that *pays* the grants) is smaller, than when alternative (B) is used. Table 1-2 shows the two sets of figures for 1902. Since federal intergovernmental payments were not important then, the percentage distribution of federal spending for civil purposes under alternatives (A) and (B) is almost identical. But the spread was to become greater as federal grants expanded.

The Intergovernmental Distribution of Expenditure and Revenue, 1902 and 1927

In the next quarter century the *absolute amount* of spending for civil purposes rose rapidly, but the *relative shares* of the levels of government—federal versus state-local—changed little. (See Chart 1-1.) The federal share declined slightly because, in the 1920's, concern over the large war-related expenditures stimulated the feeling that citizen demands for new and better public services should be directed to state and local governments.

In the years from 1902 to 1927, there was little change in the

TABLE 1-2. General Expenditure for Civil Functions by Final Disbursing Level and Originating Level of Government, 1902

(Money amounts in millions of dollars)

Level of Government	Amount Disbursed		Percentage of Total	
	Final Level (A)	Originating Level (B)	Final Level (A)	Originating Level (B)
Federal	$ 230	$ 237	18.5	19.1
State-Local	1,013	1,006	81.5	80.9
All levels	$1,243	$1,243	100.0	100.0

Source: *Historical Statistics.*

CHART 1-1. Percentage of General Expenditure for Civil Functions by Federal and State-Local Governments, Selected Years, 1902–63

A. Intergovernmental payments charged to the level of government making the final disbursement.

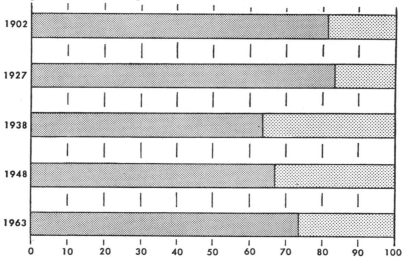

B. Intergovernmental payments charged to the originating level of government.

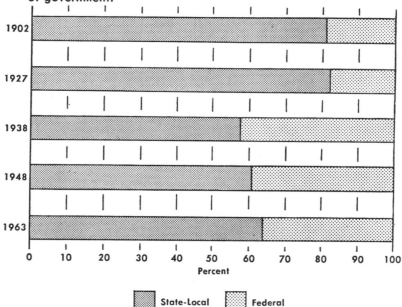

Percent

▨ State-Local   ▨ Federal

Sources: *Historical Statistics* and U. S. Census Bureau, *Governmental Finances in 1963* (1964), p 25. For actual expenditures, see Appendix Table A-1.

16

CHART 1-2. Percentage of Total Taxes Collected by Federal, State, and Local Governments, Selected Years, 1902–63

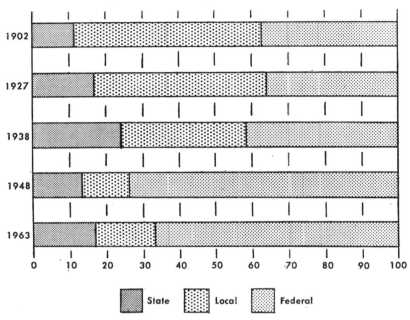

Source: Same as Chart 1-1. For specific figures, see Appendix Table A-2.

proportion of total taxes *collected* by each of the three levels of government. The state share did increase somewhat. (See Chart 1-2.) Major alterations did take place, however, in the *structure* and *composition* of taxes. (See Chart 1-3.) In 1902, *income* taxation was so small that it was not recorded separately; by 1927 it accounted for 64 percent of federal and 10 percent of state tax revenues. In 1902 taxes on *consumption* were dominant at the federal level (95 percent of the total) and important at the state level (18 percent); in 1927 their importance at the federal level was declining, and at the state level was increasing. Only at the local level was there little change in tax composition. Both in 1902 and in 1927 the property tax provided almost all of local tax revenues.

One main feature emerges from this summary of government finances before the great depression of the 1930's: with respect to expenditure for civil functions, the federal government, vis-à-vis state and local governments, played a small role, and one that seemed unlikely soon to increase. With respect to taxation, however, the federal government had been pushed by World War I to move strongly into taxes on income, both individual and corporate.

CHART 1-3. Relative Use of Types of Taxes by Federal, State, and Local Governments, Selected Years, 1902–63

(In percentage of total tax collections)

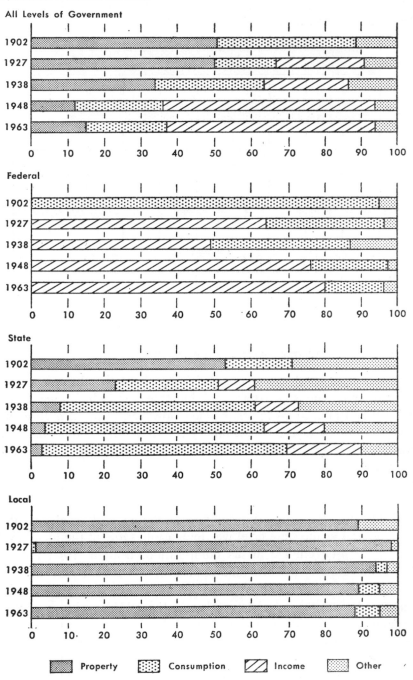

Source: Same as Chart 1-1. For specific figures, see Appendix Table A-2.

In the 1920's the rates of these taxes were sharply reduced, but there was no repeal; the framework was retained. Nonetheless, state governments had reason to be content with their prospects. They were assuming new functions and extending their control over old ones. New and productive revenues in the form of taxation of motor fuel had been discovered and developed; since federal rates were low, joint occupancy of income and death taxation with the federal government seemed practicable. For the most part, administrative decisions were left in local hands, subject to general state supervision.

The Depression of the 1930's

The decade of the 1930's brought more drastic change to the intergovernmental financial structure in the United States than had the preceding 140 years. The force behind the change was a depression without precedent in its intensity and duration. A powerful shift in social philosophy developed when it became clear that state and local governments could not cope with obvious relief and welfare needs. Local governments simply ran out of money as property tax collections declined and tax delinquencies rose, and as they found themselves unable to borrow. State governments came to the rescue, but their efforts were both laggard and inadequate. After 1933, federal intervention took place on a large scale, at first mostly by emergency programs of public works, work relief, and direct relief. Then in 1935 the Social Security Act provided a federal program of old-age insurance, a federal-state system of unemployment insurance, and an extensive plan of grants for public assistance which pushed state and local governments into these programs and reimbursed them for about half of their cost. Other governmental programs proliferated. Sometimes the new expenditure was wholly federal; quite often joint federal-state financing was provided.

Thus the 1930's brought a major intergovernmental redistribution of expenditure for civil purposes. The most remarkable change was the increase in the federal contribution. It was much larger in 1938 than in 1927, and the state-local share was correspondingly smaller. Much of this federal increase was in the form of grants, that is, money was placed in the hands of state and local governments to administer and spend. As Chart 1-1, Section A, shows, however, direct federal spending also grew.

Tax collections during the 1930's are less significant as a source of government revenue than hitherto. Federal borrowing, never before an important peacetime method of finance, took place on a large scale. Nonetheless, between 1927 and 1938 the federal and state tax shares grew, and the local share declined. (See Chart 1-2.) Consumption taxes took on greater importance, notably at the state level, where such taxes in 1938 provided 53 percent of total tax receipts. (See Chart 1-3.) Property tax as a source of state revenue continued to lose ground, but it nearly held its place as a local source.

In the 1930's judicial doctrine also showed a centralizing bias. For half a century after 1880 the Supreme Court had marked out a fairly clear boundary between federal and state activities; it stood as referee to solve jurisdictional disputes. Whether in response to shifts in social philosophy or as a reaction to contradictory precedents, a new judicial interpretation emerged in the 1930's which "accepted a reading of the general welfare clause that placed no discernible judicial limits on the amounts or purposes of federal spending. . . ."[4] The Supreme Court became unwilling also to place restraints on government regulation of economic affairs.

In the 1930's a critical chorus arose, repeating much more vehemently than in the 1880's that the states were obsolete and should be scrapped. Simeon Leland, a well known professor of public finance, believed that the states should become "administrative areas" of the national government. It was, he avowed, anomalous to have forty-eight states fumble ineffectively with similar problems. An eminent political scientist, Luther Gulick, was equally specific. The states were no longer vital organizational units; "dual federalism" was an artificial concept since state governments could not deal "even inefficiently with the imperative, the life and death tasks of the new national economy." What had they done, what could they do, about regulation of utilities, about protecting bank deposits, about social insurance? These programs were "mostly national in scope. It is extremely wasteful, and in most cases impossible, to solve them state by state."[5] No one spelled out the timing of

---

[4] Commission on Intergovernmental Relations, *A Report to the President* (1955), p. 29. This report is hereinafter referred to by its more usual designation, the *Kestnbaum Report,* so named after its chairman, Meyer Kestnbaum.

[5] These references and others of a similar tenor are given in W. Brooke Graves, *American State Government* (Heath, 1936), pp. 746-53.

the dissolution of the states; fulfillment could presumably wait on the millennium.

Three decades later, the entire analysis and indictment seem unrealistic. The economic disaster which struck the United States in the 1930's required a reallocation and also an enlargement of governmental functions. Realization of this necessity did not come easily. A period of fumbling, of debate over governmental responsibilities, and of improvisation was inevitable. Only gradually could a new alignment of functions, and especially of governmental finance, evolve.

Postwar Resurgence of State and Local Spending

Before this happened, World War II intervened. Even more than in World War I, state and local finances were put on a standby basis. As federal spending in the years from 1940 to 1944 expanded tenfold (from $10.0 to $100.5 billion), state and local spending declined (from $11.2 to $10.5 billion).

But when the war ended the federal government rapidly dismantled its military establishment and prepared to reestablish its prewar pattern of activities.[6] State and local governments prepared to catch up on deficiencies in public construction resulting from depression and war. On the surface their finances seemed strong: revenues were abundant, and never had interest rates on state and local securities been so low. Two events soon impaired the optimistic outlook: (1) a sharp rise in prices, and (2) the emergence of the cold war. The second was the more important and enduring because it brought to a halt, and then reversed, the drop in federal tax rates. State and local governments, instead of occupying sources of revenue vacated by the federal government, had to compete with the federal government for the taxpayer's dollar. Nonetheless, expenditures by all levels of government on civil functions have grown in relative, as well as in absolute, terms. (See Chart 1-4.) This trend was temporarily halted in postwar years, but by 1963 total expenditures had surpassed the 1938 peak.

Postwar state-local expenditures, considered separately, also show a sizable relative and absolute increase. They represented 6.8

---

[6] Through the Employment Act of 1946, the federal government assumed the new function of promoting economic stabilization This did not, however, require provision of new federal programs.

percent of the gross national product in 1948, and 11.1 percent in 1963. Higher standards of public demand for education, welfare, public health, highways, housing, and so forth, required state and local action. Even when intergovernmental payments are attributed to the originating level, the distribution of spending for civil purposes in 1948 and 1963 shows that state and local governments held their position. (See Chart 1-1.)

In the postwar years, 1948 and 1963, the federal share of tax collections decreased somewhat, while the state and local shares grew. (See Chart 1-2.) With respect to types of taxes used, the surprising change was the recovery of the property tax. During the 1930's, as previously noted, it lost ground precipitously. After the war it was revived and showed surprising elasticity in yield. (See Chart 1-3.)

Projections of State and Local Finance

Projections of future state-local expenditures and revenues have been made by several scholars. Inevitably the assumptions differ in detail and, for this reason, the sets of figures are not strictly

CHART 1-4. General Expenditure for Civil Functions by All Levels of Government[a] as Percentage of Gross National Product, Selected Years, 1902–63

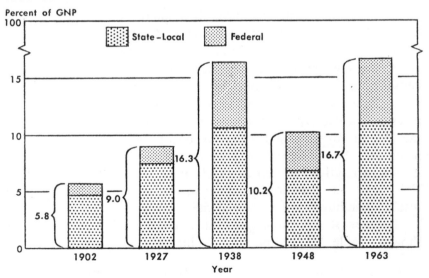

Source: Appendix Table A-3.
[a] Intergovernmental payments are charged to the level of government making final disbursement.

comparable.[7] One major assumption, which is both important and precarious, concerns the level of federal spending, especially for defense. Since defense as a function of government must take precedence over all other duties, a pessimistic assumption would limit the expansion of all government spending for civil purposes. But an optimistic assumption—that federal defense spending will shrink, or even that it will not grow quite as fast as gross national product —allows opportunity for expansion of government spending, particularly by state-local governments, for civil purposes.

Projections which premise that the growth in defense spending will not outpace the increase in gross national product expect state and local spending in ten years to be double the 1963 level. Projected expansion of state and local tax revenues, based on present rates and bases, do not match the growth in spending because the yields of the major taxes—sales and property—are not very elastic. As a result, the rates and bases of state-local taxes will have to be increased. It seems likely that the financial well-being of state and local governments in the next decade will become increasingly difficult to maintain.

No such financial problem should arise for the federal government. Its tax system is quite elastic; an increase in the gross national product will automatically bring a more than proportionate growth of revenue, with no change in present rates or bases. If full employment were attained, for example, federal revenue collections would be automatically increased by over $6 billion yearly, leaving a surplus unless federal expenditures were increased or tax rates reduced.[8]

Functional Distribution of Expenditures

This brief historical review of governmental finances indicates that while the nation has been buffeted by strong economic forces, federalism in the United States has been flexible. The division of *aggregate* governmental expenditure for civil purposes—federal vs. state and local—changed in the 1930's with growth in the federal share and decline in the state-local share. The shift is more emphatic

[7] These have been reviewed briefly in James A. Maxwell, *Tax Credits and Intergovernmental Fiscal Relations* (Brookings Institution, 1962), pp. 8-10.

[8] *Annual Report of the Council of Economic Advisers* (January 1964), p. 42.

when federal grants are reckoned as federal rather than state-local expenditure.

Division of Functions Between Federal and State-Local Governments

This section will indicate the *functions* that have been affected by these relative and absolute changes in government expenditures. Before examining the functional figures, a question should be asked. What rationale can be offered concerning the division of functions between the federal government on the one hand, and state-local governments on the other? The framers of the Constitution had a rationale; they drew lines that set limits to the powers of the national government. The lines were not clearcut in 1788, and they are much more blurred today. The scope of government has grown, and the economy of the nation is much more integrated. As a result, the concept of the separation of governmental functions, federal versus state-local, has been replaced by another concept of federal-state relations, "cooperative federalism." In 1955, the situation was summed up this way:

> Under current judicial doctrine, there are still limits on the coercive powers at both levels [National or State], but the National powers are broad and the possibilities by means of spending are still broader. The crucial questions now are questions of policy: Which level ought to move? Or should both? Or neither? What are the prudent and proper divisions of labor and responsibility between them? These are questions mainly for legislative judgment, and the criteria are chiefly political, economic, and administrative, rather than legal. The emphasis is on mutual and complementary undertakings in furtherance of common aims.[9]

The case for decentralized decision and administration remains strong, but federal participation in finance, coupled with modest federal coordination of state performance, is currently thought to be consistent with performance at the state-local level.

A modern rationale for "cooperative federalism" can be developed through analysis of the *benefits* derived by people from governmental services. Some of these services are *collective* in na-

---

[9] *Kestnbaum Report,* p. 33.

ture. The clearest instance is national defense where government considers the need of citizens in the aggregate, not individually. As a logical consequence, government raises the revenue for this expenditure by general taxes which are assessed on individuals according to standards of equity. The collective nature of the benefits dictates that this substantial expenditure—absorbing, in 1963, 68 percent of federal expenditure and 44 percent of total governmental spending—must be allocated among taxpayers according to whatever standards the legislature deems appropriate. At the other end of the spectrum, government renders services which are *semi-commercial* in nature: certain individuals are the direct beneficiaries, the government charges them prices or fees for units of the service, and individuals may choose to consume as many or as few units as they wish. A modest collective interest is present (else provision would be left in private hands), but it is veiled.[10] Examples are the Post Office, toll highways, and water supply.

Between these extremes all other governmental services may be ranged according to the relative importance of their collective, compared with their individual, interest. Thus, educational services are rendered to individuals who thereby receive direct benefits; but these services are also beneficial to the whole society. This spillover of benefits creates a strong collective interest of such importance that the cost of primary and secondary education is defrayed by general taxes, not by charges to the recipients. Many important features of public health services also have a spillover of benefit to the whole society. Welfare services form another distinguishable group of the large in-between category. Here also the benefits accrue directly to recipients, but society is collectively benefited because provision of these services satisfies deeply felt humanitarian feelings. Moreover, linkage of individual benefit with individual payment would be absurd since the recipients are, by definition, without means. In short, finance by general taxation is inevitable and appropriate; government provides the services as a collective duty.

[10] In 1958 Congress passed a law (PL 85-426) which offers an interesting example of an actual attempt to separate these "semi-commercial" and "collective" benefits. The Post Office was required to split its services into two parts: (a) those that rendered divisible benefits to recipients and should, on this account, be covered by user charges, and (b) those that rendered indivisible benefits—public services—and should be paid out of general Treasury funds. Definition of "public services" has been controversial, and computation of their cost very difficult.

How can these generalizations be applied in deciding between federal or state-local provision of a particular government service? One which is rendered to the nation as a whole (collectively)—defense, for example—is clearly federal; so also is one which, although noncollective, should be provided uniformly to individuals in all states—postal services, for example. The outlook of each state and local government is, on the other hand, circumscribed; the services each provides are for individuals in a limited geographic area. Some variation of type and level of provision is acceptable, and even desirable. Sometimes, however, the benefits from a state or local service will spill over and have an impact outside its boundaries. Primary and secondary education is one obvious example. Although the spillover undoubtedly reaches beyond the boundaries of a locality or a state, this national interest has not until recently been recognized by Congress through federal grants-in-aid. Provision is left mainly to local governments because direct benefits accrue to individuals in a locality and because local (and state) governments are strongly responsive and sensitive to the demands of citizens concerning details. The cost is provided through taxes levied at the local and to a smaller extent at the state level.

Public welfare services are another bundle of functions performed mainly at the state-local level of government. The benefits accrue directly to individuals; responsiveness of government to the variety of individual needs is vital; detailed administration is inevitable. The services are rendered mainly to needy persons, and, during the depression of the 1930's, the opinion emerged strongly that some minimum level of provision should be achieved over the nation. Since this would not result if the states were left to their own devices, federal assistance by conditional grants was enacted. Thereby, state and local governments were stimulated to offer welfare services, not indeed at a uniform level, but so that a minimum level for recipients was feasible even in poor states.

Expenditures for Civil Functions, 1902-63

What are the most important civil functions provided by government over the past sixty years, measured by the relative expenditures these have absorbed? Table 1-3 shows that four functions have consistently accounted for about half the total. Education has always been far in the lead with highways a poor second. Expendi-

TABLE 1-3. Percentage Distribution of General Expenditure for Civil Functions by All Levels of Government, Selected Years, 1902–63

Function	1902	1927	1938	1948	1963
Education	20.7	26.0	19.2	29.2	28.1
Highways	14.1	21.1	15.6	11.6	12.8
Public welfare	3.3	1.9	8.9	8.1	6.4
Health and hospitals	5.1	5.0	4.9	7.3	7.6
Other	56.8	46.0	51.4	43.8	45.1
All functions	100.0	100.0	100.0	100.0	100.0

Source: Appendix Table A-4.

ture for public welfare rose sharply in the 1930's, and remains substantial, although percentage expenditure has shrunk moderately.

What shifts have occurred in the past sixty years in the level of government providing the most important civil functions? When federal grants (intergovernmental transfers) are regarded as spent by state and local governments (which make the final disbursements), the shift appears to be very slight. (See Chart 1-5, Section A.) Except for health and hospitals, the state and local relative share is about the same in 1963 as it was in 1902.[11]

This approach conceals the growth of federal grants in recent decades. By grants, the federal level has absorbed part of the financial cost of certain functions (and it has also stimulated their performance). To emphasize the importance of grants, in Section B of Chart 1-5 intergovernmental transfers are regarded as spent by the *originating* level of government. The large contribution made by the federal government in grants for highways and welfare becomes apparent; the federal contribution to health is also substantial. Nonetheless, the shift in sixty years is not great. And the extent of federal direction which accompanied expansion of its grants was modest.

An overlapping of governmental activities now exists. Performance of certain functions remains at the state and local level, but

[11] On inspection, it turns out that 57 percent of federal spending in 1963 for health and hospitals is for veterans. A few surprising shifts over the sixty years prove to have simple and episodic explanations. For instance, the drop in the state-local share of highway expenditure in 1938 is explained by WPA spending; the drop in the state-local share of expenditure for education in 1948 is explained by the surge of federal G.I. benefits.

CHART 1-5. Percentage of General Expenditure for Selected Civil Functions Contributed by Federal and State-Local Governments, 1902 and 1963

A. Intergovernmental payments charged to the level of government making the final disbursement.

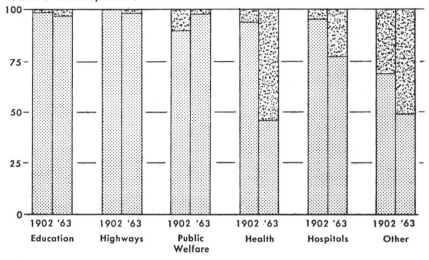

Percent of Total Expenditure

B. Intergovernmental payments charged to the originating level of government.

Percent of Total Expenditure

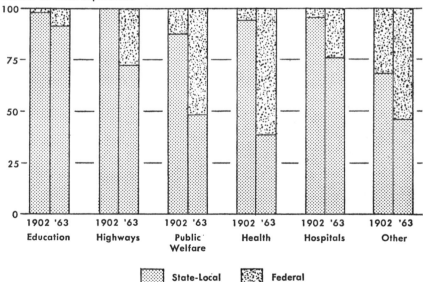

State-Local   Federal

Source: Appendix Tables A-4, A-5, and A-6. These tables also include data on other years.

the federal government participates in finances and, by specifying conditions for receipt of grants, gives a modicum of national direction. A mélange of federal grants has emerged, modifying federalism without changing its essential characteristics.

Apologia for Federalism

The situation is, then, that the expansion of federal power, so forceful a trend in the 1930's, has not continued; federalism has demonstrated a renewed vitality. The states are, so it seems, geographic units that can handle many functions more flexibly, and therefore more in accord with heterogeneous citizen demands, than the national government. State boundaries must be accepted as immutable, and while the states are diverse in population, resources, and area, this diversity is no greater than that of many sovereign nations—and not merely those newborn in the past decade.[12] Through their very existence the states, over the decades, have acquired loyalties and sentimental affection which lubricate the machinery of government.

More philosophical reasons may be advanced for a belief that, if the states did not exist, there would be need to invent them. One reason has been put cogently by Justices Holmes and Brandeis—that the states are laboratories in which limited, and therefore safe, experiments in government or administrative techniques can be

[12] In this revealing list, some American states are paired with well-established nations of approximately equal populations in 1962:

State	Population	Nation	Population
New York	17,498,000	Canada	18,600,000
California	17,029,000	Colombia	14,769,000
Pennsylvania	11,382,000	Netherlands	11,797,000
Illinois	10,098,000	Australia	10,508,000*
Ohio	10,038,000	Hungary	10,060,000
Texas	10,122,000	Belgium	9,222,000
Michigan	8,029,000	Chile	8,001,000
New Jersey	6,357,000	Sweden	7,562,000
Indiana	4,663,000	Finland	4,509,000
Tennessee	3,652,000	Norway	3,640,000
Iowa	2,774,000	Ireland	2,824,000

* 1961.

Source: *United Nations Demographic Yearbook,* 1962; U.S. Census Bureau, *Current Population Reports,* Series P-25, No. 272, September 1963.

made.[13] Such experiments, even when they fail, may have more than mere negative value. They may indicate why and what kind of federal action is needed. An illustration of this laboratory value was the experiment of Oklahoma in guaranteeing bank deposits.[14] The scheme failed, but it and similar attempts by other states disclosed defects which could be, and were, remedied by a national scheme in 1933. In the early years of the twentieth century, state and local governments experimented with techniques of government budgeting and accounting. To these experiments the Federal Budget and Accounting Act of 1921 owed a great deal. The Wisconsin income tax of 1911 preceded the federal income tax of 1913. The federal Social Security Act of 1935 grew out of much state investigation and some experimentation with old-age insurance, unemployment insurance, and public assistance. Marked progress here had to wait on federal intervention; yet with respect to unemployment insurance and public assistance, Congress chose to act through the techniques of cooperative federalism.

In a famous statement made more than three-quarters of a century ago, Woodrow Wilson wrote of the value of the states as training grounds in the practice of government. "The governorship of a State is very like a smaller Presidency; or, rather, the Presidency is very like a big governorship. Training in the duties of the one fits for the duties of the other."[15] The case for federalism, in the minds of many men, rests on a still more exalted and abstract merit: that state and local governments are bulwarks of democracy. Only where the people of a nation have adequate powers of decision can they develop a public spirit, and the specific knowledge and techniques that give life to free institutions.[16]

Despite a solid performance in postwar years, however, state governments have many structural flaws which need remedy. Nine

[13] *Black v. Hirsh*, 256 U.S. 155 (1921). Justice Brandeis wrote: "It is one of the happy incidents of the federal system that a single courageous state may, if its citizens choose, serve as a laboratory, and try novel social and economic experiments without risk to the rest of the country."

[14] In the case of *Noble Bank v. Haskill* (219 U.S. 104), Justice Holmes wrote of "the insulated laboratories of the states."

[15] *Congressional Government* (Houghton Mifflin, 1885), p. 253.

[16] George C. S. Benson, in "Values of Decentralized Government," *Essays in Federalism* (Claremont Men's College, 1961), pp. 5-16, makes an eloquent case for federalism.

years ago the Commission on Intergovernmental Relations was set up to reappraise federalism, to "study the means of achieving a sounder relationship between federal, state and local governments." Its distinguished membership of twenty-five persons included fifteen appointed by the President, five by the President of the Senate, and five by the speaker of the House of Representatives. Its report—the *Kestnbaum Report*—contained important criticisms of state government. The six members who were, or who had been, state governors did not dissent. Many state constitutions, the report declared, "restrict the scope, effectiveness, and adaptability of State and local action"; there was a "real and pressing need for the States to improve their constitutions."[17] State legislatures should provide a more equitable system of representation.[18] The power of governors was unreasonably limited by the establishment of independent agencies and boards, by the election of numerous state administrative officers, and by the lack of control over budgeting. State legislatures fettered their own power, and that of the localities, to tax and borrow; they earmarked too much revenue; they created, and should mitigate, tax conflicts.

These organizational defects impaired performance of government functions. They diverted to Washington demands from citizens which should be met at the state level; they cast doubt on the logic of federalism—that the states possess political and economic capacity appropriate to their political powers.

Another recent development, raising new doubts about the logic of federalism, has been the growth of metropolitan areas. Urban concentration of population and resources is an old phenomenon. But in postwar years disturbing trends have emerged which, if not new, strike the social conscience of the nation more forcibly and aggravate the disparities between the service and tax areas inside the metropolis.

In the metropolis a core area, embracing the central shopping

[17] *Kestnbaum Report*, pp. 37-38.

[18] On June 15, 1964, in six decisions, the majority of the Supreme Court held that the "equal protection" clause of the Fourteenth Amendment requires each state to have a legislature so that, in both houses, each member represents substantially the same number of people. The principles were set forth in an Alabama case (*Reynolds v. Sims*), and then applied in cases from Colorado, Delaware, Maryland, New York, and Virginia.

and business districts, shows signs of obsolescence. A suburban area sprawls outside, attracting business and residential units from the center. In or close to the core area fresh slums emerge which accelerate the decay and underline problems of health, welfare, and education. How should the governmental duties of the metropolis be handled? Measured in terms of per capita income, or property, or wealth, the metropolis appears to have a large fiscal potential. The difficulty lies in determining how the potential can be exercised: the metropolis is not a single governmental unit governed by one legislative body; instead, it embraces a large number of independent jurisdictions. The supply of services—such as water, sewage disposal, and law enforcement—should be organized and administered with an eye to the needs of the whole area; in fact, decisions are often obstructed or postponed while fragmented jurisdictions debate their respective fiscal responsibilities. The resources of the area cannot be mobilized for an efficient assault on its problems. Sometimes the metropolitan area is multistate, necessitating negotiation and agreement by sovereign units.

Is federal intervention indicated? If so, should it be through direct federal programs, or through conditional grants? If the latter, should the grants be funneled through state governments, or should they go directly to local units? Has American federalism the flexibility to meet and to adjust to these new stresses?

No doubt can exist that rational solution of many urban problems often requires reform of state and local political and administrative structures. If reform is postponed, or fails, centralization will be encouraged because, in present circumstances, the separate interests of the states will not be allowed to transcend a strong national interest. The federal government will not be content to act merely "as the bracket to a series of algebraic symbols."[19] The centripetal forces of modern society demand a flexible federalism. Efficient governmental administration will not, in the long pull, be sacrificed for the sake of tradition.

[19] Harold J. Laski, *Studies in the Problem of Sovereignty* (Yale University Press, 1917), p. 280.

CHAPTER II

Fiscal Performance
and Capacity

"There is a great deal of difference between Peter and Peter."
Don Quixote, Part I, Chapter 47.

THE DIVISION OF GOVERNMENTAL FUNCTIONS between a state government and the local governments which are its creatures varies widely among the fifty states. The quantitative evidence in the form of expenditures is, however, hard to interpret, most obviously because of state intergovernmental transfers. Some state governments take over and perform functions which others leave in local hands and assist by grants-in-aid. In the former case, performance of functions may, with some qualification, be regarded as centralized, that is, the state governments make a relatively large part of direct general expenditure; in the latter case, performance is decentralized. The ten state governments which in 1963 spent the highest and lowest proportions of total state-local direct expenditure are shown in Table 2-1. The two states with the highest percentages, Alaska and Hawaii, are new states where history has had little chance to entrench local units of government, and this fact explains their centralization. But no such simple explanation will serve for the other high states, or for the states with low percentages where relative decentralization seems to prevail. In terms of age, size, and

33

TABLE 2-1. Percentage of State-Local Direct General Expenditure[a] by Selected State Governments, 1963

Ten Highest States		Ten Lowest States	
Alaska	69.7	Colorado	34.4
Hawaii	68.5	Illinois	34.2
Kentucky	57.5	Maryland	32.1
Vermont	56.5	Massachusetts	29.2
Delaware	56.2	Ohio	28.5
West Virginia	53.4	Minnesota	28.0
Oklahoma	53.1	California	27.9
Louisiana	51.9	Wisconsin	25.6
Arkansas	51.8	New Jersey	25.3
North Dakota	50.9	New York	23.3

Source: U. S. Census Bureau, *Governmental Finances in 1963* (1964), p. 51.
[a] General expenditure is that for all purposes other than specifically defined utility, liquor store, and insurance trust operations. Direct general expenditure excludes intergovernmental expenditure.

population density, Delaware, New Jersey, and Maryland are quite similar; and yet Delaware falls in the group with the high percentages, while New Jersey and Maryland fall in the group with the low ones.

The fact is that interstate comparisons of state government finances (or of local government finances) are treacherous, and may be quite misleading about the relative levels of services provided by the states. More revealing comparisons can be made, state by state, of aggregates or subaggregates of state *plus* local expenditure and revenue. Such figures, when expressed per capita or per $1,000 of personal income, provide a more useful measure of state-by-state differences in governmental provision of services and collection of revenues.

A per capita measure of expenditure has limitations chiefly because population (the denominator) is an inadequate proxy for expenditure needs. Some groups in the population—for example, dependent children and the aged—require extra public expenditure. States differ in meeting their responsibilities here, and refined measurement should allow for such interstate variations. A per capita expenditure basis is rough also because it makes no allowance for price or quality differences, state by state, of public goods. Educational services may be cheaper in Mississippi than in Massachusetts, or it may be that, if account is taken of quality, the reverse is true. A similar uncertainty exists with respect to the pricing of other governmental services. Moreover, state variation in expenditure is not explicable wholly by objective needs and financial capacity; noneconomic and intangible factors, which stem from different historical backgrounds, are important.

This brief enumeration of some of the factors which might affect the levels of state and local expenditure has two purposes. One, it warns that the measure of differences used below—per capita general expenditure—is imperfect; second, it indicates that a more refined measure would be difficult to construct.

For reasons to be mentioned later, figures of state and local *revenue,* when expressed per $1,000 of personal income, are not unambiguous measures of revenue effort.

Patterns of Aggregate Expenditure

For the fiscal year 1963, state and local general expenditure for the nation averaged $343.64 per capita. All general expenditures made by state and local governments are included in this figure, whether the funds were provided from their own sources or by federal grants.

Diversity in Per Capita Expenditure

Some idea of the spread among states in per capita state and local expenditures in 1963 is given in the following list:[1]

Per Capita Expenditure	Number of States
$200–49	4
250–99	9
300–49	15
350–99	12
400–49	5
450–99	3
Over $500	2[2]
	50

[1] Derived from *Governmental Finances in 1963,* p. 45.
[2] Alaska, $670; Wyoming, $507.

TABLE 2-2. States with the Highest and Lowest Per Capita General Expenditure (Less Federal Grants), 1963

| | Highest States | | | Lowest States | |
State	Per Capita Expenditure	Expenditure Relative[a]	State	Per Capita Expenditure	Expenditure Relative[a]
Alaska	$493.54	165	North Carolina	$196.88	66
California	417.93	140	West Virginia	196.14	65
Hawaii	410.89	137	Mississippi	193.47	64
Nevada	407.57	136	Alabama	193.04	64
New York	399.22	133	Arkansas	176.86	59
Washington	377.38	126	South Carolina	173.34	58

Source: Appendix Table A-7.
[a] Expenditure relatives are computed by dividing the states' per capita expenditure by the national average. To compute the relative for California, for example, $417.93 ÷ $299.25 = 140.

These figures include funds transferred from the federal government; in order to secure figures of per capita expenditure by states from *their own sources,* federal grants should be deducted. For 1963 per capita state and local expenditure, *less federal grants,* was $299.25.[3] The six states with the highest and the lowest per capita expenditure on this basis are shown in Table 2-2. California, one of the highest states, spent $417.93 per capita in 1963; South Carolina, the lowest state, spent $173.34. The figures of per capita state-local expenditures can be made more readily comparable by assigning the value of 100 to the national average ($299.25), and computing relative numbers that express how much each state spends in relation to this national average. These expenditure relatives are shown in Table 2-2 for the six states with the highest and the lowest per capita expenditures in 1963. California has an expenditure relative of 140, and is thus spending 40 percent more than the national average; South Carolina, with an expenditure relative of 58, spends 42 percent less than the average. Twenty-eight states spend less than the average; twenty-two states more.

Efforts have been made to discover and measure the significant variables (besides population) which explain the diversity among the states. The most important other variable or "cause" is income. In general, more will be spent by state and local governments in a "rich" state, that is, one with a high per capita income, than in a

[3] See Appendix Table A-7 for detailed per capita figures for all states, before and after deductions for federal grants.

"poor" state. The state-by-state relationship between per capita income and per capita state-local government expenditure is presented in Chart 2-1. In this chart, states have been ranked according to their relative standing in both per capita income and government expenditure (less federal grants). Their per capita income rank is plotted horizontally on the chart; state-local expenditure is plotted vertically. The general pattern revealed by the points of intersection of state ranks in these two measures shows that income and government expenditure tend to rise together, with expenditure rising somewhat less sharply than income. For every 10 percent increase in a state's per capita income, state-local expenditure increases, on the average, by approximately 6 percent.

This average relationship has many exceptions. More often than not, states that rank low in per capita income have a higher rank in per capita expenditure; conversely, states that rank high in income quite often have a lower rank in per capita expenditure. And some states spend much more, and some much less, than one would expect in terms of their per capita income. For example, Connecticut and New Jersey which, in 1962, ranked third and sixth in terms of per capita income, ranked fourteenth and twenty-eighth in terms of per capita expenditure in 1963; Louisiana and New Mexico, which ranked forty-fifth and fortieth in per capita income, ranked twenty-ninth and twenty-second in per capita expenditure. This relationship is not true for *all functions;* in particular, it is not true for public welfare. Here, per capita expenditure is usually larger in poor than in rich states.

The influence of other quantifiable variables has been explored, notably *population density* (population per square mile) and *urbanization* (percentage of population living in urban places). As population density increases, per capita state-local expenditure tends to *decrease,* but not uniformly and not for all functions. Per capita expenditure for police and fire protection tends to rise with population density. Increase in urbanization has a modest tendency to increase per capita expenditure, but not for highways. Moreover, the variables, population density and urbanization, are themselves highly correlated and not independent; their effects, therefore, cannot be added.

The conclusion is justified that, except for the distinct relationship between per capita income and per capita expenditure, statisti-

CHART 2-1. States Ranked by Per Capita Income, 1962, and Per Capita General Expenditure (Less Federal Grants), 1963

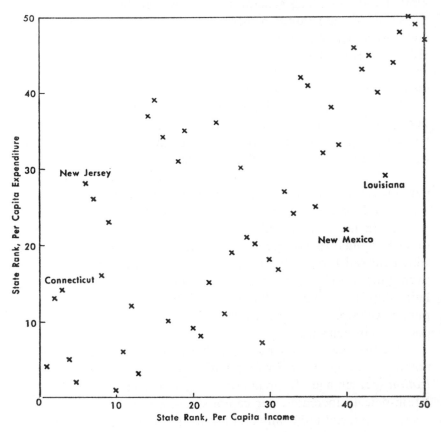

Source: Appendix Table A-8. Per capita data for all states are given in this table.

cal analysis of other factors indicates considerable diversity among the states. Explanation of the diversities is to be found in historical background or political philosophy, rather than in quantitative facts. For instance, Virginia spends much less, and Louisiana much more, on public welfare than would be expected, and it would be "a safe guess" that the explanation lies in "differences in the political philosophy of the Byrds and the Longs."[4]

Functional Distribution of Expenditure

In 1963, as Table 2-3 shows, education was by far the most important type of spending of state and local governments. It absorbed $124.49 per capita, or over 41 percent of total general state-local expenditure after deduction of federal grants. The per capita expenditure for the other functions, and the percentage spent for each, are also given in Table 2-3.

What state-by-state *variation* in functional expenditures is found, other than that attributable to differences in population and income? This is examined by first calculating the expenditure in each state for each major function as a *percentage* of total state and local expenditure. If, for example, Maine—a poor state—spent approximately the same percentage of its total expenditure (less federal grants) on education in 1963 as Connecticut—a rich state—this would indicate that the function was appraised similarly in the two states even though their actual expenditures (expressed either per

[4] Glenn W. Fisher, "Determinants of State and Local Government Expenditure," *National Tax Journal* (December 1961), p. 353. In a subsequent article ("Interstate Variation in State and Local Government Expenditure," *National Tax Journal,* March 1964), Fisher related per capita expenditure in 1960 to seven variables, and secured a higher correlation than for the three variables (per capita income, population density, and urbanization). In this study he found a high negative relation between the levels of expenditure and the percentage of low income families in a state. Seymour Sacks and Robert Harris ("The Determinants of State and Local Government Expenditures and Intergovernmental Flows of Funds," *ibid.*) used the same three variables and included federal aid and state aid per capita as additional independent variables. They found that the significant increase in federal aid in recent years, notably for welfare, had been an important determinant of state and local expenditures.

Allen D. Manvel has examined the number of state and local government *employees* per 10,000 inhabitants in an attempt to discover state patterns. He concluded that, while economic capacity provided some explanation, "traditions and geographic and demographic characteristics" were at least as influential. "Regional Differences in the Scale of State and Local Government," *National Tax Journal,* June 1964, pp. 110-20.

TABLE 2-3. Per Capita and Percentage Distribution of General Expenditure (Less Federal Grants) of State-Local Governments for Selected Functions, 1963

Function	Per Capita Expenditure	Percentage of Total Spending
Education	$124.49	41.5
Highways	42.81	14.3
Health and hospitals	23.03	7.7
Police protection	12.10	4.0
Interest	11.66	3.9
Public welfare	9.68	3.2
Sewerage	7.76	2.6
Fire protection	6.29	2.1
General control	5.42	1.8
Other functions	56.01	9.9
United States	$299.25	100.0

Source: *Governmental Finances in 1963*, pp. 46–48.

capita or per $1,000 of income) were quite different. These relative proportions of total state-local expenditure spent by the states in 1963 on their major functions have been calculated and are given in Appendix Table A-9.

The *extent of state variation* in proportionate expenditure on different governmental functions can be measured by calculating, for each function, the coefficient of variation—a percentage that expresses mathematically the degree to which states vary in their proportionate spending on a particular function. The lower this percentage, the more similar the proportionate amounts spent by the states; the higher the percentage, the greater the variance.

The coefficients of variation for state-local spending on the major functions are shown in Table 2-4. The state-by-state variation in expenditure for education is obviously modest. This expenditure falls into two parts, that for local schools and that for higher education. The low variation is explicable by the relative similarity of expenditure on local schools. Two housekeeping functions—general control (the overhead of government for legislative bodies, administration of justice, and so forth) and financial administration—also display modest variation. Examination of state expenditures for other major functions indicates that their variation is much greater than that for education or housekeeping. Apparently, expenditure

TABLE 2-4. Coefficients of Variation[a] for Functional Distribution of State-Local Expenditure (Less Federal Grants), 1963

Function	Coefficient of Variation
Education	12.9%
Financial administration	19.0
General control	23.0
Police protection	24.9
Health and hospitals	26.4
Highways	28.1
Public welfare	28.3
Interest on debt	37.0
Sanitation	44.0
Fire protection	45.8
Sewerage	47.9

Source: Derived from Appendix Table A-9.

[a] The coefficient of variation is computed by dividing the standard deviation (the square root of the average deviations squared from the average) by the average and multiplying this by 100. For example, the standard deviation of the series showing the percentage distribution of state-local expenditure on education in 1963 is 5.65 percent, while the average of all the functional deviations is 43.8 percent. The coefficient is therefore 12.9 percent.

preferences of state and local governments for most functions are quite diverse from state to state, even when the impact of differences in state income levels is excluded.

Measures of Revenue Effort

Comparisons of state expenditures gain in cogency if they are related to a measure of *revenue effort* in which the revenues collected by state and local governments *from their own sources* are referred to a relevant, uniform base. Here state personal income seems to be suitable.[5] Table 2-5 shows the revenues raised by state and lo-

[5] The income base is not unambiguous. Should it mean income produced, or personal income received by residents of a state? Both have been examined in a Staff Report of the Advisory Commission on Intergovernmental Relations, *Measures of State and Local Fiscal Capacity and Tax Effort* (1963). The Staff Report develops as another measure the *representative tax system,* which can be used to estimate the amount of revenue that state-local governments could produce, state by state, if they levied a cross-section of taxes currently in use by all state-local governments. This cross-section—established by identifying, weighting, and assigning rates to the present tax structure—can be used to estimate a state's tax capacity; when related to actual tax collections, indices of a state's tax *effort* are obtained.

These indices vary significantly from the income indices for some geographic areas. The Plains, Mountain, and Southwestern states have a higher capacity and

TABLE 2-5. States Collecting the Highest and Lowest General Revenue from Own Sources per $1,000 of Personal Income, 1963

State	Highest Revenue Collection		State	Lowest Revenue Collection	
	Per $1,000 of Income	Effort Relative[a]		Per $1,000 of Income	Effort Relative
New Mexico	$154.77	132	New Jersey	$99.99	85
North Dakota	153.68	131	Connecticut	99.63	85
Louisiana	153.14	130	Illinois	99.33	84
Wyoming	145.09	123	Virginia	99.05	84
Minnesota	142.31	121	Delaware	97.80	83
Wisconsin	141.08	120	Missouri	93.84	80
United States	117.61	100			

Source: Appendix Table A-10.
[a] Effort relatives are computed by dividing a state's revenue per $1,000 of persona income by the nationa average. Thus for New Mexico $154.77 ÷ $117.61 = 132.

cal governments from their own sources per $1,000 of personal income for the six highest and the six lowest states in 1963, as well as the national average. New Mexico, the state exerting the greatest "effort," according to this scale, collected $154.77 per $1,000 of personal income; Missouri, the lowest state, collected $93.84. Nationally, the average revenue per $1,000 of personal income was $117.61. By assigning the figure of 100 to this national average, relatives can be computed for each state that express its "effort" compared to the national average. The effort relative for New Mexico is 132, indicating that its receipts per $1,000 personal income were 32 percent above the national average; the effort relative for Missouri is 80, or 20 percent below the national average.

Examination of the effort relatives shows, as might be expected, that the revenue collections of some rich states—for example, Dela-

---

make a lower tax effort measured by the representative tax than by the personal income approach (*ibid.*, pp. 75-76). The most important factor producing the differences is high property values in comparison with property yields in these areas. The property tax component of the representative tax system, if applied at average rates, would bring in a large relative revenue. The representative tax measure may prove to be a useful measure of capacity. But the figures have been computed only for 1960, whereas yearly figures of personal income in relation to state and local revenues are available and, for this practical reason, will be used here.

TABLE 2-6. Revenue Effort Compared with Expenditure Relative of Six States with Lowest Per Capita Expenditure, 1963

State	Expenditure Relative	Effort Relative
North Carolina	66	97
West Virginia	65	99
Mississippi	64	119
Alabama	64	95
Arkansas	59	98
South Carolina	58	97

Source: Appendix Tables A-7 and A-10.

ware, Connecticut, and New Jersey—are low in relation to personal income. This does not mean that they have low *expenditure* relatives.[6] Rich states can make above-average per capita expenditure while making below-average effort. For example, the expenditure relative for both Connecticut and Delaware in 1963 was 109; their effort relatives were 85 and 83, respectively. Conversely, as Table 2-6 shows, the expenditure relatives for the six states with the lowest per capita expenditure are all appreciably below the relatives indicating their revenue effort. The conclusion obtrudes that poor states would find it difficult to achieve an average per capita expenditure. In 1963, for example, South Carolina could have lifted its per capita expenditure (less federal grants) from $114.07 to $299.25 only by lifting its revenue effort from 97 to 168.

Patterns of Tax Preference and Utilization

In examining this topic, a major difference between state and local governments should be borne in mind. *Local* governments throughout the nation show little variety in the type of tax they utilize. In 1963, 88 percent of their tax revenue was from the property tax, and in eighteen states this figure topped 95 percent (see Table 2-7). The plight of many local governments is well known. Despite strong incentives and vigorous efforts, they have been unable to diversify, and they need help from the state level.

State governments, however, show great variety in the use and the weight of their taxes. Forty years ago states relied heavily on the

[6] See Appendix Table A-7.

TABLE 2-7. Distribution of States by Percentage of Total Local Tax Revenue Collected from Local Property Tax, 1963

Percentage of Total Local Revenue	Number of States
United States average: 87.6%	
50.0–54.9	1
55.0–59.9	—
60.0–64.9	—
65.0–69.9	1
70.0–74.9	2
75.0–79.9	5
80.0–84.9	5
85.0–89.9	6
90.0–94.9	12
95.0–99.9	18
	50

Source: *Governmental Finances in 1963*, pp. 31–33.

property tax which provided more than one-third of their tax revenue. Licenses for motor vehicles and operators were a poor second in importance, death and gift taxes third, and corporation income tax fourth (see Table 2-8). By 1963 all of these had lost ground, while two old sources—motor fuel tax and individual income tax—had gained. Three new tax revenues—on general sales (usually levied at the retail level), alcoholic beverages, and tobacco products—had emerged, and the first of these won top rank over the whole field by a wide margin. The main target of state taxes now, therefore, is consumption. The pattern of major state tax revenue sources in 1963 is shown in Chart 2-2.

This pattern took shape in the 1930's. In 1927, for example, taxes on sales of specific items brought in 28 percent of state tax collections; of this revenue, however, none was from *general* sales taxes, and nearly 60 percent was from taxes on motor fuel. Property tax was losing favor as a source of state revenue, and the expectation was widespread that diminished federal reliance on income tax would bring increasing use by the states. As indicated in Chapter I, this expectation was not fulfilled. With the great depression, states did turn to taxation of individual income—six states enacted such a tax in 1933. But in these dreary years the falling yield of in-

CHART 2-2. Major Sources of State Tax Collections, 1963

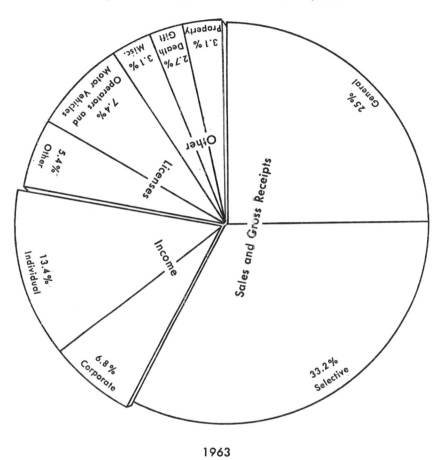

1963

Source: Table 2-8.

come tax was distressing to state governments. The unfamiliar and unpopular retail sales tax, however, did bring in the revenue, and a trend started which has not yet lost its force.

While the *number* of state governments utilizing particular types of taxes does not indicate the *weight* of the taxes, it does reveal a pattern of state preferences. Table 2-9 shows that, in 1963, only three states—New Jersey, New Hampshire, and Nebraska—

TABLE 2-8. Percentage Distribution and Rank of Major Sources of State Tax Collections, Selected Years, 1922–63

Type of Tax	1922	1938	1948	1963
	Percentage of Total State Tax Revenue			
Sales and gross receipts	14.2	54.3	59.8	58.2
General	—	14.5	21.9	25.0
Selective	14.2	39.8	37.9	33.2
Motor fuel	1.4	24.8	18.7	17.4
Alcoholic beverages	—	5.6	6.3	3.6
Tobacco products	—	1.8	5.0	5.1
Other	12.8	7.6	7.9	7.1
Income	10.6	12.2	16.1	20.2
Individual	4.5	6.9	7.4	13.4
Corporation	6.1	5.3	8.7	6.8
License	31.5	16.0	14.5	12.8
Motor vehicles and operators' licenses	16.1	11.5	8.8	7.4
Miscellaneous	15.4	4.5	5.7	5.4
Other taxes	43.7	17.5	9.6	8.9
Property	36.7	7.8	4.1	3.1
Death and gift	7.0	4.5	2.7	2.7
Miscellaneous	—	5.2	2.8	3.1
All taxes	100.0	100.0	100.0	100.0
	Rank in Importance as Source of State Tax Revenue			
Property	1	4	8	8
Motor vehicles and operators' licenses	2	3	4	4
Death and gift	3	8	9	9
Corporation income	4	7	3	5
Individual income	5	5	5	3
Motor fuel	6	1	2	2
General sales	—	2	1	1
Alcoholic beverages	—	6	6	7
Tobacco products	—	9	7	6

Sources: Advisory Commission on Intergovernmental Relations, *Tax Overlapping in the United States, 1964* (henceforth referred to as *Tax Overlapping*), p. 20; *State Government Finances in 1963*, p. 6; U. S. Census Bureau, *Historical Statistics of the United States: Colonial Times to 1957* (1960), pp. 727–28.

TABLE 2-9. Tax Pattern of State Governments, Selected Years, 1928-63

Type of Tax	Number of States[a]			
	1928	1941	1951	1963
General sales tax only	0	8	13	14
Individual income tax only	12	14	12	10
Both	0	16	19	23[b]
Neither	38	12	6	3
	50	50	50	50

Source: *Tax Overlapping*, Table 7.

[a] Hawaii and Alaska included.

[b] New Hampshire, New Jersey, and Tennessee levy partial income taxes—New Hampshire and Tennessee on interest and dividends, New Jersey on nonresident income—which are not counted here.

failed to utilize either a general sales tax or an individual income tax. The table indicates also that the number in this group has shrunk over time. In 1963 twenty-three states utilized *both* taxes, and, over time, the number in this group has grown. In 1963 fourteen states utilized general sales tax only, while ten utilized individual income tax only; the number of states in these two last categories is likely to shrink.

The Weight of State Taxes

In 1963 thirty-eight states secured more than half their tax revenues from all taxes on sales and gross receipts (see Chart 2-3 and Table 2-10).[7] In only five of the states (Oregon, New York, Delaware, Wisconsin, and Alaska) which taxed individual income did this tax yield a larger slice of tax revenue than sales and gross receipts. If a comparison is made of percentage tax receipts from individual income tax and general sales tax in the twenty-three states which, in 1963, levied both, it appears that the yield of the latter was larger in twenty states.

Conclusion

This brief survey indicates that the levels of state-local expenditure per capita are quite diverse from state to state. Even when the

[7] Three of the thirty-eight—New Hampshire, New Jersey, Nebraska—had no general sales tax. Selective sales tax provided 62.7 percent, 55.8 percent, and 55.1 percent, respectively, of their tax revenue.

CHART 2-3. Percentage of State Revenue Collected from Selected Taxes, All States,[a] 1963

Tax Revenue

Legend:
- ■ Sales and Gross Receipts Taxes
- ⧄ Individual Income Taxes
- ▨ Other

Source: Appendix Table A-11.

[a] The revenue from the partial income taxes of New Jersey, New Hampshire, and Nebraska is here reckoned as revenue from the individual income tax.

TABLE 2-10. Distribution of States by Percentage of Total State Tax Revenue Collected from Selected State Taxes, 1963

Percentage of Total State Revenue	All Sales and Gross Receipts	General Sales and Gross Receipts	Individual Income
80–89.9	3 ⎫	—	—
70–79.9	14 ⎬ 38	—	—
60–69.9	9 ⎪	—	—
50–59.9	12 ⎭	2	—
40–49.9	4	4	2
30–39.9	5	17	6
20–29.9	3	10	5
10–19.9	—	3	10
0– 9.9	—	1	9
Number of States	50	37	32[a]

Source: Derived from Appendix Table A-11.

[a] Plus New Hampshire 3.7 percent, Tennessee 1.9 percent, New Jersey 1.6 percent. The Indiana tax produced no revenue in 1963.

force of differences in the level of state income is excluded, the functional patterns remain diverse, except for expenditure on local schools and the housekeeping functions of financial administration and general control.

Is a "satisfactory" level of governmental services being provided in "poor" states, and if not, how can it be provided? One may believe that a poor state should make an above average fiscal effort to achieve a satisfactory level. But if, despite such an effort, the level of state-local services remains unsatisfactory, should financial aid be provided by the federal government? If so, in what form?

With respect to revenues, the plight of many local governments is well-known. Despite strong incentives and vigorous efforts, they have been unable to diversify, and they need help from the state level. State governments have more revenue flexibility. Most of them have found taxation of consumption both suitable and responsive to their needs, but thirty-odd tax income, individual and corporate, and all but one levy death and gift taxes. Several minor taxes are limited to a few states. Severance taxes, now important only for Texas and Louisiana, can be utilized only by states with significant mineral extraction. Document and stock transfer taxes can raise revenue only for states like New York, which have a heavy volume of transfers of intangible property.

The major sources of revenue, state and local, are examined in detail in the chapters that follow. The fact that all or most state governments utilize a tax does not mean that they utilize it in the same fashion. Diversity of practices is the rule, and diversity may be on the increase. Some part of the diversity creates interstate conflict. State governments choose forms of tax by which they hope to maximize their revenues with little consideration of the national impact. Since the future weight of state taxes seems likely to increase, so also will temptations to be predatory. Congress may intervene to specify ground rules which state governments must observe. And *within* states intervention by state governments to reform the property tax, especially local diversities in assessment, seems indicated.

For many decades neither state nor local governments have depended wholly upon revenue derived from their own sources. Annual intergovernmental transfers have been made, principally through grants-in-aid. The grants, discussed in detail in Chapter III, have served a multitude of purposes, not all of them harmonious. This growth nonetheless appears to indicate a strong legislative belief in their merits.

CHAPTER III

Intergovernmental Transfers

"As a result of many developments, the grant has become a fully matured device of cooperative government." Commission on Intergovernmental Relations, *A Report to the President* (1955).

A VERY IMPORTANT DEVELOPMENT during the past forty years has been the proliferation of *intergovernmental transfers,* especially in the form of grants and shared taxes. These transfers of funds originate either with (a) the federal government, flowing to the states and, in a smaller volume, to local governments; or with (b) state governments, flowing to local governments.[1] In 1963 federal payments totaled $8,507 million, and state payments totaled $11,885 million. The likelihood is that the scope of both flows will be enlarged both absolutely and relatively.

Federal Intergovernmental Transfers

The dominant type of federal intergovernmental transfer is the grant-in-aid which, in 1963, accounted for 96 percent of total federal intergovernmental transfers. Small amounts are in the form of shared revenues (most of which go to the states with large federal acreage), and net loans and repayable advances.[2] In the following pages attention will be focused entirely on grants.

[1] A modest flow from local to state governments—$247 million in 1963—will not be examined here.

[2] In 1963 shared revenues totaled $168.5 million; net loans and repayable ad-

Federal to State Governments

The history of federal aid for certain functions, notably road construction and education, is quite old. In 1802, when Ohio was admitted as a state, Congress declared that 5 percent of the proceeds from the sale of public lands in the state should be applied to the construction of roads, and this precedent was followed for other Western states. In 1816 Congress provided that states be given 5 percent of the net proceeds of land sales within their boundaries with the stipulation that 3 percent be used "for the encouragement of learning, of which one-sixth part shall be exclusively bestowed on a college or university." Thereafter, Congress ceded millions of acres as an endowment for public schools, and, by the Morrill Acts, gave both land and money to establish colleges in every state. These early grants were outright donations with no matching requirement and no federal supervision. Not until 1887, when the Hatch Act made grants to each state to establish agricultural experiment stations, did Congress impose the modest condition that a financial report be submitted annually, and not until 1911, by the Weeks Act, which offered grants for forest fire protection, did Congress impose advance federal approval of state plans and federal supervision of performance. Several other federal grants—vocational education (1917), highways (1916), and so forth—were provided in the next two decades.

The great upsurge came after 1932, and the end is not yet in sight. The number of programs in operation is reckoned from sixty to eighty-odd, depending on how the count is made. For the fiscal year 1963 federal expenditure on grants was $7,566 million, a sum equal to 34 percent of state tax revenue.[3] This amount will assuredly grow rapidly because thirty-seven new programs have been

---

vances $184.0 million. For a summary description of the shared revenues, see *Impact of Federal Urban Development Programs on Local Government Organization and Planning,* prepared in cooperation with the Subcommittee on Intergovernmental Relations of the Senate Committee on Government Operations by the Advisory Commission on Intergovernmental Relations (ACIR), 88 Cong. 2 sess. (1964 Committee Print), App. B, sec. QQ.

[3] One general caution is indicated in using the figures in this section. The figures show direct federal payments to state governments, but some incalculable part of these payments is passed on indirectly to local governments.

TABLE 3-1. Federal Grants to State Governments, 1963

(Money amounts in millions of dollars)

Purpose	Amount	Percentage of Total Grants
Public assistance	$2,752	36
Highway construction	2,981	39
Administration of employment security	342	5
Other	1,491	20
All purposes	$7,566	100

Source: U. S. Census Bureau, *Governmental Finances in 1963* (1964), p. 24.

enacted since World War II, many of which are not yet fully in operation.[4]

As Table 3-1 shows, however, in 1963, 75 percent of federal grant expenditure was for public assistance and highway construction. Federal grants for the latter program soared after enactment of the highway aid act of 1956, which greatly expanded federal grants for a thirteen-year period in order to cover 90 percent of the cost of the interstate highway system.

Congressional legislation concerning the annual amount to be appropriated for a grant, the allocation to each state, and the matching requirements, has become more sophisticated over the decades. In the early days Congress appropriated a sum without reckoning what might be required to meet the federal objective which, presumably, justified the grant; it made allocations to the different states according to some simple basis such as population; it specified—if any specification was made—that the states should match the grant according to a fixed ratio, 50 percent/50 percent. Over time, bit by bit, these features have changed. Estimates of the amount needed to accomplish a federal objective are often made, as well as of the amounts needed for each state. And Congress has framed a variety of matching formulas. Suppose, for example, that the annual "program need" in each of two states—one "rich" and

[4] A chronological listing may be found in *Congressional Review of Federal Grants-in-Aid*, Hearings before the Subcommittee of the House Committee on Government Operations, 87 Cong. 1 sess. (1961), pp. 26-30. A current history and description is to be found in ACIR, *The Role of Equalization in Federal Grants* (1964), Part III.

one "poor"—is $1,000,000. In the rich state the annual federal allocation might be $250,000, and the matching ratio 75 percent/25 percent; the state would have to spend $750,000 to earn all of the $250,000. In the poor state the allocation might be $750,000, and the ratio 25 percent/75 percent; this state would have to spend $250,000 to earn all of the $750,000. In this illustration the aid ratio is variable and equalizing.

Most federal grants are "closed," that is, Congress specifies the maximum annual amount to be provided for each state according to formulas which include such factors as population, area, per capita income, incidence of specific diseases, road mileage, and so on. But some federal grants are "open-end," for example, the annual amounts of old age assistance grants per state are determined by the number of needy persons 65 years and over placed on the welfare rolls, and the individual benefit payments (within specified maxima) made by each state. The annual amounts which Congress must appropriate are therefore determined mainly by the states rather than by Congress.

Federal to Local Governments

Federal intergovernmental transfers to local governments totaled $941 million in 1963. Direct federal-local aid originated, in the main, during the depression of the 1930's; it was administered by *ad hoc* agencies—the Federal Emergency Relief Administration, Public Works Administration, Works Progress Administration, and so on. Early in World War II the agencies were liquidated and the

TABLE 3-2. Federal Grants to Local Governments, 1963

(In millions of dollars)

Purpose	1963
1. Education (school operation and construction in federally affected areas)	$342
2. Housing and community redevelopment	371
3. Airport construction	51
4. Waste treatment facilities	51
5. Other grants	126
Total	$941

Source: See Table 3-1.

grants ceased. But in postwar years, as Table 3-2 indicates, a different set of grants has developed, mostly through a process of drift.

Each of the grant categories in Table 3-2 is described below:

1. Education. The federal government provides payments to localities where a marked increase has taken place in school enrollment because of federal activities, and to localities where local taxable resources have been much reduced because of federal ownership of real property.

2. Housing and Community Redevelopment. Federal capital grants finance up to two-thirds (three-quarters by an alternative computation) of the net project cost of slum clearance and urban redevelopment activities. Local housing authorities build and operate low-rent public housing, receiving an annual federal contribution which makes up the difference between the cost of operating a project and the rents.

3. Airport Construction. Most of the federal appropriation—75 percent—is apportioned among the states on the basis of population and land area; 25 percent is granted at the discretion of the Civil Aeronautics Administrator. The purpose of this aid, which may be given either to a state or a local agency, is to establish a nationwide system of public airports.

4. Waste Treatment Facilities. These grants may go to a state or local agency to provide up to 30 percent of the construction cost of sewage disposal facilities. The state pollution control agency must approve such grants.

5. Other Grants. This category includes numerous small grants which are certain to increase. Often they are for city projects, indicating congressional awareness of and interest in the problems of urbanization, and often they go to special-purpose units of government.

It is plausible to argue that direct federal-local grants are not compatible with the logic of federalism, and are, moreover, administratively awkward. To work through fifty states would appear to be better than to work through thousands of local governments. But difficult cases have operated to impair this general position. For instance, when the federal government, by extensive construction and operation of defense facilities in small geographic areas, swells the school enrollment while not adding to taxable local real property, federal grants to construct and operate schools seem justifiable. Debate over whether or not the state government should be the intermediary seems academic.

On their face, the other types of grants to local governments listed above offer less plausible grounds for direct federal-local action. But the fact is that most state governments have *not* been interested in urban renewal, low-rent public housing, and airport construction. Irresponsive to urban needs, the states did not resist federal-local action. Accordingly, a direct federal-local relationship developed, federal aid being provided on a contractual basis to numerous local agencies without an intervening state authority; the interests of the state in the activity, as well as its responsibility to its local governments, were sidetracked. The Kestnbaum Commission endorsed direct federal-local relationships "where States have failed to take positive action in the field of housing and urban renewal." But it pointed out that the federal government had "deliberately sought direct relationships with local governments in the field of housing" without attempting to bring in state governments. The Commission recommended that the federal government should "take into full partnership those States willing to assume increased responsibilities."[5]

The problems, as well as the solution favored by Congress, are illustrated by the debate in 1946 over the law authorizing federal grants for airport construction. The enabling legislation specified that any "public agency" (usually a municipality) could request federal aid for airport construction. At issue was whether the state governments should be required to establish state aviation agencies through which the request was to be channeled. Should the federal aid itself be channeled through the agencies? A precedent was the federal aid program for highway construction where such requirements had worked well for many decades. With respect to airports, however, the fact was that many states had no agency and appeared uninterested. In 1946 the airport bill passed by the House did not, and the Senate bill did, require channeling. A compromise position

[5] Commission on Intergovernmental Relations, *A Report to the President* (1955), pp. 228-29. Hereinafter referred to as the *Kestnbaum Report*.

emerged: if states chose to require the channeling of requests and federal aid through a state agency, they could; if states did *not* wish to require such channeling, direct federal-local dealing was permitted.

This remains present policy. Congress prefers to operate grants through a state program and will defer to state opinion, but it recognizes also that an overstrict and doctrinaire position would impair or destroy some desirable programs. Moreover, many city officials want direct federal-local grants, and they are supported by some interested federal administrators. For example, Patrick Healy, Executive Director of the American Municipal Association, declared that "entirely too much stress was placed in the [Kestnbaum] report on maintaining a chain of command through the States for all Federal aid or grant programs. We do feel that there is considerable merit to a direct Federal-local, that is city, relationship, and we are, by and large, satisfied with this relationship on the basis of going Federal-aid programs."[6] And recently when the Advisory Commission on Intergovernmental Relations (ACIR) recommended that federal grants for urban development programs be channeled through the states, minority dissent was expressed by Robert C. Weaver, Administrator of the Housing and Home Finance Agency; by Don Hummel, formerly Chairman of the American Municipal Association; by three city mayors; and by Senator Muskie.[7]

Problems Raised by Grants

The proliferation of grants, piecemeal, has raised problems which until recently were not perceived by Congress. Once put into operation, grants live on, even though the original national purposes behind them have altered or been achieved. Over the decades, an unforeseen and unjustifiable diversity in specific conditions to be met by the states—in mode of apportionment, in the basis for

[6] *Federal-State-Local Relations,* Hearings before a Subcommittee of the House Committee on Government Operations, 85 Cong. 1 sess. (1958), p. 109.

[7] *Impact of Federal Urban Development Programs on Local Government Organization and Planning,* p. 30. The recommendation of the majority of the ACIR was to hold only where a state "(a) provides appropriate administrative machinery to carry out relevant responsibilities, and (b) provides significant financial contributions. . . ."

matching, in administrative rules, and so forth—grew up. In the future, Congress should appraise its objectives more carefully before inaugurating new grants.

Moreover, federal grants altered the financial decisions of state governments; the bait of federal money led state legislatures to spend more in directions chosen by federal authority. The theory was that, in terms of the national interest, performance of specific services needed stimulus which federal grants would provide. It was imperfectly realized that matching requirements of federal grants would absorb larger portions of state-local tax revenues in poor than in rich states. In 1962, the portions for Delaware, Connecticut, New Jersey, New York, and California were under 6 percent; those for Mississippi, South Carolina, Arkansas, Alabama, and Tennessee ranged from 10 percent to 18 percent. And Congress did not appreciate that state legislatures, in order to finance the services eligible for federal aid, would sometimes divert state money from services not eligible for federal aid.

A notable illustration is found in expenditure for public assistance. State and local expenditure for four categories of public assistance—old age, dependent children, the blind, and the permanently and totally disabled—are eligible for, and receive, substantial federal grants; expenditure for *general assistance,* a catch-all group covering needy persons not in the four categories, is ineligible. Beyond question state and local expenditure on general assistance is skimped, especially in the poor states. Some idea of the contrast in provision of public assistance among the states in 1962 is given in the following list showing the ratio of payments for old-age assistance to those for general assistance in three poor states and three rich states.[8]

Poor States		Rich States	
Mississippi	199:1	Delaware	.6:1
Oklahoma	75:1	New Jersey	1.3:1
Tennessee	56:1	New York	1.6:1

The ratio of payments for old-age assistance to those for general assistance was very much higher in Mississippi, Tennessee, and Oklahoma—the poor states—than in New Jersey, New York and

[8] Social Security Administration, *Annual Statistical Supplement,* 1962, p. 111.

Delaware. For every dollar spent on general assistance in Mississippi, $199 is spent on relief to the aged. Recently an official in the Alabama Department of Pensions and Security, testifying before a congressional committee, agreed that potential recipients of general assistance were not adequately taken care of. Asked why this happened, she replied: ". . . It is the feeling of the legislative groups that such funds as are made available should be utilized in a manner to bring the best results to the greatest number of people. Therefore, they think they should be used for Federal matching purposes primarily."[9]

Political scientists are concerned because federal grants often impair the political powers of state legislatures and governors. Undoubtedly federal grants bring some loss of state self-government. Functions nominally in state hands come to be federally conditioned and defined; state money must be committed for purposes, and in amounts, beyond state decision; close liaisons are established between state and federal technicians to the detriment of control by state legislatures and governors.

Equalization

Inevitably federal grants redistribute income among the states, not indeed as an explicit federal objective, but as a by-product.[10] This equalizing effect is an important—and controversial—issue.

Through the use of grants, Congress has sometimes sought to enable all states to establish certain types of programs. It has therefore provided allocation and matching funds so that at least a minimum program is feasible, even for "poor" states. The interstate redistribution so produced may be called *formula equalization.*

[9] *Federal-State-Local Relations: State and Local Officials,* Hearings before a Subcommittee of the House Committee on Government Operations, 85 Cong. 1 sess. (1959), p. 1323.

[10] One common criticism is that grants simply take money away from individual residents of states, bring it to Washington, and then redistribute the money among the states (after deducting "freight charges"). One implication is that the "freight charges" are an unnecessary cost. In fact, federal costs of collection are much less than what it would cost the states to collect the same amount. Another implication is that the federal allocation belongs to the state in which it was raised. This is to misunderstand the purpose of grants. Grant expenditure, like any other federal expenditure, is aimed at national objectives; it should, therefore, be allocated to achieve these objectives.

Explicit recognition is given to differences in the fiscal capacity of states by using some variable which takes account of relative capacity as a factor to determine the allocation of federal funds, or the matching requirement, or both. The variable most frequently used is per capita income. In such case, the annual allocation of grant money to each state for a program is (within limits) inverse to state per capita income, or the matching ratio specified for a state with a low per capita income is smaller than for a state with a high per capita income. Only about one-third of the federal grant programs in operation before 1963 contained explicit equalization provisions; in 1962 the amount distributed to state and local governments in this way was only 18.6 percent of federal grants funds.[11]

Redistribution is produced also by the process of collecting, through the federal tax system, the money which is spent in grants. This may be called *tax equalization.*

A rough indication of the overall redistributive effect of federal grants is provided by grouping states into three broad categories— on the basis of high, middle, or low income per capita—and then examining the per capita grants received by each group. As Table 3-3 shows, receipt of grants in 1963 was generally *inverse* to per capita income. Thus, the richest states received $2.36 per capita from the federal government for educational purposes, and the poorest states, $3.58; the richest received $13.51 per capita for public assistance, the poorest, $19.25. This pattern did not prevail for all types of grants: in particular, grants for employment security varied directly with per capita income. Nonetheless, *aggregate* per capita grants were larger for low-income than for high-income states.

The pattern that emerges from the threefold grouping is impaired when a *state-by-state* ranking of per capita grants and per capita income is examined (see Chart 3-1 and Appendix Table A-12). Some high-income states—Nevada, Alaska, Wyoming—receive relatively *large* grants; some low-income states—Virginia, North Carolina, South Carolina—receive relatively *small* grants.[12] No sin-

[11] *Role of Equalization in Federal Grants,* pp. 71-72.

[12] The ACIR states that the correlation between state per capita income for 1961 and per capita grants by states for fiscal 1962 is —.041, that is, negative but not significantly so. When only grants disbursed on an equalizing basis are counted, the correlation is —.389. When construction grants are excluded, the negative correlation is more marked, —.601. *Ibid.,* pp. 62-63.

TABLE 3-3. Federal Grants Per Capita to State and Local Governments, 1963, for Selected Functions by State Income Per Capita, 1960–62

(In dollars)

Purpose of Grant	United States	Per Capita Grant		
		Per Capita Income		
		17 Highest States[a]	17 Middle States	17 Lowest States
Employment security	$ 1.76	$ 2.05	$ 1.41	$ 1.27
Education	2.82	2.36	2.64	3.58
Highway construction	16.23	14.09	18.99	18.30
Public assistance	14.64	13.51	12.89	19.25
Health assistance	1.79	1.33	1.93	2.72
Miscellaneous welfare services	4.74	4.19	3.96	6.92
Other	2.41	2.42	2.07	2.77
Total per capita	$44.39	$39.96[b]	$43.90	$54.80

Source: Sophie R. Dales, "Federal Grants, 1962–63," *Social Security Bulletin* (June 1964), p. 21. For further details, including state rankings in per capita income and grants, see Appendix Table A-12.

[a] Includes the District of Columbia.

[b] Due to rounding, columns do not always add up precisely.

gle explanation of the deviations is adequate, but one major cause relevant to certain high-income states is that Congress has in several instances allocated grants to the states according to criteria—area, road mileage, and public land acreage, for example—which, while relevant to certain objectives of a grant program, are unrelated to state population or income. Another major cause of deviation from the overall pattern, relevant to certain low-income states, is that these states have chosen to make relatively small welfare expenditures.

MEASUREMENT OF THE REDISTRIBUTION. A rough measurement of the relative strength, by states, of (a) tax equalization, and (b) formula equalization will be offered.

This measurement requires the use of estimates of state-by-state federal *tax incidence*. Figures which show merely where taxes were collected do not, in many cases, indicate tax burden. The true burden of the sales tax, for example, falls on the consumer, although it is the seller who formally pays the tax. Unfortunately, calculation of incidence requires assumptions which are disputable

CHART 3-1. States Ranked by Per Capita Income, 1962, and Per Capita Grants, 1963

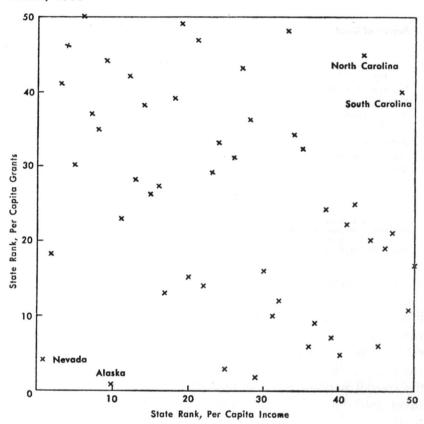

Source: Appendix Table A-12.

TABLE 3-4. Estimated Per Capita Incidence of Federal Taxes for the United States and Selected States, 1962[a]

State	Per Capita Tax Incidence	Ratio of Per Capita Tax Incidence to Average Tax Incidence
United States (average)	$ 516	1.00
Delaware	1,072	2.08
Connecticut	801	1.55
Arkansas	236	.46
Mississippi	196	.37

[a] For additional data on all states, see Appendix Table A-13.

and, accordingly, the results are approximations, dependent on the assumptions. Verification is not feasible, since the different results of estimates depend simply upon different assumptions. The figures offered here should therefore be interpreted with caution; quantitative expression does not remove limitations inherent in estimated figures.

The figures of tax incidence used here were calculated by the Tax Foundation.[13] According to these data, in fiscal 1962 Delaware was the state with the highest per capita federal tax incidence ($1,072), and Connecticut was the next highest ($801). The per capita incidence figure in Connecticut was 1.55 larger than the per capita figure for the nation ($516): when, therefore, the federal government collected $1 in taxes from the average resident of the nation, it collected $1.55 from the average resident of Connecticut (see Table 3-4). Mississippi and Arkansas were the lowest and the next to the lowest states in per capita tax incidence. When the federal government collected $1 in taxes across the nation, it collected only $0.37 in Mississippi.

Using the ratios of tax incidence, it is possible to arrive at a measure, state by state, of the redistributive effect of (a) federal grants *to* states and (b) federal taxes collected *from* states to pay for these grants. The following computation involves three steps: (1) calculating the *total* redistribution accomplished in fiscal 1963 by

[13] *Allocating the Federal Tax Burden by State*, Research Aid No. 3, Revised (1964); *Facts and Figures on Government Finance* (1962-63), p. 112.

federal tax collections *plus* grant formulas; (2) segregating the part of this total redistribution attributable to the differential granting formulas; and (3) subtracting (2) from (1) to estimate the redistribution attributable to federal taxation *alone*. With these data, state-by-state comparisons of the redistributive effect of formula and tax equalization, taken separately or together, can be analyzed.

(1) In fiscal 1963 the federal government distributed $43.85[14] per capita in grants to state and local governments; in order to provide the grants, it *collected* this amount from the average resident of the nation. (The assumption is made here that taxes collected in 1962 provided the funds for grants distributed in 1963.) Thus, it is estimated that residents of Connecticut paid $69.97 per capita ($43.85 $\times$ 1.55); in fiscal 1963 Connecticut received $36.54 per capita in federal grants. The negative differential between the two amounts ($69.97 and $36.54) was, therefore, $33.43 per capita. Mississippi, the state with the *lowest* per capita incidence of federal taxes, was in the opposite situation. Its per capita collection of taxes for the grants was $16.22 ($43.85 $\times$ 0.37). Since in fiscal 1963 Mississippi received $59.14 per capita in grants, its positive differential was $42.92 per capita ($59.14 — $16.22).

(2) The next step is to calculate the amount of redistribution in these figures attributable to the *formulas* used in the grant programs. A reasonable assumption is, perhaps, that a *neutral* formula would allocate grants according to population, that is, the amount per capita provided for each state would be uniform. Under such a scheme Connecticut and Mississippi in fiscal 1962 each would have received $43.85 per capita. In actual fact, their per capita grants were, respectively, $36.54 and $59.14. Therefore, the *allocation formulas* gave Connecticut a negative differential of $7.31 per capita, and Mississippi a positive one of $15.29.

(3) The allocation differential (2) is then subtracted from the *total* redistribution accomplished in fiscal 1963 by federal tax collections *plus* grant formulas (1). The redistribution attributable to federal *taxes* alone gave Connecticut a negative differential of $26.12 per capita ($33.43—$7.31), and Mississippi a positive one of $27.63 (42.92—$15.29).

[14] The grant figures used here and in Appendix Table A-14 exclude shared revenues. This refinement seems desirable because, for a few states, shared revenues are fairly large.

TABLE 3-5. Per Capita Redistribution of Income Attributable to Federal Grant Formulas and Tax Incidence in Connecticut and Mississippi, 1962

State	Grant Formulas	Tax Incidence	Total
Connecticut	−$ 7.31	−$26.12	−$33.43
Mississippi	+ 15.29	+ 27.63	+ 42.92
	Percentage Distribution		
Connecticut	23%	77%	100%
Mississippi	36	64	100

Source: Appendix Table A-14.

As Table 3-5 shows, the relative redistribution accomplished by federal taxes was considerably greater than that accomplished by grants for both Mississippi, a "poor" state, and for Connecticut, a "rich" state. Scrutiny of figures for all the states (see Appendix Table A-14) indicates the greater weight of tax equalization, especially for the richer states. But exceptions are frequent because, as previously noted, the distribution of grants to the states is determined by numerous variables, many of which are not equalizing. Nevada, a state with a high per capita income, receives large federal grants, and these outweigh the negative redistribution accomplished by federal taxes. South Carolina, a state with a low per capita income, receives small federal grants—less than it would receive if the grants were allocated per capita. Accordingly, the positive redistribution accomplished through federal taxes is reduced.

The interstate redistribution through taxes is, it must be emphasized, wholly an accidental by-product, since Congress shapes the tax system without consideration of any particular grant or of grants in the aggregate. Nonetheless, the knowledge that tax redistribution takes place does limit the willingness of Congress to provide much additional redistribution through grants. Moreover, the ACIR has pointed out that, while equalizing formulas are appropriate in welfare programs in order to enable "poor" states to achieve minimum service levels consistent with national objectives, they are inappropriate for grants aimed at encouraging planning and experimentation.[15] And when grants are developmental, such as those

[15] *Role of Equalization in Federal Grants*, pp. 56-60 and 74-75. The ACIR points out that other federal expenditures, when allocated by states, greatly exceed the amounts of federal grants (p. 52).

for highway construction, allocation of funds by states should
not be on an equalizing basis, although equalizing matching-ratios
may be appropriate. Highway construction, for example, should be
determined by traffic needs. If, on this basis, approved highway
projects in two states—one rich and one poor—are estimated each
to cost $1 million, the federal grant might, say, be set at 30 percent
of cost for the former and 60 percent of cost for the latter.

One other factor should be considered here. Federal grants are
an alternative to federal assumption of responsibility for an activity.
Use of grants means that *some part* of the cost of the activity remains with state and local governments, and they provide this part
through a regressive tax system. Such a procedure brings about less
interstate redistribution of income than would complete federal assumption of the activity.

Fiscal Effort as a Condition of Receiving a Grant

In the future development or reform of granting procedures,
Congress might well set requirements for eligibility by specifying (a)
the minimum level of program provision that would be acceptable
even in low-income states, and (b) the *fiscal effort* required of state
and local governments in a state as a condition and determinant of
the amount of the federal grant. How fiscal effort should be defined
has not been adequately explored. Not long ago academic opinion
seemed prepared to express it as a percentage of personal income
per state, but possibly this simple concept is inadequate. A recent
staff report prepared for ACIR explored this problem, showing in
particular that dissimilar results are obtained when capacity is measured by the "representative tax system"[16] and by income received
by residents of a state. The report does not attempt to resolve the
relative merits of the different approaches. It simply declares that
"fiscal capacity and tax effort indexes can be constructed that would
materially facilitate the formulation of public policies."[17]

Appraisal of Types of Grants

In spite of faults, the device of federal grants has been strongly

[16] See Chap. II, note 5, pp. 41-42.

[17] *Measures of State and Local Fiscal Capacity and Tax Effort,* p. 93. Several
recommendations for reform of the equalization features of federal grants are made
in *Role of Equalization in Federal Grants,* pp. 75-81.

endorsed. The Hoover Commission in 1949 declared that, "in addition to decreasing inequalities of service [grants had] raised the level of all aided services, without transferring functions entirely to the National Government."[18] The Kestnbaum Commission declared that "the grant has become a fully matured device of cooperative government." It went on to state "broad principles" to guide future use of grants. Grants should be confined "to fairly small segments of broad activities" in order to secure a clearer definition of objectives, as well as closer supervision.[19] The Commission was, therefore, not in favor of unconditional grants or even of *block* grants, that is, those for a broadly defined function or activity of state and local governments.

The Committee on Government Operations of the House of Representatives in 1958 took a similar stand. It declared: "While aware of the administrative difficulties caused by the use of special categories within some programs, the subcommittee, nevertheless, is appreciative of the strong legislative reasons for confining grants to narrow segments of a general activity."[20] Narrow definition allowed precise application of a stimulus by the federal government, and any tendency toward rigidity could be offset by allowing "transfer of up to 20 percent of Federal apportionments between the special categories of any program, when such transfer is requested by a governor and approved by the responsible Federal agency as being in the public interest."[21] On the other hand, the Hoover Commission favored block grants "based upon broad categories—such as highways, education, public assistance, and public health—as contrasted with the present system of excessive fragmentation."[22]

On what grounds might a choice be made between use of conditional specific grants and block grants? The former, as the name indicates, have conditions and controls by which the granting government defines the activity to be aided and guides the performance by the recipient government. Most obviously the *conditional* grant

---

[18] *Federal-State Relations,* Report to the Congress by the Commission on Organization of the Executive Branch of the Government (1949), p. 30.

[19] *Kestnbaum Report,* pp. 120 and 133.

[20] *Federal-State-Local Relations,* p. 51.

[21] *Ibid.,* p. 43.

[22] *Federal-State Relations,* p. 36. See also H. F. McClelland, "Financing Decentralization," in *Essays in Federalism* (Claremont Men's College, 1961), pp. 79-82.

is meant to stimulate performance of specific activities. The assumption of the granting government—say the federal—is that an activity is being underperformed at the state-local level. To some extent a national judgment is substituted for a state-local one, since more government resources are pulled toward the activity than would occur without federal intervention. If the outcome is that the "right" total amount comes to be devoted to the activity, all is well. But sometimes distortion occurs—more is spent on the aided activity than on similar and other state-local activities, and indeed sometimes the latter may be deprived of state-local expenditure altogether. As noted above, for instance, federal grants for old-age assistance have induced poor states to overspend on it in relation to the unaided activity of general assistance. Nonetheless, the conditional grant is aimed directly at definable and defined national objectives, and performance can be checked. The appeal of these features to Congress is great. Moreover, the pressures on Congress for grant programs come from groups interested in specifics.

A block grant, for example, one appropriated for public assistance as a whole rather than for specific categories of public assistance, would eliminate detailed provisions concerning categories in favor of broad provisions; it would also remove the stimulus to spending on specific categories in favor of spending on a group of categories. Allocation of expenditure within the group would be a *state* decision: each state could, within limits, apply its own set of priorities. Since some interstate variations in need, as well as variations over time, are to be expected, a block grant could provide flexibility of adjustment. The federal government could forego the provision of specific stimuli, and the imposition of specific standards. Indeed, the main advantage of a block grant, with a minimum of conditions, might be to lighten the financial load borne by some state-local budgets, rather than to stimulate larger expenditure on the function. To persons interested in applying a stimulus, this is a fault, but to those who only wish to shift part of the burden of functions from state and local shoulders, it is not. Block grants seem especially indicated as a technique to consolidate old grants for functions no longer in need of stimulus.

An unconditional grant is simply a block grant not tied even to a broadly defined state-local function. In the United States the federal government has eschewed this type of grant, but in Canada and Australia it has long been in use. In the most recent versions of unconditional grants in these countries, the federal government does not manifest an interest in specific state and local functions; rather it provides revenue which state and local governments may use as they choose. The logic of the grant is that the federal government has an interest in enabling all standard state and local functions to be performed at a foundation (or average) level.

This can be clarified with a simple illustration. Suppose, as in Australia, examination indicated that the governments of two states, even by exerting a tax effort somewhat greater than the other four states, could still only provide their citizens with governmental services somewhat below the average of the other states. The gap would be bridged by an unconditional grant to the two states. Technical decisions concerning relative tax efforts and expenditure standards are made annually by the Commonwealth Grants Commission. While Congress has, in the past, been unreceptive to the unconditional grant, the rationale behind it—limited fiscal equalization among governmental units—is worth attention.[23]

The Number and Structure of Local Governments

Before examining the second broad stream of intergovernmental transfers—the flow from state to local governments—a résumé of the number and structure of local governments will be relevant.

Local governments, constitutionally, are the creatures of the states, and the states have spawned a large progeny. When the first count was made, thirty years ago, the total number of all types of governmental units in the United States was approximately 180,000. By 1942 it had fallen to 155,116 and by 1962 to 91,236, as a result of a steep decline in the number of school districts. (See Table 3-6.) Undoubtedly, in many parts of the United States the number of governmental units is still excessive.

[23] In the summer of 1964 President Johnson created a Task Force on Intergovernmental Fiscal Cooperation to develop ways to strengthen the finances of state-local governments. According to press reports, the task force recommended the use of unconditional grants, to be distributed among the states according to population. *New York Times,* Oct. 28, 1964.

TABLE 3-6. Number and Type of Governmental Units in the United States, Selected Years, 1942–62

Unit of Government	Number			Change	
	1942	1957	1962	1942–57	1942–62
U. S. Government	1	1	1	—	—
States	48	48	50	—	+2
Counties	3,050	3,047	3,043	− 3	−7
Municipalities	16,220	17,183	17,997	+ 963	+ 1,777
Towns and townships	18,919	17,198	17,144	− 1,721	− 1,775
School districts[a]	108,579	50,446	34,678	−58,133	−73,901
Special districts	8,299	14,405	18,323	+ 6,106	+10,024
Total	155,116	102,328	91,236	−52,788	−63,880

Sources: U. S. Census Bureau, *1957 Census of Governments,* Vol. I, No. 1, "Governments in the United States," p. 1; *1962 Census of Governments,* Vol. I, "Governmental Organization," p. 1.

[a] This counts only the so-called "independent" school districts. Another 2,341 "dependent" school systems were in operation in 1962, administered by county, city, or town governments. In four states (Virginia, Hawaii, North Carolina, Maryland) there are no independent school districts; in twenty-three states independent districts are responsible for all public schools; in the remaining twenty-three states, the situation is "mixed." *Ibid.,* p. 4.

An important characteristic of many local governments is the overlapping of three or four—and occasionally seven or eight—layers of governmental units in the same geographic area. There may be school districts, sanitary districts, counties, soil conservation districts, drainage districts, and so on. The diversity among governmental units is apparent in Table 3-7 listing the five states with the lowest and the highest average population per unit, and square mileage per unit.

In terms of public finance, this diversity seldom makes sense. In *rural* areas, small and overlapping units often lack the resources to perform any function with efficiency. State governments have an important responsibility for these situations; certainly they should be careful not to waste resources and perpetuate inefficiency by grants to archaic governmental units. In *urban* areas, governmental units of very unequal financial strength cannot provide a uniform level of service; the infirm ones cannot even provide the minimum level needed for the whole of the urban community.

The problems are most acute and intractable in *metropolitan* areas, which are composed of a central city or cities and a variety of suburban units. In 1962 the 212 Standard Metropolitan Areas

TABLE 3-7. States with Highest and Lowest Population and Square Mileage per Governmental Unit, 1962

Average Population per Governmental Unit			
Lowest		*Highest*	
North Dakota	212	Hawaii	33,000
Nebraska	290	Virginia	10,963
Mississippi	291	Maryland	9,065
Kansas	410	Rhode Island	8,826
Montana	511	Massachusetts	8,792
Average Square Mileage per Governmental Unit			
Lowest		*Highest*	
New Jersey	5.6	Alaska	10,287.7
Pennsylvania	7.3	Nevada	806.9
Illinois	8.7	New Mexico	397.6
Delaware	9.9	Hawaii	305.9
Rhode Island	12.4	Arizona	300.5

Source: "Governmental Organization," pp. 27–28.

of the nation contained about two-thirds of the total population; they had 18,442 units. The Chicago metropolitan area alone contained 1,060 units distributed as follows:[24]

Counties	6
Townships	114
Municipalities	246
School districts	340
Special districts	354
Total	1,060

While unification is understandably difficult, problems of sanitation, water supply, police, and transportation do need coordination. Sometimes functional intergovernmental schemes which do not change the existing governmental structure have been put into operation, for example, the Metropolitan Water District of Southern California. But more complete structural integration is often desirable even though annexation, the technique favored a few decades

[24] "Governmental Organization," p. 124.

ago, has been halted in many states by the opposition of suburban areas.

In recent years a new type of local unit, the *special district,* has grown in numbers—from 8,299 in 1942 to 18,323 in 1962. These districts have peculiar features: they are created usually to perform a single function; they overlap geographically; except for school districts, most of them do not depend on taxation. Their growth, which is symptomatic of the local government's weakness in performing an activity, injures local government. While most of the blame is to be placed on the states, the federal government must bear a share because a good many special districts have been created through its "direct advocacy."[25] Specialists in the Department of Agriculture prefer to deal with officials of soil conservation districts (2,461 in 1962) rather than with county officers. Federal specialists in housing prefer to deal with officials of housing and urban renewal districts (1,099 in 1962) rather than with city officers. The pragmatic tendency of federal agencies to develop local counterparts has complicated local government structure and encouraged isolation of units within an urban area. Against the short-run convenience of special purpose districts must be set the long-run confusion arising out of uncoordinated area development.

The organization of local governments is not, to be sure, merely a matter of administrative and fiscal efficiency. In a democracy a wide variation in performance is—and should be—tolerated. The present variation, however, far exceeds acceptable limits. Moreover, the obstacles to change here are patent and powerful: local loyalties, vested interests, urban-rural antagonisms, the inertia of status quo. States have often made change difficult by constitutional and statutory provisions. Some state constitutions, for instance, prescribe a pattern of local government. Debt and tax limits for local governments are widespread, and their operation sometimes reinforces the maintenance of overlapping units because the pyramided separate limits of all the units in a given geographic area add up to a total beyond what might be allowable by the electorate if consolidation were put into effect.

Yet the record of recent years proves that, given the will, much

[25] John C. Bollens, *Special District Governments in the United States* (University of California Press, 1961), p. 250.

can be done. In the twenty years from 1942 to 1962 the number of school districts declined by two-thirds.[26] A forward step would be for the states to remove the self-imposed constitutional and statutory inflexibilities which stand in the way of governmental reorganization. Another would be for them to make enlargement of financial aid to local governments conditional upon progress in structural reorganization. More efficient local governments would allow a larger measure of local financial responsibility in provision of local services. And it is a truth, as well as a truism, to say that only when local governments are strong does democracy flourish.

Intergovernmental Transfers from State to Local Governments

There are two basic types of intergovernmental transfers from state to local governments: (a) grants, that is, appropriated funds, and (b) shared taxes, that is, portions of tax yields. The nature of the distinction between the two is important, even though (for reasons that will become apparent) no specific figures can be offered. State-local *grants* need no special explanation. In the case of *shared taxes,* one level of government—the one most fitted to make efficient collection—assigns all or part of the collections on some basis to the governments which give up the tax. For example, a state government might assume the sole right to tax the income from intangible property, promising to distribute all or some share of the proceeds to local governments according to the place of residence of the owners; or it might assume the sole right to tax motor vehicles as property, promising distribution of the proceeds to local governments according to where the vehicles were principally garaged.

Shared taxes frequently began when a state government withdrew from the base of the general property tax some types of property which could not be efficiently or equitably taxed by local governments. A *quid pro quo* as revenue was assigned to local governments to make the move palatable. In the first instance the states tended to use such criteria as location of the property, prior assessed value of the property, and prior local revenue from the prop-

---

[26] See Table 3-6.

erty. Quite frequently it turned out that because of the greater
efficiency of state administration, the amounts collected by the state
were much in excess of the prior collections of the local governments. Moreover, distribution according to origin of the revenue
favored rich localities. Accordingly, the basis for sharing was shifted,
usually toward some measure of local government need, and
specific directions for use of the revenue were added. A variety of
formulas was framed, the particular outcome depending on the tug
and pull between those local governments wanting to retain a favorable allocation and those wanting a change appropriate to their
needs. As a result, the original basis for tax-sharing has been over-
laid by numerous modifications which usually tend (a) to allocate
the proceeds according to some measure of local need, and (b) to
commit them to designated purposes.

In these two respects the original logic of the shared tax has
been impaired and shared taxes, as now used, have come to resemble conditional grants. An important difference is, however, that the
annual amount shared depends on the amount collected. It is therefore unstable, being larger in boom and smaller in recession years.
This is awkward for local governments, since their spending has the
opposite variation. Moreover, in many states, the criteria for sharing different taxes are varied and complicated. They have grown *ad
hoc* over the decades. At the very least it would make sense to pool
the state collections, to distribute them according to a single formula,
and to reduce earmarking. In such case the shared taxes would
become an unconditional grant *except* that the annual amount
would depend on collections, whereas the amount of a grant would
depend on an annual legislative decision.

The distinction between shared taxes and grants has become so
blurred that the Bureau of the Census does not provide separate
figures for them. Instead, figures for state intergovernmental payments to local governments are offered, split into two categories,
those for *general* local government support and those in support of
specific functions such as education, highways, and welfare. In
terms of the amount of revenue, state sharing is important for income taxes, liquor store profits, motor vehicle licenses and registration fees, gasoline taxes, sales taxes, tobacco taxes, and pari-mutuel
taxes.

State Intergovernmental Expenditures

Intergovernmental expenditure by states on a significant scale is a phenomenon of the 1930's, although a structure had been built up earlier. In 1902, the first year for which the Bureau of the Census supplies figures, this state intergovernmental expenditure was $52 million. It is a mark of the limited scope of state governmental activities that $52 million amounted to 38.8 percent of total state direct general expenditure (see Table 3-8). Local governments were then relatively much more important, and the $52 million received by them from state governments comprised only 6.1 percent of their general revenue. By 1927, state intergovernmental payments had risen to $596 million—totalling 43.2 percent of total state expenditures and 10.1 percent of local general revenue. The 1930's and the postwar period brought further absolute increases. For some years state intergovernmental expenditure has been more than half of state direct general expenditure and nearly 30 percent of local general revenue.

The Functional Distribution of State Aid

Significant changes have taken place, over the decades, in the *functional* distribution of state aid (see Chart 3-2). In 1902 educa-

TABLE 3-8. State Intergovernmental Expenditure, State Direct General Expenditure, and Local General Revenue, Selected Years, 1902–63

(Money amounts in millions of dollars)

Item	Year				
	1902	1927	1938	1948	1963
State intergovernmental expenditure	$ 52	$ 596	$1,516	$ 3,283	$11,885
State direct general expenditure	134	1,380	2,576	6,186	22,491
Local general revenue	854	5,903	6,651	11,373	41,218
State intergovernmental expenditure as a percentage of state direct general expenditure	38.8	43.2	58.8	53.1	52.9
State intergovernmental expenditure as a percentage of local general revenue	6.1	10.1	22.8	28.9	28.8

Sources: U. S. Census Bureau, *Historical Statistics of the United States: Colonial Times to 1957* (1960), p. 728; *Governmental Finances in 1963*, pp. 22–24.

CHART 3-2. Percentage Distribution of State Intergovernmental Expenditure, by Function, Selected Years, 1902–63

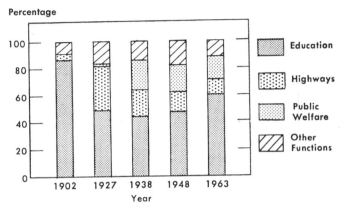

Source: Appendix Table A-15.

CHART 3-3. State Intergovernmental Expenditure as a Percentage of Local Expenditure, by Function, Selected Years, 1902–63

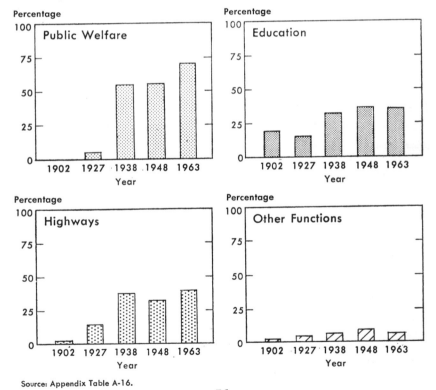

Source: Appendix Table A-16.

76

tion was the major recipient—87 percent of the total; in 1963 it was still the function receiving by far the largest slice—59 percent. But public welfare began to secure important state aid in the 1930's and by 1963 accounted for 16 percent of total state aid.

These developments mean, of course, a great increase in state-local collaboration. Chart 3-3 shows that state governments now provide a good slice of the finance of important functions of local government—over two-thirds of public welfare and over one-third of education and highways—and they give a good deal of direction as well. In some states centralization has gone farther, with complete control of a function assumed by the state government.

The Need for Reform

A major fault of state transfers has been that, by accepting the existing government organization, they have sometimes perpetuated the lives of inefficient units and placed barriers in the way of desirable reforms. In many parts of the United States school districts, for example, have been, and still are, too weak in resources and too small in area and number of children to provide effective educational units. Their boundaries were drawn in the light of conditions —especially transportation—which no longer exist. Some logical reconstitution of units would reduce inequalities in revenue resources and provide a school population relevant to effective organization. Against such a step local loyalties and all the forces of *status quo* will often be ranged, and, as a result, state legislatures have sometimes preferred to distribute state aid without requiring local governmental reorganization. The effect is to strengthen the power of inefficient units to resist reform. State aid is dissipated without accomplishing the objectives which are its justification.

An alternative to state aid is a reallocation of governmental functions so that provision and administration of education, public assistance, and roads (or some designated portion of them) become a state responsibility. Centralization of this sort has progressed in recent decades, especially with respect to highways and public assistance. An improved reallocation of functions would reduce administrative expenses by reducing overhead and duplication. It is, however, no cure-all since centralization at the state level has faults as well as virtues. It runs counter to the idea of "home rule"—that local governments need autonomy in performance of some activities because they are aware of, and responsive to, the variety of local needs. Indeed, the insensitivity of state legislatures to urban needs is so patent that state control over cities should often be weakened rather than strengthened. State aid offers a middle course: it leaves performance of the specific governmental activity in local hands, while providing state financial assistance and a modicum of overall direction.

In postwar years many students have urged that state governments reform their system of intergovernmental transfers. Indeed, usually no *system* exists. Driblets of shared taxes and grants go to local governments for fragmented functions, and by an amazing variety of formulas. Consolidation—pooling of aid and distribution by a simplified formula—would be a clear gain.

The question arises about how much *equalization* is desirable and how it is to be secured. The granting of state aid is moving toward an approach—now only dimly perceived—that first defines the *local need* for different government programs. The second major task is the definition of the *local ability* to finance a foundation program from its own sources. For example, the need for primary and secondary education is often measured in *dollars per pupil in average daily attendance*. Local ability is indicated by what it can raise through taxation at a specified rate on equalized property valuations. Thus, if a minimum program for primary education requires $300 annual expenditure per school child in average daily attendance, and if the local unit could raise $150 per child by levying a property tax at a specified rate (uniform for a type of unit), the indicated grant would be $150 per child. The reader should understand that adequate and objective evidence upon which to base such a quantification of need and ability is not easy to secure. Further, there are objections to expressing the need for some functions, such as education, in money terms.

In any reform of intergovernmental transfers the states should provide some aid as general or unconditional grants—grants without strings and for no specific local function. New York in 1946 moved in this direction by the so-called Moore plan which, among other things, replaced certain volatile shared taxes with a per capita grant for general municipal purposes. The change provided the localities with a stable revenue which they could use for whatever purposes they chose, thereby promoting local autonomy. This promising instance has, however, not been enlarged in New York or imitated elsewhere. State legislatures seem to prefer to provide aid for specific purposes.

CHAPTER IV

State Taxes on Individual Income and Sales

"Whoever hopes a faultless tax to see,
Hopes what ne'er was, or is, or e'er shall be."
McCulloch after Alexander Pope.

BEFORE THE TWENTIETH CENTURY, taxation of individual incomes by the states had a long and unsuccessful history. So marked was the failure that many eminent students of public finance expressed the opinion that failure was inevitable. The key to the failure was ineffective administration. One economist, T. S. Adams, believed that "past failure did not preclude future success," and his faith was justified by the marked success of the Wisconsin tax of 1911. This success rested upon "two administrative innovations": centralized administration and use of information-at-source returns.[1] And the Wisconsin tax, be it noted, antedated the Sixteenth Amendment to the Constitution which made a federal income tax possible.

Taxes on Individual Incomes

Despite the enactment of a federal tax on individual incomes in 1913 and the remarkable extension of federal coverage and rates during World War I, state income taxes at this time experienced a

[1] Clara Penniman and Walter W. Heller, *State Income Tax Administration* (1959), pp. 5-6.

80

wave of popularity. By 1919 nine states and Hawaii were levying the tax. In the next decade five more states were added; by 1937 the total was twenty-nine states plus Hawaii. Thereafter, additions slowed almost to a standstill. Alaska joined the ranks in 1949, West Virginia in 1961, and Indiana in 1963. The total at present is, therefore, thirty-three states.[2] Over one-third of the population is free from individual income tax in its home state, and this population lives mostly in the older industrial states—Connecticut, Illinois, Michigan, New Jersey, Ohio, and Pennsylvania. More and more these states turned to taxing consumption by motor fuel taxes, excises, and general retail sales taxes.

A simple count of the number of states using the individual income tax overstates its importance as a state revenue. In the 1920's it was never better than fifth among the major sources of state tax revenue (see Chapter II). In the 1950's and 1960's, however, it rose to third place, and in 1963 produced 13.4 percent of state tax collections. The improvement is due partly to higher rates, broadened base, improved administration (especially through adoption of withholding), and partly to the great responsiveness of the tax to a rise in gross national product (GNP). According to a recent calculation, every 1.0 percent rise in GNP increases the yield of state individual income taxes by 1.7 percent.[3] But the high elasticity of the individual income tax has a two-way stretch, so that collections decline sharply when GNP declines. As a trend, GNP may confidently be expected to rise, but over the cycle it will rise and fall. This cycle-instability is a worry to state governments because their ability to finance operating deficits by borrowing is limited.

Diversity in State Yields

Although the aggregate yield of the state individual income taxes is unimpressive, the yield in some states is striking. For Oregon in 1963 it was 44.3 percent of all tax collections and, as Table

[2] Plus the District of Columbia, which enacted an income tax in 1939. In addition, New Hampshire and Tennessee levy a tax on interest and dividends, and New Jersey one on the income of nonresident commuters.

[3] Dick Netzer, "Financial Needs and Resources over the Next Decade: State and Local Governments," *Public Finances: Needs, Sources and Utilization,* A Conference of the Universities-National Bureau Committee for Economic Research (1961), pp. 37-38. The elasticity of general sales taxes was reckoned at 1.0 percent, that of state corporate income taxes at 1.1 percent.

TABLE 4-1. State Individual Income Tax Collections, Highest and Lowest Six States, 1963

Percentage of Total State Tax Collections				Dollars per Capita			
Highest Six States		Lowest Six States		Highest Six States		Lowest Six States	
Oreg.	44.3	W. Va.	7.6	Del.	$76.98	N. D.	$9.70
N. Y.	40.6	Ark.	7.4	N. Y.	57.53	Ala.	9.30
Del.	37.5	Ariz.	6.7	Oreg.	54.73	Ariz.	8.69
Wisc.	36.5	Okla.	5.2	Wisc.	53.87	Ark.	7.56
Alaska	33.2	Miss.	3.6	Alaska	52.44	La.	5.42
Minn.	32.7	La.	3.6	Hawaii	45.49	Miss.	3.39

Source: Advisory Commission on Intergovernmental Relations, *Tax Overlapping in the United States, 1964* (1964) (hereinafter referred to as *Tax Overlapping*), Table 49. See also Appendix Table A-17 for additional details. Years are fiscal unless otherwise noted.

4-1 shows, it was 32 percent or more for five other states. On the other hand, the table shows that for some states the yield was very modest.

This same diversity is displayed also by per capita figures (Table 4-1). Per capita collections for the highest state, Delaware, were more than twenty times those of the lowest state, Mississippi. The six states with the highest per capita collections collected 48 percent of total collections—Delaware, New York, Oregon, Wisconsin, Alaska, and Hawaii—although their population was only 21 percent of the total population of the thirty-three states. Per capita figures do not, of course, take account of the inequality of the states in tax base, rate structures, exemptions, deductions, and so on.[4]

Some Characteristics

In two states, Vermont and Wisconsin,[5] the *personal exemption* is lower than that of the federal tax ($600); twelve states have the same personal exemption as the federal tax,[6] while twenty states

[4] *Tax Overlapping*, Tables 51-53, provides information on these matters.

[5] Vermont: $500 for a single person, $1,000 for a married couple, and $500 for each dependent; Wisconsin: tax credits of $10, $20, and $10 on the final tax are equivalent to exemptions of $435, $870, and $405 for a single person, married couple, and dependent, respectively.

[6] One of them, North Dakota, has an exemption for a married couple of $1,500 rather than $1,200.

TABLE 4-2. Distribution by States of Personal Exemptions in State Income Taxes, 1964

Single Person		Married Couple or Head of Family		Dependents	
Amount of Exemption	Number of States[a]	Amount of Exemption	Number of States[a]	Amount of Exemption	Number of States[a]
$ 435	1	$ 870	1	$ 0	1
500	1	1,000	1	200	1
600	13	1,200	12	300	3
750	1	1,500	2	333	1
800	2	1,600	2	400	3
833	1	1,700	1	405	1
1,000	7	2,000	7	500	4
1,200	1	2,333	1	514	1
1,500	4	2,400	1	600	16
1,750	1	2,500	1[b]	750	1
2,000	1	3,000	3	800	2
2,500	1	3,250	1	1,000	1
5,000	1	5,000	1		
		7,000	1		
	35		35		35

Source: *Tax Overlapping*, p. 118.
[a] Includes the District of Columbia. New Hampshire and Tennessee, which tax income from intangibles only, are not included. New Hampshire allows a $600 exemption to single and married persons, but no credit for dependents; Tennessee allows no personal exemptions or credit for dependents.
[b] In Massachusetts the minimum exemption allowed against earned and business income is $2,500. In the case of a joint return, the exemption is the smaller of $4,000 or $2,000 plus the income of the spouse with the smaller income.

(and the District of Columbia) have a higher one (see Table 4-2). Usually the additional exemption for dependents in these twenty is less than the personal exemption for a single person. For example, the personal exemptions for a single person and a married couple in California in 1964 were $1,500 and $3,000, while the exemption for each dependent was $600.

Twenty-three states (and the District of Columbia) allow an additional exemption on account of age, and twenty-eight (and the District of Columbia) on account of blindness. Five states—Arkansas, Iowa, Kentucky, Minnesota and Wisconsin—provide the personal exemption by a *tax credit*. For example, in Wisconsin, a single person has a tax credit of $10. Since the rate of tax on the first $1,000 of net income is 2.3 percent, this tax credit is equivalent, for the first bracket, to a personal exemption of $435. A $10 tax credit for a spouse is equivalent to an additional personal exemption of $435 —a total of $870.

The variety of personal exemptions can be explained partly on the basis of history. States, when they first enacted their tax, would adopt an exemption acceptable at the time. Thereafter different sets of forces and needs would operate on them and on the federal government, making for diversity.

The statutory rates of the state taxes are graduated[7] to a modest level, the highest being 11 percent (Delaware). Usually there are seven or eight brackets, the top one including a wide range of income, for example, in New York, "over $15,000," in Oregon, "over $8,000." The lower brackets are, therefore, narrow (often with $1,000 intervals) and the effective rates of progression, at first quite steep, flatten out or turn down for incomes above $15,000.[8]

A good many federal practices find their way, with a considerable lag, into the state laws. Thus, in 1963, thirty-one states (and the District of Columbia) allowed a variety of *standard deductions* as an alternative to itemizing; twenty provided an *optional tax table;* twenty-seven (and the District of Columbia) had adopted *withholding* and twenty-one complement it with *declarations of estimated tax.* The very important step of withholding was pioneered by Oregon in 1948 and now only Arkansas, California, Iowa, Kansas, Mississippi, and North Dakota are without it. In all adopting states the increase in collections was strong in the first year because of the transition to current payment coupled with nonforgiveness, so that the taxpayer was liable for any overlap between what was

[7] Except for Massachusetts and Maryland, where income is classified by source, a higher rate being applied to investment income. The effect is to produce rough progression because larger incomes will usually contain more investment income than small. A good many small incomes, nonetheless, are chiefly or wholly from investment, and a few large incomes are chiefly "earned."

[8] *Tax Overlapping,* Table 50, indicates that for 1964 in a "median state" the effective rate of tax for a married couple with two dependents and an adjusted gross income of $5,000 would be 0.5 percent; with an adjusted gross income of $25,000, the rate would be 2.5 percent. In nineteen states some deductibility of federal tax payments is allowed in calculating the state liability. The effect is to reduce progression of the state taxes in the lower brackets and to bring about regression in the higher ones. See Emanuel Melichar, *State Individual Income Taxes,* Storrs Agricultural Experiment Station, Monograph 2, July 1963.

due for the previous year and the current year.[9] A significant long run increase—10 percent on the average—was also experienced. Withholding serves to locate taxpayers who otherwise might not file; it reduces delinquency by keeping taxpayers current; it collects without lag from a growing tax base. Recently compliance has been eased in fourteen states by adoption of the federal tax base (with modifications). Starting with adjusted gross income from the federal return, the taxpayer will deduct interest on federal securities (since, constitutionally, this is not taxable by a state), and add interest on securities of other states and of local governments in other states. Before 1963-64, the state tax in Alaska was approximately a flat 16 percent, and in West Virginia, 6 percent, of the federal tax liability.[10] The federal tax cut of 1964 caused a change. In West Virginia, effective January 1, 1963, the state established a rate schedule of its own designed to yield the same revenue as would have resulted if no federal tax cut had been made. Similarly, in Alaska, effective March 5, 1964, a state schedule was enacted with the same objective.

The moves toward conformity with the federal law should not be overstressed. Important differences exist between the federal and the state definitions of taxable income, of which the most important arise out of the allocation of interstate income and definition of residence. Less vital differences occur with respect to income splitting, dividend credits, capital gains, variation in allowed deductions (for example, Minnesota allows campaign contributions and expenses). Much of the variation rests on no better basis than inertia; some is an expression of state experimentation; some, especially with respect to income arising outside the state, grows out of the insoluble problem of state boundaries and a desire to define taxable income so as to tax nonresidents. The cost of the variation in terms of taxpayer inconvenience receives slight consideration.

Residence and Origin of Income

This question arises for the federal tax only with respect to foreign income, since the federal definition of income applies over the nation. But for the states the question of residence is important.

---

[9] Only three states (New York, Minnesota, and Wisconsin) and the District of Columbia provided any significant forgiveness.

[10] Technical qualifications of this statement are disregarded.

The classic solution, proposed in the Model Plan of the National Tax Association in 1919, was that residence of the taxpayer should govern; individuals should be taxed on their entire net incomes by their home state.[11] A state would not tax *nonresidents* on income earned within the state; it would tax *residents* on income earned outside the state. The other approach, pioneered by Wisconsin, was to levy a tax on all income arising in Wisconsin whether earned by residents or nonresidents; it did not tax income accruing to residents from outside Wisconsin. Either plan would eliminate most discriminatory taxation of individual income. The former would favor states where the residents had large investments outside the state; the latter would favor states in the opposite situation.

In law and in practice neither approach has been accepted. In law, most states claim the right to tax the total income of a resident, whatever its origin, and also to tax income originating in the state and going to nonresidents. In practice, the states, while casting a wide net, have moderated the discrimination inherent in their laws through *crediting and reciprocity* provisions by which they allow a credit for income taxes paid by their residents to other states or exempt, on a reciprocal basis, each others' residents.[12]

As indicated in Chapter II, seventeen states have not enacted taxes on individual incomes, and some of the thirty-three utilizing such taxes have employed them sparingly. Most states have chosen

[11] *Proceedings of the National Tax Association,* 1933, pp. 365-74.

[12] *Tax Overlapping,* Table 55, pp. 128-29. Crediting for residents is widespread; that for nonresidents is less usual. Some (currently ten) states require reciprocity as a condition. An illustration of the meaning of reciprocity and crediting is offered for California. There a person is allowed to deduct from his state tax the same proportion of the tax paid in another state as income taxable in the first state bears to total income upon which a tax is paid in the other state, provided the other state reciprocates. California provides a credit to nonresident taxpayers for the tax paid in the other state on the common income—that is, the portion of the income taxed by both states. The amount of the credit is calculated by multiplying the tax paid in the *state of residence* by a fraction, the numerator of which is the income taxed by *both* states and the denominator of which is the income taxed by the state of *residence.* For example, suppose a resident of State X to have a total taxable income in that state of $10,000, of which $2,000 is earned in California. His tax liability in his state of residence is $900. The credit allowed against his California tax would then be $2,000/$10,000 × $900. The result is subtracted from his California tax liability.

to cultivate other sources of revenue, especially taxation of consumption.

Taxes on Sales

Taxation of consumption has taken the form of taxes on particular commodities (selective sales), and on general sales, mostly imposed at the retail level.

Selective Sales Taxes

Selective sales, or excise, taxes are predominantly of two types: (a) benefit taxes, notably those on motor fuel, and (b) sumptuary taxes, for example, those on liquor, tobacco, and pari-mutuels. The rationale of *benefit* taxes is that they are levied *quid pro quo* as indirect prices for public services that yield particular and measurable benefits to individuals. Failure to levy them would be to allow receipt of particular services without particular payments; the cost of such services would then be borne by the community as a whole through general taxes (this subject is examined in greater detail in Chapter VII). The rationale of *sumptuary* taxes on liquor, tobacco, and pari-mutuels is more illusive. The taxes penalize consumption of these things and should fulfill the sumptuary purpose of diminishing their consumption. In fact, in an affluent society the taxes are pushed not hard enough to secure much diminution but hard enough to secure a large revenue. The compromise rationale for this situation seems to be that if particular consumers care to pay a penalty tax, the proceeds to be used for collective purposes, they may continue to consume.

In 1963 more than four-fifths of the state collections from selective sales taxes was sumptuary and benefit (Table 4-3). Taxation of motor fuel is common to all the state governments, and so is taxation of liquor. Three states—Oregon, North Carolina, and Colorado[13]—do not tax tobacco products, and of the twenty-four states that tax pari-mutuels, only a handful secure much revenue thereby. A description of the major groups of state excise taxes follows.

[13] Colorado imposed a tax, effective July 1, 1964.

TABLE 4-3. State Revenue from Selective Sales Taxes, 1963

(Money amounts in millions of dollars)

Tax	Amount	Percentage of Total Selective Sales Tax Collections
Motor fuel	$3,851	52.5
Alcoholic beverages	793	10.8
Tobacco products	1,124	15.4
Pari-mutuels	319	4.4
Other taxes[a]	1,247	16.9
Total	$7,334	100.0

Source: U. S. Census Bureau, *Compendium of State Government Finances in 1963* (1964), p. 12.
[a] Includes excises on insurance ($639 million), public utilities ($437 million), amusements ($23 million), and miscellaneous items ($148 million).

MOTOR FUEL. The first taxes on commodities widely used by the states were on gasoline and tobacco products (especially cigarettes). In 1919 Oregon imposed a gasoline tax, and so productive and acceptable did it prove that by 1929 it was used by every state in the union. During the 1930's and early 1940's it was the most important tax source of state governments, yielding one-quarter or more of their tax revenue (see Chapter II). Gasoline rationing during World War II cut the yield, and taxes on *general* sales became the leading revenue producer, a position that they have not relinquished.

The rates at which the states tax motor fuel are fairly diverse, as shown in the following distribution of states by their gasoline tax rates in January 1964:[14]

Cents per Gallon	*Number of States*
5	6
$5\frac{1}{2}$	1
6	21
$6\frac{1}{2}$	4
7	17
$7\frac{1}{2}$	1
8	1
	51

[14] *Tax Overlapping*, Table 76. Includes the District of Columbia.

There is, moreover, diversity concerning exemptions and refunds. In seven states (particularly Alabama and New Mexico, and to a lesser extent, Florida, Hawaii, Mississippi, Nevada, and Wyoming) local gasoline taxes are also levied, usually at the rate of one cent per gallon.[15]

Federal use of the gasoline tax began in 1932 amid strong state protest at federal trespass. This time the protest rang true: the states had made vigorous use of the tax; their administration of it was reasonably efficient and had brought no significant jurisdictional conflicts. The issue of federal trespass was therefore a real one, and state pressure for federal withdrawal had merit. The issue was, however, sidetracked when Congress, in 1956, not only enlarged federal aid to highway construction, but also provided that, for sixteen years, large slices of revenue from the federal motor fuel tax (as well as from other highway user taxes) be placed in the new Highway Trust Fund and spent for an expanded program of highway construction.

TOBACCO. In 1921 Iowa enacted a cigarette tax, and by 1929 seven other states had followed suit. The depression of the 1930's accelerated adoption of this tax (or a tax on tobacco products). By 1964 forty-eight states and the District of Columbia (all except North Carolina and Oregon) taxed cigarettes, and seventeen imposed excises on other tobacco products. In eight states some local governments tax cigarettes.[16]

In taxing cigarettes the states encountered important administrative difficulties because they had to collect from wholesalers and jobbers within their jurisdiction rather than—as does the federal Treasury—from a small number of manufacturers. Evasion of a state tax took two forms: (1) smuggling, and (2) purchase in interstate commerce.

An early device to defeat evasion was enactment of a state *use tax,* that is, a levy on commodities purchased outside a state but brought into it for use. Applied first to the gasoline tax and then extended to other commodities, the tax gave tax administrators a

[15] *Ibid.,* Table 77.

[16] Of the five hundred municipalities taxing cigarettes, over three hundred were in Florida where the local tax is collected by the state and credited against the state tax. For details concerning the local taxes, see *ibid.,* Table 83.

legal base for enforcement, leaving unsolved the task of finding the commodities on which the tax had not been paid.

The states turned to interstate cooperation, especially by providing lists of consignees to tax administrators in states to which cigarettes were shipped. This device was, however, inoperative when the sellers were located in states that did not tax these items, since no basis for reciprocity existed. Moreover, cigarettes could be shipped by parcel post (as gasoline could not), and dealers, protected by the privacy of the United States mails, did not declare such shipments. The Post Office resisted schemes which would have required it to provide information to the states concerning shipments of tobacco products.

But after World War II, as the number of states imposing taxes on tobacco products grew, pressure for federal help mounted, and in 1949 Congress required sellers of tobacco in interstate commerce to send to tax administrators copies of invoices of every tobacco shipment into their state. This effectively closed a major loophole.

Tobacco taxes have been increasingly productive in the postwar years. In 1963 they produced 5.1 percent of state tax revenue collections, with the top state, New Jersey, securing 12.9 percent and the bottom one, Hawaii, 1.8 percent (Table 4-4).

ALCOHOLIC BEVERAGES. The third bundle of commodities subject to state excises is liquor. After repeal of prohibition the states chose two different methods of controlling, and gathering revenue from,

TABLE 4-4. Distribution of States by Percentage of Total Tax Revenue Collected from Tobacco Taxes, 1963

Percentage of Total	Number of States
0–1.9	2
2.0–3.9	8
4.0–5.9	19
6.0–7.9	13
8.0–9.9	3
10.0–11.9	1
12.0–13.9	1
Total	47

Source: Derived from State Government Finances in 1963, p. 12.

the liquor business. In 1963 thirty-two had chosen the "license" system, raising revenue mostly from a gallonage excise and license charge; sixteen had chosen the "monopoly" system of state stores, raising revenue chiefly from profits.[17] No details of the state-by-state variation in pattern can be offered here. For 1962 the revenue summary was as follows: state excises on alcoholic beverages, $740 million; licenses, $91 million; state monopoly system, net contribution to general funds, $236 million. Local governments secured $100 million.[18]

The intricate problem of interstate tax conflict and trade barriers will only be mentioned. The states used the freedom given them by the Twenty-first Amendment to the Constitution, which excluded alcoholic beverages from the protection given to interstate commerce, to levy liquor taxes and license charges as trade barriers in order to protect local producers and distributors. A counter-agitation developed against such practices which halted further growth of discrimination, although it did not remove that already in existence.

General Retail Sales Taxes

DEVELOPMENT. The success of selective excises (particularly on motor fuel) as revenue producers held back state taxes on general retail sales. The states were, besides, afraid that taxation of sales might cause migration into tax-free states, and conscious that the Supreme Court had been zealous in barring taxation of all transactions of an interstate character. Sales made by merchants to customers outside a taxing state, and sales made by merchants who were outside a taxing state to customers in a taxing state, could not be taxed. The effect of this strict Court interpretation was to discriminate in favor of interstate commerce.

The depression of the 1930's broke through some of the obstacles, and it turned out also that the Supreme Court relaxed its constitutional interpretation. The states perceived that a general sales tax was a source of revenue which, unlike income taxation, held up

---

[17] In North Carolina the stores are county-operated under state supervision. Mississippi is officially "dry."

[18] Details concerning state and local taxes are provided in *Tax Overlapping*, Chap. 13.

in bad times. Moreover, Congress indicated clearly in 1931-32 that
a federal sales tax was unacceptable. The states, worried by the col-
lapse of the property tax and the desperate plight of local governments, saw sales taxes as a means of financial salvation. In 1933
thirteen states enacted a general tax on retail sales, and by the end
of 1938 eleven more states had followed suit—a total of twenty-
four. World War II halted the swing, but afterward, as states prepared to finance the backlog of demands bottled up during the war,
there came a second wave of sales taxes. In 1944 the general retail
sales tax became the most important tax source of state governments, and its lead has widened in the years since. By 1963 thirty-
seven states (and the District of Columbia) imposed the tax, and it
accounted for 24.5 percent of their tax collections.

Chart 4-1 and Tables 4-5, 4-6, and 4-7 give an indication of
the interstate variation in the significance of the tax. For thirty
states in 1963 it produced more than one-quarter of their tax revenue; for twenty-eight it yielded over $30 per capita. The range of

**CHART 4-1. Distribution of States by General Sales Tax and Individual
Income Tax Collections Per Capita, 1963**

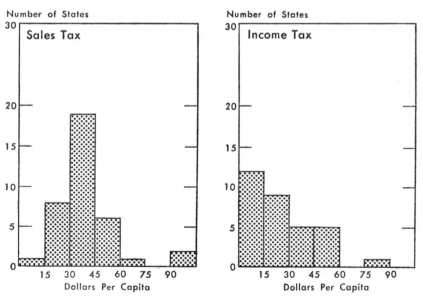

Source: Table 4-5.

TABLE 4-5. Distribution of States by General Sales Tax and Individual Income Tax Collections Per Capita, 1963

Dollars Per Capita	Number of States	
	Sales	Income
Under $15.00	1	12
15.00–29.99	8	9
30.00–44.99	19	5
45.00–59.99	6	5
60.00–74.99	1	0
75.00–89.99	—	1
90.00 or over	2	0
	37	32

Source: *State Government Finances in 1963*, p. 47.

rates—from 2 percent to 5 percent—is shown in Table 4-7.

Meanwhile, *local* governments have utilized the tax, following the examples of New York City in 1934 and New Orleans in 1938 (see Chapter VII). After the war local sales taxes spread to California, Illinois, Mississippi, Utah, and, in small degree, to a few other states. In 1963 about 2,000 local governments imposed the tax, most notably in California and Illinois.[19] In six of the thirteen states with local general sales taxes, collection is facilitated by state-local coordinated action; in seven the tax is locally administered. While the aggregate revenue secured—$1,065 million or 4.8 percent of local tax revenue in 1963—may seem modest, to the great cities of New York, New Orleans, and Los Angeles the tax brings in over one-quarter of their total tax collections.

SOME CHARACTERISTICS. The state (and local) governments chose retail sales as the base of their tax. Some states have few manufacturing concerns, and others many, which ship across state lines. If a state were to tax sales at the manufacturing level, this would burden these concerns compared with competitors outside the state; it would, besides, raise complications concerning interstate commerce. Taxing at the retail level avoids or limits these difficulties.[20]

[19] See *ibid.*, Table 45 for the number in each state, and the rates.
[20] In Chap. V difficulties with respect to interstate commerce through *use taxes* are examined.

TABLE 4-6. Distribution of States by Percentage of Total State Tax Revenue Collected from General Sales Tax, 1963

Percentage of Total	Number of States
Under 10.0	1[a]
10.0–19.9	4
20.0–24.9	2
25.0–29.9	8
30.0–34.9	12
35.0–39.9	5
40.0–44.9	2
45.0–49.9	1
50.0 or over	2[a]
	37

Source: *Tax Overlapping*, Table 42.
[a] Wisconsin, 9.2 percent; Illinois, 50.5 percent; Hawaii, 50.8 percent.

The tax as employed is, therefore, approximately a single-stage tax on retail sales. Sales for resale are excluded from the base, and so also are most sales to industrial consumers. The latter exclusion is provided imperfectly by two common tests, the *ingredient* test and the *direct use* test. The ingredient test removes from the tax base property that becomes an ingredient of a product to be sold; the direct use test removes property used directly in producing goods to be sold. But neither rule excludes completely from the tax base sales of supplies used in industrial processes. Sales of office supplies and of fuel, for example, are included in the base. While complete

TABLE 4-7. Distribution of States by General Sales Tax Rate, 1964

Tax Rate	Number of States
2%	9
$2\frac{1}{4}$	1
$2\frac{1}{2}$	1
3	19[a]
$3\frac{1}{2}$	3
4	4
5	1
	38

Source: *Tax Overlapping*, Table 43.
[a] Includes the District of Columbia.

exemption of goods that have a consumption and a production use would not be justified, the result of inclusion in the base is multiple taxation. The tax on the goods used in production is shifted forward and becomes a cost of the relevant consumer goods which, in turn, are taxed when sold at the retail level. In addition to a tax at the retail level of 3½ percent and 3 percent, respectively, Hawaii and Mississippi levy fractional rates on wholesale transactions; Hawaii levies a fractional rate at the manufacturing stage.[21]

A general retail sales tax should logically include *services* in the base. In fact, most services are excluded, and thereby a considerable slice of consumers' expenditures is not taxed. It is, however, common to include in the base admissions, transient lodging, meals served in restaurants, and some public utility services (sales of gas and electricity, telegraph, and telephone services). Some states, on grounds of equity, exclude specific categories of tangible consumer goods—medical supplies and food for home consumption in ten, and medicine only in three more. Three states exempt clothing.

In almost two-thirds of the states the tax rate is uniform (commonly 3 percent) for all taxable items. All the sales-tax states have supplementary *use* taxes, applicable to goods bought outside the state and brought into it for consumption. In 1937 the Supreme Court in *Henneford et al v. Silas Mason Co.* (300 U.S. 577) upheld the use tax, declaring that the tax was not on interstate commerce, but on the privilege of use after commerce had ended. Since then the constitutional basis of sales and use taxes has been so greatly broadened that serious concern is now expressed that the states will put *discriminatory* burdens on interstate trade.

Information concerning administrative and compliance costs of sales taxes is faulty. Compliance costs fall mostly on retailers, rather than on consumers, and about half the states compensate them for their costs to the extent of 2 to 3 percent of the tax obligation; administrative costs reported by the states run less than $2 per $100 of sales tax revenue.[22] State governments spend too little in seeing that firms remit payment of tax at the required time. A more

---

[21] See *Tax Overlapping*, Table 44 for state rates on services and nonretail businesses.

[22] See Clinton V. Oster, *State Retail Sales Taxation* (1957), pp. 160-62; John F. Due, *State Sales Tax Administration* (Public Administration Service, Chicago, 1963), pp. 225-30. Due provides a careful description and analysis of all aspects of administration.

serious administrative weakness is inadequate audit. The audit staffs are usually inadequate in size, in technical training, and in compensation.

THE CHARGE OF INEQUITY. Beyond question the most weighty criticism of the sales tax has been its inequity. The tax is on consumption, and since consumption must absorb a higher percentage of income for poor than for rich persons, a tax which rests on consumption is *regressive*. Its rate, as a percentage of income, is higher for the poor man than for the rich. The extent of the regression depends on the coverage of the sales tax. Exemption of food, medicine, and clothing reduces regression simply because low-income persons have relatively high expenditure for these items. But exemptions narrow the tax base, and discriminate in favor of persons who consume relatively large amounts of the exempt items. This discrimination may accord with social policy, but it complicates administration and therefore induces or allows evasion. A firm that sells exempt and non-exempt articles must distinguish between them in its accounts. Besides, definition of food, medicine, and so on, raises borderline cases which require arbitrary decisions. Are candy, coffee, and Coca-Cola to be defined as "food"? In Ohio the answer for coffee is "yes," for Coca-Cola "no." Every exemption is, in effect, a subsidy to consumers of the untaxed product, and therefore requires justification.

A recent Wisconsin study reckoned the incidence or burden of three alternative sales taxes with approximately the same aggregate yield despite a different rate or base. Table 4-8 shows the "effective" rates of these alternative taxes for different classes of residents (families and unrelated individuals)—that is, the rates as percentages of adjusted gross income. For all three alternative taxes, the effective rate pattern is consistently and moderately regressive, with not much difference in the degree of regression. The decline in effective rates is abrupt from the first bracket of adjusted gross income ($0-999) to the second, but thereafter the decline is gradual.[23]

---

[23] The severe regressivity of the first bracket is, to some extent, a statistical mirage. Some of the income-receivers in this group are not genuinely and regularly low-income receivers. They may be "supplementary family earners" who earn small sums, but belong to families in higher-income brackets, or persons who have a small income for a year because of temporary factors.

TABLE 4-8. Effective Sales Tax Rates for Wisconsin Residents Under Three Alternative Rate and Exemption Plans[a]

(In percent)

Adjusted Gross Income	Effective Rate		
	A	B	C
$ 0–999	4.54	4.24	4.15
1,000–1,999	2.18	2.17	1.98
2,000–2,999	1.80	1.83	1.66
3,000–3,999	1.59	1.67	1.49
4,000–4,999	1.49	1.58	1.41
5,000–5,999	1.41	1.54	1.35
6,000–7,499	1.30	1.48	1.24
7,500–9,999	1.19	1.37	1.16
10,000 and over	.79	.98	.76
All classes	1.37	1.50	1.30

Source: University of Wisconsin Tax Study Committee, *Wisconsin's State and Local Tax Burden* (1959), pp. 85–86.
[a] (A) A typical or common sales tax which includes in its base most tangible personal property, but exempts most services. The rate is 2 percent.
(B) A similar base except that off-premise food purchases are exempt. The rate is 3 percent.
(C) A similar base, but with inclusion of many services. The rate is 2 percent.
A fourth alternative (D) is examined in the Wisconsin study. Its base is identical to (A), but the effect of a credit or refund of $15 per Wisconsin resident is calculated. The yield of (B), because of the higher rate, was largest (p. 87).

The typical sales tax—alternative A—has, however, the fault not only that the effective rate increases somewhat with the *size of the family,* but that the spread in effective rates is largest for low-income families. When food is exempt, these inequities largely disappear.[24]

How seriously should the regression of the sales tax be regarded? J. K. Galbraith in his widely-read *The Affluent Society*[25] viewed it lightly. He argued that liberal opposition to a more extensive and intensive use of sales taxation was an instance of "conventional wisdom," irrelevant to problems of the present. In an affluent society where most spending by most persons is far above subsistence, moderate regression is unimportant.

A very different position was taken in the AFL-CIO booklet, *State and Local Taxes,* which declared that the most important stan-

[24] Reed R. Hansen, "An Empirical Analysis of the Retail Sales Tax with Policy Recommendations," *National Tax Journal* (March 1962), pp. 1-13.
[25] Pp. 316-17.

dard of judgment in deciding on the goodness or badness of a tax is
equity. By this standard "the most unfair taxes of all . . . are the
sales taxes." Taxes "based on ability to pay and the progressive
principle . . . are the only really desirable taxes."[26]

The reader will be left to weigh the merits of both positions and
to make a choice between them.

The equity argument, whatever weight is given to it, should be
placed in perspective by relating it to the total tax burden borne by
taxpayers. The fact that one tax is regressive or progressive has
significance only with respect to its weight in the total system of
taxes. The sophisticated and abstract argument which has been developed by economists concerning tax sacrifice among individuals
assumes a summation of the sacrifices imposed by the whole system
of taxes. For decisive practical reasons, local governments utilize
regressive taxes. State governments have more freedom, but their
choice concerning tax progression is narrowly limited because taxpayers subjected to high rates in one state can move to others where
the rates are lower. The national government has very much more
freedom, since movement outside the national boundaries for the
purpose of tax avoidance imposes other costs, many of them non-
monetary, of great weight.

The relevant issue, then, is the incidence on individuals of *total*
taxes—federal, state, and local. In pursuit of overall equity, the
regressivity of particular taxes—notably sales taxes, or even the
total taxes of state and local governments—is not very significant.
The results of a recent estimate of tax incidence on families with
different incomes show that while aggregate state and local taxes
are regressive, federal taxes are progressive. *Total* federal, state,
and local taxes impose a proportional burden on all income levels
up to the $15,000 bracket; thereafter, they are progressive (see
Table 4-9).

The arguments and conclusions just presented leave unan-
swered some awkward, if abstruse, questions. Should it be assumed
that Congress determines the progression of the federal tax system

[26] AFL-CIO Publication No. 80 (1958), pp. 10, 70, and 105.

TABLE 4-9. Taxes[a] as a Percentage of Family Personal Income, Calendar Year 1958

Income	State and Local Taxes	Federal Taxes	Total
Under $2,000	11.3	9.6	21.0
2,000–3,999	9.4	11.0	20.4
4,000–5,999	8.5	12.1	20.6
6,000–7,999	7.7	13.9	21.6
8,000–9,999	7.2	13.4	20.6
10,000–14,999	6.5	15.1	21.6
15,000 and over	5.9	28.6	34.4
Total	7.5	16.1	23.7

Source: George A. Bishop, "The Tax Burden by Income Class, 1958," *National Tax Journal* (March 1961), p. 54.
[a] Excluding social insurance taxes.

after consideration of the evidence concerning the incidence of state and local taxes? Does Congress use the federal tax system as an instrument to secure the "right"—the desired—*total* incidence? Evidence in support of the opinion that Congress does so act would be hard to produce, and yet no harder than evidence concerning how Congress resolves many major decisions concerning spending and taxing.

Another difficult, if more niggling, question is: How can Congress make an adjustment in the progression of federal taxes so as to fit the different tax systems of fifty states? A scale of federal progression suitable as an instrument of adjustment to the tax systems of Illinois and Indiana, where taxes on consumption are dominant, would be less suitable for Oregon or Delaware, where they are not. Congress must, it seems, be assumed to aim at adjusting to a hypothetical *average* state and local tax system. This interpretation of the procedure adopted, of necessity, by Congress brings to light a fault of a markedly regressive (or progressive) state tax system. If Congress adjusts the progression of federal taxes to an "average" state system, citizens in a state with a system which diverges markedly from this average secure an imperfect adjustment. The *overall* incidence of taxes for citizens in Illinois will be quite different from that in Oregon.

Sales Tax or Income Tax?

The equity argument over income and sales taxes interweaves with many of the other arguments about the relative merits of these taxes.

Revenue Productivity

Proponents say that sales taxation produces more revenue than income taxation. A 1959 Wisconsin study estimated that a "typical" sales tax at the rate of 2 percent would yield more annually than the existing normal income tax with rates running from 1 percent to 7 percent[27] and tax credits of $7 (single) and $14 (married). Opponents of sales taxation retort that the high revenue productivity grows out of a tax base which leaves no minimum of consumption free from tax. Spending by a worker out of unemployment compensation, or by an aged recipient of old age assistance, is taxed. Only income that is saved, or perhaps spent on services, is not taxed. Opponents usually then extend the attack by declaring that all taxes, regardless of form, are paid out of income. Whatever tax revenue a state legislature wishes to raise could therefore be secured via an income tax which would gauge and allow for individual and family needs on a rational and aboveboard basis.

This logical rationale often fails to persuade the state legislature. The income tax structure which would have to be enacted in order to yield a revenue equal to a sales tax seems likely to raise severe voter opposition and possibly to stimulate migration out of state. Opportunism concerning the form of taxation is bound to be a characteristic of legislatures, not because they are "reactionary," but because they aim to minimize the adverse reactions of voters. Payments of sales tax are somewhat concealed, and even when overt and known the payments are little by little. A taxpayer is always current and never in arrears; a large lump of sales tax is never due at deadlines. Withholding of income tax does, to be sure, capture some of this feature, but each bite is still sizeable. The sensible

[27] *Wisconsin's State and Local Tax Burden,* p. 96. A flat rate earnings tax with no exemptions, as is now levied by some large cities, would yield more than a retail sales tax at the same rate. See Robert A. Sigafoos, *The Municipal Income Tax: Its History and Problems* (1955), pp. 137-39.

opinion that tax burdens on citizens should be explicit, and that concealment is a fraud, seems overstrict to the legislator concerned with short-run responses.

Interstate Mobility and Federal Deductibility

A practical issue of some consequence is the comparative effect of sales and income tax on interstate movement. A state income tax on top of a heavy and steeply progressive federal income tax may seem oppressive and even confiscatory to a high-income person. Shift in domicile to avoid the state tax might result. Proponents of state income taxes sometimes brush aside this possibility by demonstrating the ameliorative effect on progression and on total income tax of federal deductibility. The federal income tax allows payments of state income tax to be deducted from the base of the federal tax. In short, the base of federal tax is income *after* deduction of state income tax payments (and of many other deductible items). The federal Treasury, therefore, collects less federal tax from a taxpayer in an income tax state. If, for example, a taxpayer in 1962 had a taxable income of $3,600 in State A, which had no income tax, his federal tax would be $720 (20 percent of $3,600); a similar taxpayer in State B, which collected $35 in income tax from him, would find his federal tax reduced to $713 (20 percent of $3,600 minus 35), and he, therefore, really paid only $28 more as a result of the state income tax. Similarly, a taxpayer with a taxable income of $27,600 would pay a federal tax of $8,348 in State A; in State B a state income tax of $1,965 would reduce his federal tax to $7,503, making his combined payment only $1,120 more than the single payment in State A. In the face of this situation, why have states been reluctant to use progressive income taxes? Have they failed to appreciate the effects of deductibility?

This illustration, while wholly valid, is defective and unrealistic. State A, *without* an individual income tax, must raise, from alternative taxes, a revenue equivalent to that of State B *with* an income tax. Moreover, the federal income tax law allows individuals the right to deduct state and local sales and most other taxes. If, therefore, State A, which has no income tax, does have a sales tax, taxpayers there can reduce their federal income tax by deducting their state sales tax payments. The relevant comparison is between the aggregate tax levels (federal and state) of taxpayers in States A and B. Is it favorable to one or the other?

Table 4-10 below summarizes the results of an illustrative calculation for two such states, assuming approximately the same total revenue to be produced in each, in one case by an income tax and in the other by a sales tax. For a married taxpayer with two dependents and an income of $3,600 the combined tax bill (state income tax plus federal income tax) in State A is $748; the bill for a similar taxpayer in State B (state sales tax plus federal income tax) is $828, that is, a differential of $80 favorable to residents in State A. But for a taxpayer with an income of $27,600 the combined tax bill in State A is $9,468, compared with a bill in State B of $8,524, that is, a differential of $944 favorable to residents in State B. High-income persons are those most likely to migrate for purposes of tax avoidance. Therefore, a state legislature might choose to enact a sales tax rather than an income tax: it might worry more about interstate migration than equity.

Other Considerations

With respect to *costs of administration,* probably the income tax has a modest advantage over the sales tax—1 percent to 1½ percent of receipts as a cost compared to 1½ percent to 2 percent. With respect to *compliance,* the income tax puts costs chiefly upon the payers of the tax, while the sales tax puts them on retailers.

TABLE 4-10. Combined Federal and State Tax Liability of Married Taxpayer with Two Dependents in States with Income Tax and Sales Tax, 1960

Taxable Income[a]	(A) State Income Tax Plus Federal Income Tax	(B) State Sales Tax Plus Federal Income Tax	Column (A) Minus Column (B)
$ 1,600	$ 320	$ 396	$— 76
3,600	748	828	— 80
7,600	1,748	1,753	— 5
27,600	9,468	8,524	+944

Source: James A. Maxwell, *Tax Credits and Intergovernmental Fiscal Relations* (1962), p. 102.
[a] Before deduction of state tax or other allowed deductions.

Sales taxation has sometimes been favored because part of it can be shifted out of state—to tourists, visitors, and out-of-state buyers of the products of a state. But states also use the income tax to tap nonresidents, as when New York levies on the income earned in the state by commuters from New Jersey and Connecticut. While some states have more ability than others to exact tribute of this sort, one may guess that the net amount of the tribute is exaggerated.

Sales tax and income tax differ significantly in *revenue stability*. The yield of a progressive income tax will vary more over the business cycle than that of a general sales tax. The reasons are twofold: (1) the base of the income tax is the more variable, and (2) its rates are progressive. State (and local) governments favor taxes with stable yields because, in recession, they cannot easily borrow to finance deficits. And yet an income tax with a high built-in revenue flexibility promotes *national* economic stabilization.

Current Trends

In the 1930's and postwar, when sales taxes were being adopted by many states, controversy arose which viewed sales taxation and income taxation as *alternatives*. The debate is still often couched in these terms, even though it has come to be quite unrealistic. In 1963 only three states (Nebraska, New Hampshire, and New Jersey) had neither a general retail sales tax nor an individual income tax, and therefore only this select group is free to make a choice (see Chapter II). Fourteen states eschew an individual income tax and have only a general sales tax; ten have made the opposite choice and have only an individual income tax. State use of income tax might increase if decreased federal use of the tax took the form of credits to taxpayers for payments of state income tax.[28] Without some such push state legislatures seem likely to favor sales tax for several reasons, not least because it is unutilized by the federal government. In 1963 twenty-three state governments utilized *both* income and sales tax. The prospects are for additions to this number. Certainly it is unlikely that states with both taxes will drop one, or that states with one will shift to the other.

[28] Analysis of such a move, and of other federal credits, is provided in Maxwell, *op. cit.*

CHAPTER V

Other State Taxes

"But you must confine yourself within the modest limits of order."
Twelfth Night, Act I, scene 3.

THE IMPERFECT RATIONALE for state taxation of business income is some version of a benefit theory. Business, it is held, owes taxes because of benefits received from the jurisdictions where business is carried on. The states have utilized this rationale to levy an amazing variety of taxes, most of them financially insignificant. Attention here will be confined to income taxes on corporations.[1]

Corporation Income Tax

The modern version of a state tax on corporate income, like that on individual income, started with the Wisconsin tax of 1911. Thereafter, most states, when they enacted income taxes, taxed both individual and corporate income.[2] By 1963 thirty-seven states (and the District of Columbia) had a corporation income tax (Table 5-1).

[1] Of the states that levy no corporation income tax, a few (Ohio, Michigan, and Texas) raise considerable sums by annual *license taxes* on *corporations in general,* and the others raise modest amounts using these taxes. Some states (Delaware, Massachusetts, and New Jersey) with corporate income taxes raise significant additional amounts in a similar way.

[2] In 1963, however, five states—New Jersey, Connecticut, Pennsylvania, Rhode Island, and Tennessee—taxed corporate but not individual income (the New Jersey tax on commuter income, and the Tennessee tax on income from intangibles are not counted); two—New Mexico and West Virginia—taxed individual and not corporate income.

TABLE 5-1. Adoption of State Corporation Income Taxes, 1910–63

Year	Number of States
1910–19	9[a]
1920–29	8
1930–39	15
1940–49	2
1950–63	3
Total	37

Source: Advisory Commission on Intergovernmental Relations (ACIR), *Tax Overlapping in the United States, 1964* (1964), p. 22. Years are fiscal unless otherwise noted.
[a] The Hawaii tax, enacted in 1901, is included here.

Twenty-nine states (and the District of Columbia) use flat rates—2.0 percent to 10.5 percent—and eight, graduated rates. In twenty-three states the tax is on net income; in eight a franchise or excise tax, measured by net income, is levied on the corporation for the privilege of doing business in the state; and in six states both types of corporate taxes are used. These taxes in fiscal 1963 produced 6.8 percent of total state tax collections, a percentage that has been stable in recent years. As usual, variation among the states was appreciable (see Table 5-2), with Iowa having the lowest percentage (1.6 percent) and New York the highest (16.9 percent). The distribution of collections per capita by states for fiscal 1963 is also shown in Table 5-2: South Dakota is at the bottom with $0.67 and New York at the top with $23.90.

TABLE 5-2. Distribution of States by Percentage of Total State Tax Revenue and Dollars Per Capita Collected from State Corporation Income Taxes, 1963

Percentage of Revenue	Number of States	Collections Per Capita	Number of States
0–2.9	3	0–$4.99	8
3.0–5.9	11	5.0–9.99	17
6.0–8.9	12	10.0–14.99	6
9.0–11.9	7	15.0–19.99	4
12.0–14.9	2	20.0–24.99	1
15.0–17.9	1		
	36[a]		36[a]

Source: Derived from U. S. Census Bureau, *Compendium of State Government Finances in 1963* (1964), pp. 11 and 47.
[a] Indiana tax not effective until 1964.

According to the Advisory Commission on Intergovernmental Relations (ACIR) in 1964, the states are "moving toward greater reliance on the Federal tax base for State corporate income taxes as well as for individual income taxes."[3] Fifteen now use the federal base, with some adjustments. For nine of these states, the federal base is a moving one, that is, account is taken of amendments over time; for the other six, the federal base is static, that is, the reference is to definitions in effect at some date in the past. The remaining twenty-two states (and the District of Columbia) define net income in a manner independent of the federal definition. This creates obvious problems of compliance, since the taxpayer has to consider not only the federal provisions, but also those of the state. The problems are compounded for the corporation that earns income in several states. The existing diversity is rooted in historical, constitutional, and policy reasons. The weight of these reasons needs current appraisal because the advantages of uniformity, through approximate conformity to the federal definitions, are very strong. At present the level of compliance is poor when departures from the federal base are complex. Conformity means also that a state secures the benefits of federal enforcement with little or no state expense.[4]

All payments of state corporation income taxes are deductible by corporations in computing net income for federal corporation income tax purposes. The federal tax is, of course, much heavier than the combined state taxes; in 1963 the former yielded $21.6 billion and the latter $1.5 billion. Since the federal yield is so high and the rate so nearly proportional, tax differentials from corporate income taxation, state by state, are not large.

Interstate Allocation of Income

The most persistent and acute problem in state use of this tax concerns the allocation of interstate income. At present over 120,000 companies in the nation do business and earn income in more than one state. On what basis should states reckon their tax

[3] *Tax Overlapping,* p. 142.
[4] *State Taxation of Interstate Commerce,* Report of the Special Subcommittee on State Taxation of Interstate Commerce of the House Judiciary Committee, H. Rept. 1480, 88 Cong. 2 sess. (1964), Chap. 17.

share of the net income base? Three rules for division are used: (1) formula apportionment, (2) specific allocation, and (3) separate accounting. *Separate accounting,* while permitted by most states, has only limited application.[5] It assumes that the operations of a multistate business can be split into pieces; in fact, most such businesses are "unitary." *Specific allocation,* provided by all except six states, means that some items of income are regarded as non-apportionable—for example, dividends and interest—and must be allocated *wholly* to one state or another. The states differ concerning the *kinds* of income which are to be allocated, and also concerning *where* a particular kind of income has its source.[6] Specific allocation, it should be appreciated, applies only to part of the income of a business; it is used mainly as an adjunct to formula apportionment.

FORMULA APPORTIONMENT. The states have devised many formulas, and not infrequently the aim has been to secure a tax advantage for a state without consideration of what is fair for a corporation doing a national business. A simple hypothetical example will show how inequities may exist. Assume a corporation with an annual net income of $600, with property of $1,200 distributed in three states, and with sales of $3,000 distributed among four states. In this example, each of the states levies taxes on the basis of an allocation formula that represents the proportion that the corporation's sales and properties *in its state* bears to the corporation's *total* property and sales. Each state gives equal weight in the formula to both property and sales. Thus, in State A the allocation fraction is 5/12 ($800/$1,200 plus $500/$3,000) divided by 2 and its share of income is $250 (5/12 of $600). The other states calculate their tax base similarly (see Table 5-3). If, however, each state were to use either property or sales alone, taking care to choose the one which is more favorable to it, the results would be as shown in the last column of Table 5-3, where the aggregate tax base adds up to more than the corporation's net income.

No easy way exists to show the diversity of state apportionment of interstate corporate income. In 1963 the following eleven sets of

[5] *Ibid.,* pp. 160-67.
[6] *Ibid.,* pp. 197-217.

TABLE 5-3. Illustration of Inequities in Formula Allocation of Taxable Income of a Hypothetical Corporation with Interstate Property and Sales

(Money amounts in dollars)

State	Amount of Property	Amount of Sales	Proportional Allocation Formula		"More Favorable" Formula	
			Allocation Fraction	Taxable Income	Allocation Fraction	Taxable Income
State A	$ 800	$ 500	$\frac{5}{12}$	$250	$\frac{8}{12}$	$400
State B	300	1,500	$\frac{3}{8}$	225	$\frac{1}{2}$	300
State C	100	200	$\frac{3}{40}$	45	$\frac{1}{12}$	50
State D	—	800	$\frac{2}{15}$	80	$\frac{4}{15}$	160
Total	$1,200	$3,000		$600		$910

factors were being used by the states in determining their apportionment formulas:[7]

Apportionment Formula	Number of States Using
1. Property, payroll, and sales	26
2. Property, manufacturing costs, and sales	3
3. Property and sales	3
4. Sales	4
5. Property and business (payroll, purchases, and sales)	1
6. Property and payroll	1
7. Manufacturing assets, manufacturing payroll, and sales	1
8. Property, expenditures, and sales	1
9. Inventory, payroll, and sales	1
10. Investment capital in securities	1
11. Property, sales to in-state buyers, and sales from in-state offices	1
	43[8]

[7] *Ibid.*, p. 119.

[8] Some states are counted more than once, since they employ alternative formulas.

But the mere listing of these combinations of factors does not fully indicate their diversity, since definitions of each component differ. For example, seventy-five definitions of receipts (sales) are used. A somewhat less confusing situation prevails with respect to property and payrolls.

The difficulties and costs created for business—especially small business—by the differences are important. The Council of State Governments has pointed out that the states pay an administrative penalty

due to the diversity among their corporate income tax laws. For example, cooperative auditing by States of returns filed by multistate businesses would appear to be desirable in the interests of efficient tax administration. But the States are largely foreclosed from using this device because of the differences in their laws and the tax forms required. Exchange of information among States and comparison of returns filed by taxpayers can have only limited value under present conditions. Greater uniformity among the States with respect to formulas and other key features of their corporate tax laws would make interstate cooperation in this field more feasible and thus increase the efficiency and effectiveness of State tax administration.[9]

A UNIFORM FORMULA. A uniform apportionment formula would make available for taxation 100 percent of the income of a corporation, assuming its use by all states. At present, since the states use different bases, selecting factors favorable to them, the bases (and the income) add up to more than 100 percent.[10] Moreover, some states use "catch-all" sales factors that require all sales destined to the state to be counted in a formula even though some will later be shipped out to other states.

Three factors currently in use are worth notice: property, payroll, and sales. The Massachusetts formula gives equal weight to each. Two major variants exist, one defining sales according to *origin,* that is, the state in which the goods are produced; the other according to *destination,* that is, the state in which the goods are consumed or used. In recent years, the trend has been toward increased

[9] *State Income Taxation of Mercantile and Manufacturing Corporations,* Hearings before the Special Subcommittee on State Taxation of Interstate Commerce of the House Judiciary Committee, 87 Cong. 1 sess. (1962), p. 514.

[10] Thirteen states do not tax corporate income.

use of "destination of sales" as a revenue-raising measure by states that are—or think they are—net importers. In some states, however, use of the destination factor was meant to favor locally-based firms that sold outside the state. The tax bill of such a firm in the home state would be lower when the sales factor is destination rather than origin. To be sure, the tax base apportioned out of the home state should be added to the tax base of the state of sales destination.

Substantial justice could be achieved by any one of several formulas, provided only that the states could agree. Fractional allocation might then be based upon factors which are easy to ascertain, enabling both the taxpayer and the tax administrator to respond promptly in an economical and equitable manner. At one time the Massachusetts formula, mentioned above, was used quite widely. But in postwar years, encouraged by laissez-faire decisions of the Supreme Court, some of the states displayed anarchical tendencies, and the feeling arose that Congress should intervene.

In 1959 the Supreme Court upheld a Minnesota tax on a corporation which solicited orders in Minnesota but owned no real estate and warehoused no merchandise there. Three justices dissented, and one, the late Justice Felix Frankfurter, declared forcibly that a situation was emerging that required congressional remedy. As a result of the decision, he argued, state governments would place new burdens on interstate commerce. Many small corporations would become subject to a separate income tax in each state. They would "have to keep books, make returns, store records, and engage legal counsel, all to meet the diverse and variegated tax laws of forty-nine States, with their different times for filing returns, different tax structures, different modes for determining net income, and different, often conflicting, formulas of apportionment."[11] The courts could not provide a remedy; indeed, reliance on them "only aggravates the difficulties and retards proper legislative solution. . . . The solution . . . ought not to rest on the self-serving determination of the States of what they are entitled to out of the nation's resources. Congress alone can formulate policies founded upon economic realities. . . ."[12]

[11] *Northwestern States Portland Cement Co. v. Minnesota*, 358 U. S. 450, 474.
[12] *Ibid.*, at 477.

Congress did act. Public Law 86-272, which was enacted on September 14, 1959, restricted the authority of the states to impose taxes on interstate commerce. Income taxation of a corporation was not allowable if the only activity of a corporation within the state was the solicitation of orders. Such an activity did not constitute doing business in a state. The law left uncertainties concerning what was or was not prescribed. But it was meant to be temporary, since it ordered Congress to study and propose legislation concerning the taxation of interstate commerce. The first results of the study, dealing with corporation income taxes, were released in June 1964.[13]

THE ECONOMIC LOGIC. On economic grounds, which formula is to be favored? The nub of the argument here concerns *where income is earned,* that is, where is the location of the factors that create income? C. Lowell Harriss argues as follows:

Income is created by human and material resources. The resources utilized by a business as a whole in producing its income can be measured reasonably well by what is paid for them. Moreover, the places where the resources have been producing during a year can be determined on a consistent, though not completely unambiguous, basis.[14]

Property and payrolls should count. Differences of opinion exist concerning what property should be included and what standard of valuation should be used; differences exist also concerning the composition of payrolls, and the state in which payrolls are located. But these issues can be resolved without great difficulty.

Such a formula would not give sales any separate or distinct place. Sales effort would be represented merely by the *cost* of the economic resources used in selling; it would not be represented by

---

[13] *State Taxation of Interstate Commerce.* A report on state sales and use taxes was promised for the end of 1964. Congressional appraisal and legislation may follow.

[14] "Interstate Apportionment of Business Income," *American Economic Review* (June 1959), p. 400. A very similar argument is spelled out in more detail by Charles E. Ratliff, Jr., *Interstate Apportionment of Business Income for State Income Tax Purposes* (1962), Chap. V. A very different basis would be to measure the relative extent to which a multistate company "has caused the various States to incur governmental costs." For a discussion of this method of allocation, see *State Taxation of Interstate Commerce,* pp. 158-59.

the value of sales made in a state. Proponents of the value of sales destination as a separate component argue that selling effort is an essential part of the economic process, and that without sales no income would be created; they argue also that out-of-state sellers "exploit" the market of a state. The first argument leads only to the conclusion that the cost of sales effort should count to the extent that is a part of cost. To imply that since sales are necessary, they should count in their totality is a fallacy. Property is necessary; so are management, materials, and skilled and unskilled labor. Each factor and subfactor makes a contribution appropriately measured by its cost, and no economic justification exists for overweighting one type of cost. The second argument assumes that selling is *exploitation* of a market. This also is a fallacy unless important monopoly features are present. In a free market neither buyer nor seller is exploited; exchange is a two-sided and mutually beneficial process. If, indeed, important monopoly features are present, exploitation may exist. But surely inclusion of a sales destination factor in a formula has no logical bearing on such a situation.[15]

REVENUE PRODUCTIVITY. A major practical difficulty is that change to a uniform formula might decrease the revenue of some states. Attempts to measure the potential revenue effects have been made, and they indicate that most states greatly exaggerate the revenue advantages to them of their particular formulas.[16] The study made

[15] Readers should be warned that dissent from these opinions exists. (See particularly Jerome R. Hellerstein, "Allocation and Nexus in State Taxation of Interstate Business," Tax Symposium of the Tax Institute of America, October 1964.) The dissent emphasizes, first, that the federal government in income taxation regards income as arising where the sale is effected, and second, that a sales destination factor is the major way by which a significant share in the tax base can be allocated to "market" states. While deploring the present disorder, the opinion is advanced that a federal prescription of *uniformity* of methods of dividing interstate income would go a long way toward simplifying compliance and administration, especially if a quantitative minimum limit (for example $100,000 of receipts from sales in a state) is set for establishment of nexus (jurisdiction to tax). The argument offered in this monograph is, however, that distinct rules for apportionment and nexus are neither necessary nor desirable; a simultaneous solution of jurisdiction and apportionment is best.

[16] See, for example, *Report of Survey of Effects on State Revenues of Various Proposed Uniform Apportionment Formulas* by the Council of State Governments, Chicago, 1956, mimeographed; other surveys are reported in *State Income Taxation of Mercantile and Manufacturing Corporations.*

for the Special Subcommittee of the House Committee on the Judiciary in 1964 provided definitive answers. It measured the comparative revenue effects of three uniform formulas: (1) a two-factor formula including only property and payrolls, (2) a three-factor one in which a sales-origin factor is added, and (3) a three-factor one in which a sales-distribution factor is added. The revenue consequences to the states of a changeover to any one of the three formulas would be modest:

For only two States do the staff's estimates indicate that changeover to any of the three formulas studied could produce a loss in total tax revenues of as much as 1 percent; for two States a gain of more than 1 percent of total tax revenues could be produced. The vast majority of the income tax States could adopt any of the three uniform formulas studied with either a gain in revenue, no change in revenue, or a loss of less than one-half of 1 percent of total tax revenues. Even these estimates are based on the assumption that the States are able today to collect all revenues assigned to them by the relentless application of the formulas currently in use, and thus take no account of the limitations imposed by jurisdictional rules and enforcement problems. If it may be assumed that any uniform system for division of income would be designed in a fashion to mitigate these problems, the losses would certainly be smaller in fact, and in some cases a revenue gain might be produced even though the staff's estimates suggest a loss. In short, as a factor to be weighed in choosing among alternative uniform schemes for the division of income for tax purposes, revenue considerations are very minor.[17]

COMPLIANCE COSTS. What other considerations come to mind? One is "the cost to taxpayers of remitting their State income payments." A large compliance cost is inefficient in itself, and it also impairs the *quality* of compliance. Computation of a property factor is, the study finds, "relatively simple if property is valued either at original cost or at the adjusted basis for Federal tax purposes . . . ," and computation of payroll factors is "generally quite simple."[18] But a sales factor, especially for smaller companies, is costly to compute and these compliance costs are "wholly disproportionate to the tax

[17] *State Taxation of Interstate Commerce*, p. 562.
[18] *Ibid.*, pp. 562-63.

liabilities involved." Indeed, any formula which attributes income to a large number of states—as a sales destination factor must often do—is bound to bring either high costs of compliance, or else noncompliance.

Many companies involved in interstate commerce are quite small, and most of them, even though their markets are spread over many states, have a place of business in only one state. The recent tendency of state governments to demand that tax returns be filed by a company wherever it has a sales office, or inventories, or itinerant employees, has induced a low level of compliance.[19] The picture which emerges is of a tax system "which works badly for both business and the States. It is the picture of a system in which the States are reaching farther and farther to impose smaller and smaller liabilities on more and more companies. It is the picture of a system which calls upon tax administrators to enforce the unenforceable, and the taxpayer to comply with the uncompliable."[20] The legal requirements and the world of facts are far apart. Broad assertions of jurisdiction, even when constitutionally valid, have not been accompanied by fulfillment.

The likelihood is that formulas with a sales destination factor more often lead to under- than to over-taxation. A company that makes shipments into states where it has no business location is permitted by the formula to reduce its tax base in the states where it has places of business. The company will, however, often fail to report this base in states where it makes the sales. In short, jurisdictional rules bring about a shrinkage of the base in the home state, while actual compliance does not bring this income into the base in the sales destination states.

TAX CREDIT OR TAX SHARING. Other and much less satisfactory forms of congressional intervention would be provisions for tax credit or tax sharing. By the former, Congress might state that some defined part of a state income tax payment could be credited by a

---

[19] "Thus among 819 instances studied in which companies had salesmen soliciting and accepting orders, returns were filed in 21 cases. Among 130 instances in which companies maintained sales offices, only 44 returns were filed. And among 234 instances in which companies owned goods in public warehouses, only 91 returns were filed. In each of these cases, the States involved required filing on the basis of the activity considered." *Ibid.*, p. 597.

[20] *Ibid.*, p. 598.

corporation against its federal income tax payment in states that tax corporations according to specified conditions. Such a step would, in effect, force the thirteen states without a corporation income tax to enact one; it would, besides, favor the richer and more industrialized states in which most corporation income is created. Neither of these results is appealing. *Tax sharing* would require state withdrawal from taxation of corporate income in return for receipt of some predetermined slice of federal collections. On what basis should the share of each state be determined? State-by-state federal collections now reflect where the federal return was filed and the federal tax paid. Usually a single federal return is made at the principal place of business of the company. Therefore the figures of federal collections by states give no accurate report of where income was earned; they overstate the income earned in the states where corporations have their headquarters. State governments attempt to tax all corporate income derived within their own borders, and the nonindustrial states, therefore, collect much of their revenue from corporations that make their *federal* income tax payments elsewhere.

As a result, if state-by-state collections of revenue from corporate income tax are expressed as percentages of the federal collections reported by the Commissioner of Internal Revenue, the percentages are usually high for the nonindustrial states. According to Laszlo Ecker-Racz's calculations, based on the years from 1953 to 1958, Mississippi has by far the highest percentage (43.8 percent), with Arkansas in second place (25.8 percent).[21] On the basis of these figures, a negotiation that sought the voluntary substitution of federal-state sharing of tax collections for the present situation would have to concede a generous share to states like Mississippi and Arkansas. Any sharing based on origin of income is sure to favor the richer states; sharing based on other criteria—origin of sales, destination of sales, payrolls, and so forth—might be more favorable to the poorer and less industrialized states. But so long as the economic criterion of origin of income is utilized, such sharing will be advantageous to the richer states.[22] Moreover, sharing would be a

[21] *Public Finances: Needs, Sources, and Utilization* (1961), pp. 154-57.
[22] See James A. Maxwell, *Tax Credits and Intergovernmental Fiscal Relations* (1962), pp. 146-47.

centralizing step which—if it is to be taken—should have a much stronger justification than is provided by the need for a uniform apportionment formula.

FEDERAL INTERVENTION. Erecting unreasonable tax obstacles to interstate trade is a serious matter. Commerce should flow freely because, more than ever before, the United States is economically one nation. The jurisdiction of the state governments in taxing commerce should stop at state lines, and reasonable rules are available to define the proper tax base of each state in the net earnings of a multistate business. But many of the states have been unwilling to accept the rules, and the result has been discrimination, excessive costs of tax administration, multiplication of litigation, costly compliance and victimization of "exposed" businesses—and noncompliance by other businesses. These costs are not easily perceived by the public, but they are serious in their effect on the national economy.

Efforts to persuade the states to adopt a uniform rule for division of corporate income have been made for decades. As of today the results have been negligible, and no hope can be affirmed of better progress in the future. Rather would realism predict a worsening situation as the upward trend of state tax rates continues. Congressional intervention seems, therefore, to be an indicated and desirable step. How the income of a multistate company should be divided, for tax purposes, among the states is a question which demands one answer. The diversity of present answers provided by state laws is a perversion for which no rationale can be found in the theory of federalism.

The Use Tax

The *use tax* is a state levy on commodities purchased outside a state, but brought into it for use. As state retail sales taxes grew in number, the strong protection then given by the Supreme Court to interstate commerce was annoying to tax administrators and to retailers in sales tax states. These states discovered a remedy in the form of the use tax which, in 1938, the Supreme Court held to be constitutional. Designed merely as a supplement to the sales tax, its rates, application, and so forth, are identical.

Enforcement and Interstate Commerce

A major problem has been enforcement. Application to residents in one state who buy out-of-state is obviously awkward except where, as in the case of automobiles, the article must be registered. More and more the states have ordered out-of-state sellers to collect the use tax for them. In 1941 the Supreme Court upheld the right of Iowa to require a mail-order house to collect a use tax on its sales to residents of the state. Since then the Supreme Court has liberalized its interpretation, the culmination coming in 1960 with *Scripto, Inc. v. Carson.*[23] A Georgia corporation with no office or place of business in Florida shipped goods there pursuant to orders from jobbers. The Court held that Florida was within its rights in requiring the Georgia corporation to be responsible for the collection of a use tax on products shipped to Florida. Thereafter many states were prompt to impose use tax collection on out-of-state manufacturers and vendors, and soon agitation developed to place some restrictions on the states parallel to those of PL 86-272, mentioned above, concerning multiple taxation of income.

One line of argument was that sellers who had no office or place of business in a taxing state should not be required to collect the state's use tax on sales in the state. Compliance here, so ran the contention, was even more complex than in the case of state income taxes because the bases of state sales and use taxes were more complex and more subject to frequent change. State officials argued, in rebuttal, that collection through out-of-state sellers was essential to enforcement, and that application of the exemption of PL 86-272 would bring a serious reduction in state revenue.

The fact is, then, that interstate sales currently raise serious problems not only with respect to corporation income taxes, but also state sales and use taxes. Should Congress allow the state where a purchaser resides to require out-of-state sellers to collect the use tax for it? Should Congress *limit* this obligation to those sellers who have some definable business connection with the taxing state? Or should Congress in effect prohibit use taxes by declaring that only the state in which the seller is located should collect taxes on interstate sales? This last step would reduce compliance costs,

[23] 362 U. S. 207.

since sellers would have to comply only with the laws of the states from which goods were shipped. It would, however, be favorable to the producing states. Whatever choice is made, the case for some clear congressional delineation is strong.

Death and Gift Taxes

Death and gift taxes are not an important source of state tax revenue—in 1963 they provided only 2.7 percent of total state tax collections. Most of the states levy inheritance rather than estate taxes, although no summary description of the variety is accurate. Twelve states levy taxes on gifts as complements to their death taxes.

There is, of course, a marked variation in yield among the states, as Table 5-4 shows. For twenty-five states death and gift taxes in 1963 provided less than 2 percent of tax revenue, but for eight states—Connecticut, Delaware, Massachusetts, New Hampshire, Pennsylvania, New Jersey, Rhode Island, and Maine—they supplied over 4 percent and for one of these—New Jersey—8.5 percent. The states that rank high in percentage tax collections seem to levy death taxes that are more severe than average, since the yields they collected in 1960 were higher than what they would have col-

TABLE 5-4. Distribution of States by Percentage of Total Tax Revenue Collected from Death and Gift Taxes, 1963

Percentage of Total	Number of States
0– .9	11
1.0–1.9	14
2.0–2.9	10[a]
3.0–3.9	7
4.0–4.9	5
5.0–5.9	1
6.0–6.9	0
7.0–7.9	1
8.0–8.9	1
	——
	50

Source: *State Government Finances in 1963*, p. 11.
[a] Includes District of Columbia.

lected from a representative estate tax system, that is, one that is an average of actual state tax structures.[24] It happens also that all except Maine and New Hampshire are rich states. But *some* rich states—Ohio, Maryland, and Illinois—choose to levy light taxes. So also do *most* poor states. Mississippi, Georgia, Alabama, Arkansas, Kentucky, and South Carolina all collected less in 1960 than they would have by a representative or average set of rates and exemptions.

The Federal Tax Credit

The state governments have used death taxes much longer than the federal government. On three occasions before 1916 a federal tax was used as an emergency device—1798-1802, 1862-70, and 1898-1902—and repealed when the emergency need had passed. A few state governments levied inheritance taxes early in the nineteenth century, but by 1891 only nine states were using these taxes, all of them with low flat rates. Thereafter the need for revenue and an agitation against concentration of wealth combined to popularize the tax. By 1916 forty-two states levied it (all but Florida, Mississippi, New Mexico, Nebraska, South Carolina, and Alabama), usually at low progressive rates, raising $30.7 million or 8.4 percent of their tax revenue. All but one of the taxes were on inheritances, that is, on the portions of a decedent's estate passing to each individual heir.

In 1916 the federal government imposed an estate tax, that is, one on the *entire net estate* left by a decedent. The state governments, by virtue of long prior occupancy, regarded death taxation as their preserve, and they resented federal intrusion. Further, the states advanced the legal theory that they—and *not* the federal government—had the right to regulate the descent and distribution of property at death. In the 1920's, when federal finances eased and those of the state governments tightened, agitation for federal repeal mounted. In 1924, a curious compromise emerged. Congress raised the rates of the federal estate tax, but it also provided for a credit of up to 25 percent against the federal tax for death taxes paid to the states. If, for example, the federal tax on an estate was

[24] ACIR, *Measures of State and Local Fiscal Capacity and Tax Effort*, p. 148.

$100 and the state tax $25, the total tax, after credit, would be $100 rather than $125.

At this time (1924) three states—Florida, Nevada, and Alabama —were without a death tax. Florida had never had such a tax, but in November 1924, by constitutional amendment, it forbade enactment of either inheritance or income taxes. The purpose of this move was only too apparent: by supplementing the attractions of its climate with the establishment of a tax haven, Florida hoped that rich people would domicile themselves within its borders. Since domicile for the purpose of taxation was easy to establish, the other states had reason to fear the migration of estates beyond their jurisdiction. Nevada promptly met the threat, or rather imitated Florida, by passing a similar constitutional amendment in July 1925; California, which had up to this time been the natural competitor of Florida as a domicile for retired millionaires, discussed the need for parallel action.

Nothing more was needed to bring home the realization that the future of death taxes as a source of state revenue was in serious jeopardy. At the very time when many state officers were urging federal withdrawal from the field, here were signal illustrations of the inability of the states to use a system of death taxation with success. And the most casual survey indicated that there were other weaknesses in the state taxes. Rates, exemptions, definitions, and administrative practices were diverse. While complete uniformity in these matters was not to be hoped for, the existing variation was beyond reason. Even more dangerous were the discriminatory practices which had grown up, particularly in the taxation of nonresident decedents.

Some attempt to clean house was imperative, and at the meeting of the National Tax Association in September 1924, a resolution was adopted recommending that the Association assemble a conference of federal as well as state representatives to consider remedies for the existing difficulties over death taxation. In February 1925 the conference met at Washington. Delegates appointed by the governors attended from twenty-five states, and President Coolidge, addressing the conference, promised his "cordial cooperation." After thorough discussion it was voted that the chairman, Dr. T. W.

Paige, should appoint a committee of investigation to report recommendations to a second national conference. A committee of nine members was named with F. A. Delano as chairman, and it reported in November 1925.

The committee had a twofold objective. It wished to stifle the anarchistic moves of Florida and Nevada, and also to apply some pressure on the states generally to reform their taxes. Accordingly it recommended increase of the federal tax credit from 25 percent to 80 percent, and repeal of the federal tax in six years if, meanwhile, the states had cleaned house. At this same time, in 1926, the Ways and Means Committee of the House of Representatives was holding hearings on revenue revision. It decided to accept one of the recommendations of the Delano Committee—enlargement of the federal credit to 80 percent. By this step the tax advantages sought by Florida and Nevada were largely canceled out, since the estate of a decedent in those states would pay the full federal tax.

This was the turning point of the movement for repeal of the federal tax. Many state officials were, on the one hand, pacified by the 80 percent credit, and on the other hand, timid about the prospect of federal withdrawal. For a few years progress toward reform was made.[25] In 1931 federal credits for state taxes offset, on the average, 75.6 percent of the federal tax liability; the number of states using the estate tax only had risen from two in 1925 to seven in 1932, and the number using estate and inheritance taxes jointly had risen from three to twenty-seven.

But in 1931-32 all such progress stopped because of the depression. Congress underscored this retreat when, in 1932, it enacted a supplementary estate tax (with an exemption of $50,000) against which no credit for state taxes was provided. The 80 percent credit enacted in 1926 was retained, but the idea of repeal was no longer contemplated. On several later occasions Congress increased the federal rates and altered the exemptions in order to increase federal collections. As a result, the federal tax credit, which in 1931 came to

---

[25] The reform came through decisions of the Supreme Court which limited the situs of intangibles to the domicile of the decedent, and through adoption of reciprocity (that is, State A would exempt intangibles of nonresident decedents provided that State B reciprocated).

nearly 76 percent of the federal tax liability, has declined to 10 percent. The aim of providing the states with a larger share of death tax revenue was sidetracked.

So also was the aim of *tax coordination*. Disintegration of state death taxation through interstate tax competition was indeed averted and at present only Nevada has no death tax. But in other respects coordination has not been achieved. State governments differ in type of tax, definitions, rates, exemptions, deductions, exclusions, and administrative practices. The Advisory Commission on Intergovernmental Relations in 1960 found many types of state taxes.[26] Five states (Alabama, Arizona, Arkansas, Florida, and Georgia) had pure "pick-up" taxes modelled on the federal statute, and designed to impose a tax liability equal to the maximum allowable credit. For example, if the federal tax on an estate under the 1926 provisions was $100 and the credit $80, the state tax would be $80 and the total tax $100. Two states (North Dakota and Utah) had estate taxes only; four (Mississippi, New York, Oklahoma, and South Carolina) had estate and pick-up taxes; thirty-five (and the District of Columbia) had inheritance taxes with pick-up taxes as supplements in order to secure "unused" federal credits.[27] Effective rates are quite divergent. For instance, on net estates of $50,000 and $100,000 the tax of the top states is nineteen times higher than that of the low ones; on larger estates the tax is four to six times higher.

Federal-State Coordination

The ACIR recommended that Congress increase and modify the federal credit in order to spur the states toward coordination and to provide a modest increase in state revenues. In place of a flat percentage, a two-bracket graduated credit was proposed that would make available a relatively larger share in the lower tax brackets and a smaller share in the higher brackets. For example, a credit of 80 percent of the gross federal tax liability might be allowed on the first $250,000 of taxable estates, and 20 percent on the balance. Thereby the aggregate credit would be increased from about $132 million to $640 million. Such a credit would be somewhat more favorable to the non-industrialized states, and would

[26] ACIR, *Coordination of State and Federal Inheritance, Estate, and Gift Taxes* (1961), p. 25.

[27] *Tax Overlapping*, Table 66.

provide a more stable revenue. The Commission recommended, however, that *two conditions* be attached to the new credit: (1) revenue maintenance, and (2) a shift to estate taxes.

State death taxes over the last decade have averaged 2.8 times the amount credited under the 1926 law. Thus many estates paid state death taxes in excess of the amount that could be credited against the federal tax. If the maximum federal credit were to be increased, these estates could claim larger credits. For this reason the ACIR believed that "the immediate effect of an increase in the Federal credit, especially in the lower brackets, would be Federal tax reduction, not increased State collections."[28] Unless a state felt an urgent need for additional revenue, it might be loath to take action depriving its residents of the federal reduction. The Commission felt strongly that it was no part of its duty to recommend a tax decrease (or increase). Accordingly, it declared that the new credit should be conditional upon revenue maintenance, that is, "certification by the Governor to the Secretary of the Treasury that the estimated annual revenue level of his State's death taxes has been raised in an amount corresponding to the estimated aggregate increase in the tax credits on Federal estate returns filed from his State. This commission further recommends that the States be required to maintain these higher tax rate levels for a period of five years."[29]

While the new credit, coupled with revenue maintenance, would provide the states with additional revenue, it would in itself do nothing to alleviate the complexity of death taxation, a complexity "due largely to the prevalence of inheritance type taxes among the States." Tax simplification was an important objective, and therefore the ACIR recommended "that the higher Federal estate tax credit . . . be limited to estate type State taxes, as distinguished from inheritance taxes."[30] So far Congress has not acted on the recommendations of the Advisory Commission.

Conclusion

The weight of the arguments in favor of federal withdrawal from death taxes has diminished over the decades. After nearly fifty

[28] *Coordination of State and Federal Inheritance, Estate, and Gift Taxes*, p. 76.
[29] *Ibid.*
[30] *Ibid.*, p. 20.

years of unbroken federal occupancy, the historical plea of prior state occupancy seems unconvincing, and while property does pass at death under state law, the constitutional right of the federal government to tax transfer of property at death is now beyond dispute.

The argument that the fiscal need of the states exceeded that of the federal government was persuasive in the 1920's, and it has weight today. Here the question is whether or not death taxation is a logical or promising source of state revenue. Death tax revenue from its very nature is unstable for the nation as a whole. This instability increases when the taxing unit is a state because, in such case, the yearly number of returns is small and the composition of taxable estates is highly variable from state to state. Rates for this tax should not be significantly different from one state to another, because decisions concerning where to do business and where to reside should not be affected by such factors. The sources of private wealth recognize no state lines, and the basis on which the states mainly rest their right to tax—domicile of the decedent—is often quite unrelated to the geographic origin of a decedent's wealth. In short, for most states the death tax is not now, and cannot be, a satisfactory revenue source. Uninhibited attempts to apply the tax, which overlook the national interest, may distort decisions concerning economic activity.

CHAPTER VI

The Property Tax

"A tax as ancient as that on property tends to become an institution and to accumulate fondly clinging traditions as it evolves over the years." Advisory Commission on Intergovernmental Relations, *The Role of the States in Strengthening the Property Tax*, Vol. 1, p. 3.

DURING MOST OF THE HISTORY of the nation, the property tax has been, by a wide margin, the most important tax revenue source. Table 6-1 shows that in 1902 it provided over 51 percent of total federal, state, and local tax collections. No other tax even approached it in importance. As late as 1940 the property tax provided nearly 35 percent of total tax collections; the second-ranking tax, on corporation income, provided 10 percent. With World War II, however, the property tax lost ground. By 1944 it provided only 9.4 percent of total collections, and was outranked by the revenue from taxes on individual and corporate income. The reason for the shift was, of course, the vast expansion of *federal* tax collections to which the property tax made no contribution, since it was, and always had been, wholly a source of state and local funds.[1] Recently the property tax has regained some ground and in 1963 it provided 15.3 percent of total tax collections.

---

[1] The so-called direct tax levied by the federal government in 1798, 1814-16, and 1861, might be regarded as a property tax, since it was levied chiefly against property. See Paul Studenski and Herman E. Krooss, *Financial History of the United States* (1952), pp. 50-51, 76, and 141.

125

Significance to State and Local Governments

The significance of the property tax as a source of state and local tax revenue is indicated in Table 6-1. Completely dominant

TABLE 6-1. Property Tax Collections in Relation to Total Federal, State, and Local Tax Collections, Selected Years, 1902–63

(Money amounts in millions of dollars)

Year	Total Tax Collections			Property Tax Collections as Percentages of	
	Federal, State, and Local	State and Local	Property Tax	Federal, State, and Local Tax Collections	State and Local Tax Collections
1902	$ 1,373	$ 860	$ 706	51.4	82.1
1913	2,271	1,609	1,332	58.6	82.8
1927	9,451	6,087	4,730	50.0	77.7
1938	12,949	7,605	4,440	34.2	58.3
1944	49,095	8,774	4,604	9.4	52.5
1948	51,218	13,342	6,126	11.9	46.0
1962	123,785	41,523	19,056	15.4	45.3
1963	131,078	44,281	20,089	15.3	45.4

Sources: U. S. Census Bureau, *Historical Statistics of the United States: Colonial Times to 1957* (1960), pp. 722 and 726; *Governmental Finances in 1962* (1963), pp. 15 and 28; and *Governmental Finances in 1963* (1964), p. 22. Years are fiscal unless otherwise noted.

in 1902 and 1913, and only slightly less so in the 1920's, the property tax lost relative ground in the 1930's and during World War II. In postwar years it has provided about 46 percent of state and local tax revenues. The reason for the decline was that state governments replaced the property tax with other revenue sources.

State Governments

This step was taken because the states found new and more attractive taxes, and because the administrative machinery of the property tax was local. State governments did not assess and collect property tax through state officers; instead they apportioned to their local governments yearly a sum which the local governments were

TABLE 6-2. Distribution of States by Percentage of State Tax Revenue from General Property Tax, 1963

Percentage of Total	Number of States
0.0– 4.9	19
5.0– 9.9	5
10.0–14.9	1
15.0–19.9	1
20.0–24.9	—
25.0–29.9	1
	27

Source: Advisory Commission on Intergovernmental Relations (ACIR), *The Role of the States in Strengthening the Property Tax* (1963), Vol. I, p. 71.

instructed to secure and turn over to the state treasury. This procedure was not popular and when in the 1930's delinquency in property tax payments became large, the state tax was bitterly resented. As a measure of relief to local governments, many state governments discontinued their tax; collections, which were 23.0 percent of state taxes in 1927, fell to 6.8 percent in 1942. The downward trend has continued and, in 1963, the figure was 3.1 percent. The general property tax has become a local tax. The proposition that state and local sources of taxation should be separate, rather than overlapping, found practical application here. Table 6-2 shows the percentage of state tax revenue from the general property tax in 1963. The tax was important to the governments of three states— Nebraska (28.6 percent), Wyoming (18.0 percent), and Arizona (13.3 percent)—and minor to twenty-four.

Local Governments

Not only has the general property tax become local, in terms of revenue productivity it is almost the *only* local tax. In 1963, it provided 88 percent of local tax revenue. The efforts of local governments during the past thirty years to develop other taxes have borne fruit only in large cities (see Chapter VII). Additional nontax revenues have, however, been found, notably state and federal aid and collection of charges. As Table 6-3 shows, these nontax revenues provided about one-quarter of local funds in 1927; by 1963,

TABLE 6-3. General Revenue of Local Governments, 1927 and 1963

(Money amounts in millions of dollars)

Source of General Revenue	Amount		Percentage of Total	
	1927	1963	1927	1963
Tax revenue				
Property tax	$4,360	$19,401	73.9	47.0
Other taxes	119	2,764	2.0	6.7
Nontax revenue				
State and federal aid	605	12,689	10.2	30.8
Charges and miscellaneous	819	6,365	13.9	15.5
Total	$5,903	$41,218	100.0	100.0

Sources: *Historical Statistics*, p. 728; and *Governmental Finances in 1963*, p. 30.

they provided almost half. If, therefore, attention is concentrated on all *general revenue,* the importance of the property tax to local governments has diminished in recent decades.

Local governments are of many types, and the property tax is not of the same importance to all of them. As Table 6-4 shows, the dependence of school districts is nearly complete—it provides 99 percent of their tax revenue—and that of counties, townships, and special districts is almost as great. Municipalities, however, have managed to secure more than one-quarter of their tax revenue from other sources.

The extreme dependence of local governments on the property tax rests upon one ineluctable fact—lack of option. No other tax is available for productive use. Local taxation of income, sales, or business would induce shrinkage in the tax base and, therefore, bring serious injury to the locality. But real property is quite immobile; differential taxes of some severity will not induce migration out of a local geographic area. Workers must reside close to their work; retail outlets must locate close to consumers; manufacturing establishments, once committed, tend to stay put, since even severe property taxes are a modest part of their total costs. In short, real property offers a base upon which local governments can safely levy taxes.

The yield of the tax in postwar years has been quite elastic, responding well in the aggregate to increases in gross national product, as well as to increases of population in areas of local govern-

TABLE 6-4. Local Government Property Tax, Tax Revenue, and General Revenue by Type of Governmental Unit, 1963

(Money amounts in millions of dollars)

Governmental Unit	General Revenue	Tax Revenue	Property Tax	Property Tax	
				As Percentage of General Revenue	As Percentage of Tax Revenue
All units	$41.2	$22.2	$19.4	46.5	87.4
Counties	9.1	4.4	4.1	45.0	93.2
Municipalities	14.0	8.3	6.0	42.8	72.3
School districts	15.3	7.9	7.8	51.0	98.7
Townships and special districts	3.6	1.6	1.5	41.7	93.7

Source: *Governmental Finances in 1963*, p. 30.

ment and an increased proportion of school children in the population. Jesse Burkhead concludes that, on the basis of its statistical record in the 1950's, "the property tax is a far better fiscal instrument than most of its critics have allowed. There is every reason to believe that it will continue to hold its relative importance in state-local public finance structures."[2]

Is the property tax administered with efficiency? Is it equitable in its incidence? As will appear hereafter, both questions must be answered with qualified negatives. Complaints against the tax on these grounds have been voiced for eighty years, ever since the property tax began to be a significant burden. Proposals for reform have been advanced for nearly as long a period, and, while some of these proposals have passed into limbo, some are very current. The failure to apply remedies, despite reiterated complaints, must mean that remedies are difficult to implement.

Should a renewed effort at reform be made? Is the property tax worth refurbishment? An affirmative response must lean heavily upon the belief that local governments should have a major source of revenue of their own.

[2] *State and Local Taxes for Public Education* (Syracuse University Press, 1963), p. 70. In Chap. IV Burkhead reviews the measurement of property tax elasticity made by others, and presents his own investigation of elasticity over time with special reference to the State of New York.

Incidence and Economic Effects

How should the property tax be rated in terms of the principles of taxation? Does it conform to standards of equity? How does its incidence compare with that of other taxes? What are its economic effects? To make this appraisal, let it be assumed that administration of the property tax conforms to good current practice (as seen below, now achieved in one-third of all local areas). In particular, let the assumption be made that the assessment of real property (the mainstay of the tax) is quite uniform *within* each taxing jurisdiction and levied on the gross value of real property.

This definition itself brings into view some obvious faults. Not only is ownership of important kinds of wealth excluded (intangibles and tangible personal property), but no account is taken of mortgages on real property. The base of the tax is gross value, rather than net, and this is characteristic of an impersonal tax that is levied against things. Against this gross value a *proportional* tax rate is levied. If equity is held to indicate that tax payments be proportional (not to say progressive) in relation to net wealth, the property tax is defective.

Incidence

One estimate of the actual incidence of the property tax indicates that it is regressive with respect to income, although not so regressive as aggregate state and local sales taxes.

The effective rates in 1954, according to income groups, for both the sales and property taxes are shown in Table 6-5. The figures in the last two columns of this table show, for each tax, the range of variation—in either direction—from the average. These figures were calculated by assigning the value of 100 to the average effective tax rate, and then expressing the tax rates for each income group as a percentage of this figure. Thus, the effective rates for the property tax range from 91 percent to 120 percent of the average; those for sales and excise taxes diverge more widely—from 58 percent to 139 percent of the average. This reckoning rests upon a number of assumptions about the shifting of the tax burden of different types of property, because the property tax is "a bundle of taxes on a bundle of elements":[3] that the tax on the value of land held vacant, or used for owner-occupied residences, or for business, is on the owner; that the tax on rental or leased housing is shifted to

TABLE 6-5. Estimated Effective Rates of Property and Sales Taxes, 1954

(In percent)

Income	Effective Rate		Rate as Percentage of Average	
	Property	Excise and Sales	Property	Excise and Sales
0–$2,000	4.2	5.0	120	139
2,000– 2,999	3.9	4.6	111	128
3,000– 3,999	3.8	4.2	109	117
4,000– 4,999	3.7	4.0	106	111
5,000– 7,499	3.5	3.9	100	108
7,500– 9,999	3.4	3.5	97	97
10,000 and over	3.2	2.1	91	58
Average	3.5	3.6	100	100

Source: R. A. Musgrave, "The Incidence of the Tax Structure and Its Effects on Consumption," in Joint Committee on the Economic Report, *Federal Tax Policy for Economic Growth and Stability,* 84 Cong. 1 sess. (1955), p. 98. On the other hand, George Bishop's estimates make the property tax the more regressive ("The Tax Burden by Income Class, 1958," *National Tax Journal,* March 1961, p. 54). Musgrave's assumptions concerning shifting and incidence of the property tax seem more relevant than those of Bishop.

the tenant, and that on owner-occupied homes is borne by the owner; that the tax on business property (except land) is shifted to the consumer.

This analysis is based on data for 1954. The results would be modified by more recent data. Assessment of property has improved since 1954 (as will be shown later), and this improvement has moved the figures toward proportionality.

Moreover, doubt has been cast upon the regressivity belief by two recent studies. One study found that, contrary to the usual belief, relative spending for housing tends to rise somewhat as long-term income increases;[4] the other found that when money in-

[3] University of Wisconsin Tax Study Committee, *Wisconsin's State and Local Tax Burden* (1959), p. 131.

[4] Margaret G. Reid, *Housing and Income* (1962), p. 398. "The findings of this monograph . . . show higher housing-income ratios for the rich than the poor. In other words, the ratio of housing to income tends to rise with normal income." "Normal" income is long-run or "permanent" income.

come is adjusted in certain ways the property tax is not regressive. One such adjustment imputes an amount for rental income to home owners; this increases the income of low income families by a greater proportion than that of higher income families. Another adjustment deducts federal income tax payments from gross income; the payments are, of course, greatest for those with high incomes. The result of these and other minor shifts in the income base is to make the incidence of the property tax on residential property roughly proportionate.[5]

Some writers have argued that the property tax is not levied according to the ability but rather according to the *benefit* principle: if so, the tax should be regarded as a payment by individuals for services rendered. This argument is most plausible with respect to such local governmental services as fire protection, street improvements, sewerage construction and operation, street lighting, and so forth. But even here *general* benefits, which spill over to the community, are present. And education expenditure, the most important component of local budgets, is not related in any meaningful sense to property taxes. The benefits from primary and secondary education spread far beyond the recipients, and assessment of property tax for it is, moreover, quite unrelated even to the direct benefits which accrue to recipients. The general property tax is, then, only partially a benefit tax. This benefit does, however, serve to leaven the nonprogressivity of the tax.

Economic Effects

What, finally, are the economic effects of the property tax? Since it is levied on ownership of property (especially real property), rather than on current economic effort, it does not adversely affect labor incentives. But the tax must discourage private spending for housing and thus reduce the housing supply by some unascertain-

[5] Survey Research Center, University of Michigan, *Income and Welfare in the United States* (1962), pp. 292-308. A summary quotation is as follows: "The regressive nature of the property tax, so long accepted as fact, is not upheld by an analysis which includes renters and takes account of the imputed rental income resulting from the owner's equity in his own home, of Federal income tax liability, and of family size and structure, in assessing ability to pay. The property tax is not particularly inequitable between high and low value residential properties. Nor does it represent a higher proportion of incomes of lower income than higher income families."

able amount. Similarly, it may have adverse effects on business investment in taxable property. In urban areas the property tax, combined with fragmentation of governmental units, may have a distorting effect on land-use patterns. Heavy taxes on property in core cities may induce business to move to the suburbs, leading to fiscal imbalance in a metropolitan area.[6]

Judged, therefore, in terms of equity and economic effects, the property tax cannot be awarded a high position. As a source of state income, it has no attraction, because other broad-based and productive taxes are in successful use. But no alternative *local* taxes are in sight. For local governments the property tax provides a large, predictable, certain, and elastic revenue.

The Base of Property Taxation

During colonial times and the early years of the Republic, property was taxed selectively and at nonuniform rates. But with the nineteenth century a strong swing began toward inclusion of all property in the tax base, and toward taxation within each jurisdiction at a uniform rate. The two rules of *universality* and of *uniformity* were widely accepted and, indeed, often embodied as requirements in state constitutions. Governmental property was, however, exempt, and so also was the property of religious, charitable, and educational establishments. The main component in the tax base was real property—land and its improvements. But personal property—tangible and intangible—was another component. *Tangible* personal property includes machinery, inventory, livestock, motor vehicles, furniture, jewelry, and so on; here the significant split is between business property (including farms) and household effects. *Intangible* personal property consists of legal rights to valuable things—stocks, bonds, mortgages, bank deposits, and the like. Most of these are "representative" of real property or of tangible personal property; a few—such as patents and copyrights—are nonrepresentative; and sometimes intangibles are mixed. Inclusion in the tax base of both the representative property and the real property on

---

[6] Burkhead, *op. cit.*, offers optimistic conclusions concerning trends. He suggests that "although imperfections remain, property tax resources do tend to be more uniformly distributed among the municipalities within a given metropolitan area over time" (p. 106).

which the representative property rests is clearly duplicative. Yet if the real property—a farm—is in one taxing jurisdiction and the mortgage is located in another jurisdiction, a problem arises concerning the relative rights of each jurisdiction to levy and collect the tax.

Shrinkage of Personal Property Components

In the years before the Civil War, when property tax rates everywhere were low, personal property was a substantial part of the base. In Boston, for example, the tax rate in 1850 was $6.80 per $1,000, and personal property accounted for about 40 percent of total assessments. While the amount of personal property in the form of intangibles is unknown, C. J. Bullock concluded that at this time nondeclaration was not usual.[7] But when, in the 1870's, the property tax rate in Massachusetts rose sharply, assessment of personal property diminished and real property came to be almost the only component in the tax base. This was the pattern nearly every-

TABLE 6-6. Gross Assessed Value[a] of Locally Assessed Property, 1956 and 1961

(Money amounts in billions of dollars)

Type of Property	Assessed Value		Percentage of Total	
	1961	1956	1961	1956
Real property				
Residential (nonfarm)	$163.3	$113.5	48.2	44.0
Acreage and farms	32.7	29.1	9.6	11.2
Vacant lots	7.0	4.8	2.1	1.9
Commercial and industrial	75.0	58.0	22.0	22.5
Other and unallocable	3.8	4.4	1.1	1.7
Total real property	281.9	209.8	83.0	81.3
Personal property	57.6	48.3	17.0	18.7
Total assessed property	$339.5	$258.0	100.0	100.0

Sources: U. S. Census Bureau, *1957 Census of Governments*, Vol. V, "Taxable Property Values in the United States," p. 6; *1962 Census of Governments*, Vol. II, "Taxable Property Values," pp. 7 and 28.
   [a] Before exemptions.

[7] "The Taxation of Property and Income in Massachusetts," *Selected Readings in Public Finance* (1924), p. 308.

TABLE 6-7. Assessed Tangible Personal Property Subject to Local General Property Tax, Four States, 1961

(Money amounts in millions of dollars)

State	Commercial and Industrial	Agricultural	Household	Motor Vehicles	Other	Total
Arkansas	$ 95	$ 40	$ 44	$ 93	$ 22	$ 293
Illinois	3,793	291	403	938	299	5,724
Nebraska	311	292	40	210	9	862
North Carolina	1,491	87	209	710	160	2,655
	$5,690	$710	$696	$1,951	$490	$9,534
Percentage of total	59.6	7.4	7.3	20.5	5.2	100.0

Source: *1962 Census of Governments*, Vol. II, p. 154.

where. In some states the facts of the situation were recognized by legal enactment, and in others by administrative practice that disregarded the law.

Table 6-6 shows that in 1961, 83 percent of locally assessed property was real ($281.9 billion out of a total of $339.5 billion). Personal property was assessed at $57.6 billion, of which almost the whole was tangibles. *Tangible* personal property was legally exempt in four states (Delaware, Hawaii, New York, and Pennsylvania), general coverage prevailed in sixteen states, and partial coverage elsewhere. The disappearance from the assessment rolls of some kinds of tangible property, such as household effects, is notorious, even though state law has not always recognized this fact. Assessors cannot ascertain the existence of such property by acceptable administrative techniques, and they cannot accurately value it when ascertained. Commercial and industrial tangible personal property was legally taxable in forty-six states, household personal property in thirty-three states, and motor vehicles in twenty-two states. This listing exaggerates the taxation of household personal property, since more than half of the thirty-three states provided partial exemptions. But it *underestimates* the taxation of motor vehicles, since eight states that exempt them from local general property tax apply a special property tax, and most of the remaining twenty apply some other form of taxation. Table 6-7 indicates the relative importance in 1961 of the different types of tangible personal property in four of the sixteen states where the general property tax is applicable. Commercial and industrial property made up nearly 60 percent of the total. Valuation of this kind of property is often based upon an agreement between owner and assessor, rather than on appraisal. Some states *classify* tangible personal property, taxing it at specified rates lower than the rate on real property, and sometimes—in Ohio, for example—this method works fairly well.

There are two kinds of tangible personal property used in business: (a) machinery and equipment, and (b) inventory. The former has been a more satisfactory component of the property tax than the latter. Inventory is moveable, its amount is often highly variable over the year, and its turnover is different from industry to industry (and even among firms in the same industry). Inventory can, therefore, be manipulated for the purpose of tax avoidance and its removal from the property tax base has considerable appeal.

Intangibles were legally part of the local general property tax base in nine states (plus Alaska at local option), and the *1962 Census of Governments* provides figures for seven of them. In West Virginia, so it appears, the locally assessed value of intangibles was nearly 71 percent of that of all personal property; in Wyoming, Montana, and Arkansas it was less than 5 percent. In twenty states special property taxes were legally provided, and in fifteen of these the coverage was comprehensive.[8]

This brief survey indicates that the base of the property tax is no longer general; intangibles have been legally or administratively removed. The reason is not, of course, that their value is unimportant, since intangibles account for perhaps one-third of the value of all property. Removal stems from two facts: (1) Most intangibles are representative property; to tax them as property is obviously "double" taxation. (2) Intangibles are easy to conceal; they can elude the most persistent assessor, and they will display this quality unless the rate on them is very low. Devices to detect ownership of intangibles have been suggested. None of them is feasible on a local, or even a state basis, because intangibles are so easily shiftable in location. When, some decades ago, a classified property tax

[8] *1962 Census of Governments,* Vol. II, pp. 6 and 29.

was in favor, the argument gained credence that the rate on intangibles in all localities should be $3 per $1,000, that is, approximately 5 percent of a yield of $60. A number of states chose to follow—and still do—this technique of taxing intangibles at a special low rate, uniform for the whole state.[9]

Compared with other types of property, discovery and assessment of real property is relatively easy. Adam Smith observed that "the quantity and value of the land which any man possesses can never be a secret, and can always be ascertained with great exactness."[10] While the history of property taxation in the United States makes this generalization seem oversanguine, the fact remains that real property can more readily be discovered and assessed than other kinds of property. In this area, administrative abuse is least defensible; and here abuse must be rooted out if the property tax is to be retained as the mainstay of local revenues.

Assessment

The most publicized and the most serious administrative fault of the general property tax is inaccurate assessment. The inaccuracy is of two types: (a) underassessment, and (b) deviation of individual property values from the general assessment ratio of the taxing jurisdiction.

Underassessment

Although the laws of two-thirds of the states contemplate full value assessment, deep underassessment is the practice. The *Census of Governments* in 1957 and 1962 prepared incisive and cogent materials, on a national basis, concerning the valuation of real property. As has been indicated, this property is the most important component of the general property tax, and the Census Bureau has developed extensive tabulations of assessment and sales ratio data. The numerator of the ratios is assessed value, "as shown on local tax records prior to sale"; the denominator is "measurable sales,"

[9] *Ibid.,* Table 25. The classified property tax usually classified property into three groups: real estate, tangible personal property, and intangible personal property. Different rates were applied to each group.

[10] *The Wealth of Nations,* Book V, Chap. II, Pt. II.

that is, the sales prices for properties "changing hands on an ordinary market basis."[11] The 1962 Census disclosed that, for the nation, the assessed value of locally assessed taxable real property was, on the average, 29.5 percent of market value as indicated by measurable sales during a six-month period in 1961 (Table 6-8). The ratios ranged from 5.6 percent in South Carolina to 65.5 percent in Rhode Island.[12] In seventeen states, to be sure, the law provides for assessment at specified percentages of full value.[13] But in these states the actual level is below the specified fractional level, except for Oregon and Arkansas where the law has recently been adjusted to fit existing local practice. In the other thirty-three states, assessment practice is quite out of line with the legal requirement of full value.

Undervaluation in itself is not inequitable. If all property were assessed at some uniform percentage of true value (or fair cash value, fair value, actual value), the result would be simply a higher rate of tax. In practice, however, general undervaluation has two major faults: (1) it induces inequity in individual assessments, and (2) it impairs or defeats the objectives of other state financial legislation.

[11] *1962 Census of Governments,* Vol. II, p. 9.

[12] The ACIR has calculated the average effective rate of the property tax by states for 1960 by relating tax liability to the actual value of the taxed property. The distribution of states by their effective property tax rates is:

Percent	Number of States
0.5-0.9	16
1.0-1.4	21*
1.5-1.9	9
2.0-2.4	5
	——
	51

Average: *1.4%*

* Includes the District of Columbia.

Source: ACIR, *Measures of State and Local Fiscal Capacity and Tax Effort* (1962), p. 125. It appears that, with few exceptions, states with low effective property tax rates have low per capita total state and local taxes.

[13] Alabama, 60%; Arkansas, 18%-20%; Hawaii, 70%; Indiana, 33⅓%; Iowa, 60%; Kansas, 30%; Nebraska, 35%; Oklahoma, 35%; Oregon, 25%; South Dakota, 60%; Utah, 40%; and Washington, 50%. Maryland, Minnesota, Montana, and Ohio specify various fractions for different classes of property. ACIR, *The Role of the States in Strengthening the Property Tax,* Vol. 1, p. 43.

TABLE 6-8. Distribution of States by Ratios of Assessed Value to Sales Price, 1956 and 1961

Simple Sales-Based Average	Number of States	
	1956	1961
0.0– 9.9	2	3
10.0–19.9	16	15
20.0–29.9	16	13
30.0–39.9	4	6
40.0–49.9	7	10
50.0–59.9	2	2
60.0–69.9	1	1
	48	50
Average	30.0%	29.5%

Source: *1957 Census of Governments*, Vol. V, p. 81; 1962, Vol. II, p. 94.

Inequity in Individual Assessments

More than half a century ago, C. J. Bullock diagnosed the failure of uniform and general undervaluation as follows:

If the practice is to assess realty at its true value, the assessor has a definite mark at which to aim, and the citizen a definite standard by which he can compare his assessment with his neighbor's; but when the opposite practice prevails, assessor and taxpayer alike are left in uncertainty. Absolute accuracy, of course, is not to be expected, but errors can be more readily detected if the standard is full valuation. If two buildings worth $100,000 each are assessed, the one for $20,000 and the other for $18,000, the discrepancy seems to be but $2,000; in reality it is $10,000, since it represents one-tenth part of the tax burden.[14]

Statistical evidence in support of this generalization is supplied by the ratios of assessed value to sales price secured by the *Census of Governments* for 1957 and 1962, and especially by ratios collected in 1,356 "selected areas" for nonfarm houses, a class of

[14] *Selected Readings in Public Finance*, p. 293.

TABLE 6-9. Illustrative Calculation of a Coefficient of Dispersion for Nine Properties

	Assessed Value	Assessment Ratio	Deviation[a] from Median Ratio (50.0)
A.	$ 6,400	32.0	18,0
B.	7,400	37.0	13.0
C.	8,000	40.0	10.0
D.	8,800	44.0	6.0
E.	10,000	50.0 (median)	0.0
F.	11,000	55.0	5.0
G.	11,600	58.0	8.0
H.	12,800	64.0	14.0
I.	13,200	66.0	16.0
		Total	90.0

$$\text{Average deviation} = \frac{90.0}{9} = 10.0$$

$$\text{Coefficient} = \frac{\text{Average deviation} \times 100}{\text{Median ratio}} = 20\%$$

Source: Frederick L. Bird, *The General Property Tax: Findings of the 1957 Census of Governments* (1960), p. 54.
[a] Negative and minus signs are disregarded here.

property that is large and "relatively homogeneous."[15] The Census reckoned a median ratio for each area. Individual item ratios would, of course, differ from the median, and an average of the differences can be computed. For example, in illustrative Table 6-9 the median assessment ratio of nine items of property is 50.0, and the average deviation is 10.0.

Another area might, however, have the same average deviation (10.0) but a much lower median ratio, say 25.0. To secure comparability in the ratios of assessed values to sales prices in different areas, the deviation from the median ratios within an area should be expressed in *relative*—not absolute—terms. This is accomplished by dividing the average deviation by the median assessment ratio. In the two examples previously considered, this measure—the *coefficient of dispersion*—is 20 percent for the series of properties with a median assessment ratio of 50.0 and an average deviation of

[15] *1962 Census of Governments*, Vol. II, p. 12.

TABLE 6-10. Coefficients of Intra-Area Dispersion in Relation to Median Assessment Ratios for Nonfarm Houses, Selected Areas, 1956 and 1961

Median Assessment Ratio	Coefficient of Intra-Area Dispersion	
	1956	1961
Under 20.0	37.3	32.7
20.0–29.9	32.0	26.8
30.0–39.9	25.1	23.3
40.0 or more	22.2	19.4

Sources: *1962 Census of Governments*, Vol. II, Table 17; *1957 Census of Governments*, Vol. V, Table 17.

10.0, and 40 percent for the properties with a median assessment ratio of 25.0 and the same average deviation. The relative dispersion in the latter instance is greater than in the first.

Table 6-10 shows the median assessment ratios for nonfarm houses and their coefficients of dispersion for selected local areas in 1956 and 1961. Clearly, the relationship is inverse: as assessment ratios rise—that is, as assessments come closer to sale prices—the coefficients decline—that is, relative deviation from the average diminishes. It seems then that severe undervaluation is unlikely to be uniform, and for this reason it engenders inequities in individual assessments.

Undervaluation has other faults. It obscures unequal assessments and thereby prevents a taxpayer from being aware that his assessment is out of line with that of other properties. He may suffer from an undervaluation illusion. Since the assessed value of his property is below market value, he may fondly believe that he is especially favored and therefore be silent. Even if this illusion is not present, he will have difficulty in securing a review of his assessment. When the law specifies full value, acceptable evidence of undervaluation in support of an appeal for adjustment is not easy to obtain.

Impairment of Other Financial Objectives

Assessed valuations of local governmental units have often been incorporated into state financial legislation. In the days when state governments allotted local shares of a state general property tax according to local assessed valuation, local units perceived that an easy way to cut their shares was to reduce their valuation. Such a move was, of course, easily imitated, and a rash of competitive undervaluation resulted. Discontinuance of the state tax in most states eliminated this pressure for undervaluation, but the property tax continues to be allotted on the basis of assessed valuation to raise revenue for county governments and a miscellany of other units with no tax resources of their own. State governments have also distributed some grants-in-aid and some state-collected taxes to local governments, using assessed values as an indicator. For example, state governments in allocating educational grants have often assumed that a low assessed value per child of school age indicated a low financial ability. But unless inter-area valuations are uniform, this is faulty evidence. In short, assessed value has been and is an elastic measuring stick.

State governments, perceiving these defects, have instituted state equalization of local assessments as a remedy. No attempt is made to value individual properties, but state officers estimate *aggregate* property values for each local unit, using these to secure a more equalized inter-area standard for allocation. This technique, whatever its merits, does nothing to rectify inaccurate values of particular properties or to push localities toward full-value assessment. The two broad uses of assessed valuation by the state governments pull local governments in opposite directions. A locality is tempted to set a low valuation in order to reduce its share of county tax assessment and to set a high valuation in order to secure larger shares of state grants or of state distributions of taxes.

The state equalization process has often been crudely executed, resting upon subjective and personalized decisions of a few state officers. In recent years, the sales-sampling technique has been developed. The ratios of sales price to assessed value are determined for a sample of recently-sold properties, and these ratios constitute the basis for updating and equalizing the assessments of different localities. If the sample is adequate and representative, this method has merit.

State governments should recognize that a good central assessment is important not only to provide more accurate guidelines for distribution of state grants and tax collections for counties, but also as a foundation upon which an effective state review of local assessment may be built.

Local assessed valuations have been used widely in state constitutions or in state legislation as the base for *ceilings on local debt and property tax rates*. Extensive and variable underassessment means that

regulatory policy is determined by the assessor rather than by constitution or statute. When the level of assessment declines from, say, 50 to 25 percent (a not untypical trend over the past several years) while the tax and debt limit ratios remain unchanged, the assessor has reduced effective taxing and borrowing power by one-half.[16]

Frederick L. Bird has given specific instances in his analysis of 1957 Census data. In Alabama the constitution sets the local tax ceiling at 1.25 percent of assessed valuation. The average assessment in 1956 was 18 percent (18.6 percent in 1961), and therefore the effective ceiling was 0.225 percent of full value. Such a situation helps explain why the property tax is a relatively weak source of local revenue in Alabama. In Washington the state constitution specifies a local tax ceiling of 4 percent of assessed valuation. Since the average assessment was 17 percent (14.3 percent in 1961), the effective ceiling was 0.68 percent of full value. In Indiana the debt limit for municipal corporations is 2 percent of assessed valuation. Since average assessment for the state in 1956 was 21 percent (20.8 percent in 1961), the effective limit was 0.4 percent of full value. In Pennsylvania the debt of local governments (except Philadelphia) may not exceed 7 percent of assessed valuation. An average level of assessment in 1956 of 33 percent (32.2 percent in 1961) reduced the effective limit to 2.31 percent of full value. Bird thinks that circumvention of the limitation—by the creation in Pennsylvania of school authorities and in Indiana of school building corporations —has been the outcome. The effect of tax ceilings coupled with extreme underassessment is "to compel hand-to-mouth operations and to discourage any long-range financial planning. . . . The perversion, by underassessment, of limitations on local borrowing power may be

[16] *The Role of the States in Strengthening the Property Tax*, Vol. 1, p. 45. Other less important and less familiar applications could be cited. In Wisconsin assessed valuations "serve more than 80 statutory uses."

even more detrimental to local government."[17] It has made long-term borrowing necessary to meet minor and recurring capital requirements that should be financed from current revenues; it has debarred sound capital programing and budgeting.

Tax exemptions are another instance in which the apparent objective of state legislation is distorted by general undervaluation. The homestead and the veterans' exemption—the two common types—are usually specified in dollars; for example, in Massachusetts the veterans' exemption is $2,000. In 1961 the average assessment ratio in the state for nonfarm houses was 37.5 percent, and therefore the exemption was worth $5,333. In Florida a veterans' exemption of $5,000, constitutionally provided, was worth $10,350.[18] The effect of the Florida exemption is to remove more than one-third of locally assessed real property from the tax rolls. Obviously the greater the underassessment in a state, the more valuable is an exemption stated in dollar terms.

The remedy for the defects discussed in this section is, in principle, quite obvious. Assessed values should be used only as the base for property taxes; constitutional and statutory requirements that they be used for other purposes should be abolished. A less sweeping remedy, assuming that state governments wish to continue partial property tax exemptions as well as local tax and debt limits, would be to specify that *full* value, rather than assessed value, should be the base.[19]

Uniformity of Intra-Area Assessments

While deep underassessment appears to induce inequitable assessments, full value assessment is not a practicable goal. As already indicated, when taxpayers are uninformed concerning relative underassessment, they suffer from the illusion that underassessment

[17] *The General Property Tax,* p. 42; 1961 data derived from *1962 Census of Governments,* Vol. II, Table 13.

[18] *1962 Census of Governments,* Vol. II, Table 8. The computations are as follows: with 100 percent valuation (as the law specifies) the exemption is $2,000; with 37.5 percent valuation, the exemption is worth $\frac{\$2,000}{37.5} \times 100 = \$5,333$; in Florida, $\frac{\$5,000}{48.3} \times 100 = \$10,350$.

[19] *The Role of the States in Strengthening the Property Tax,* Vol. 1, pp. 60-61.

TABLE 6-11. Distribution of Selected Local Areas by Coefficient of Intra-Area Dispersion of Assessment Ratios of Nonfarm Houses, 1956 and 1961

(In percent)

Coefficient of Intra-Area Dispersion	Percentage of Areas		Cumulative Percentage	
	1956 (1)	1961 (2)	1956 (3)	1961 (4)
Under 15.0	7.9	13.7	7.9	13.7
15.0–19.9	12.5	16.2	20.4	29.9
20.0–24.9	15.1	17.7	35.6	47.6
25.0–29.9	14.6	14.3	50.2	61.9
30.0–34.9	10.4	10.4	60.6	72.3
35.0–39.9	10.7	8.3	71.3	80.6
40.0–49.9	11.6	8.8	82.9	89.4
50.0 and over	17.1	10.6	100.0	100.0
Total	100.0	100.0		

Source: *1962 Census of Governments*, Vol. II, Table 19; *1957*, Vol. V, Table 19.

of their property is a favor. But even when free of this illusion, taxpayers feel that full value assessment would not be accompanied by reduction in the nominal rate of the property tax. They suspect, instead, that it would bring an acceleration in expenditures. Assessors also are motivated to favor undervaluation. They are aware that it blunts objections from taxpayers. Assessors suspect also that current property values are inflated, and they fear that full valuation would, in the event of deflation, bring overvaluation. Modest undervaluation is a cushion against this possibility. Some assessors are also conscious of the power over local borrowing which undervaluation puts in their hands.

The goal should, therefore, be assessment uniformity within an area at some figure not much below fair value. Since perfection here is an aspiration only, the question arises: What standard of uniformity is achievable? What coefficient of dispersion is tolerable within each assessment area? Bird has suggested a figure of 20.0 percent.[20] Table 6-11 shows the national distribution of coefficients

[20] *The General Property Tax*, p. 54. The general property tax has the peculiarity that its base, and therefore the amount of the tax liability, is determined by

TABLE 6-12. Distribution of States by Coefficients of Intra-Area Dispersion for Nonfarm Houses, 1956 and 1961

Median Area Coefficient of Intra-Area Dispersion	Number of States	
	1956	1961
Under 15.0	1	1
15.0–19.9	2	6
20.0–24.9	5	12
25.0–29.9	10	15
30.0–34.9	11	11
35.0–39.9	11	4
40.0 and over	5	0
	45[a]	49[b]

Source: Same as Table 6-11.
[a] Not computed for Arizona, Delaware, Nevada, Hawaii, and Alaska in 1956.
[b] Not computed for Alaska in 1961.

of dispersion for nonfarm houses in select local areas in 1956 and 1961. In 1956 only 20.4 percent (see Column 3), and in 1961 only 29.9 percent (see Column 4), of the areas met Bird's suggested standard. The table does, however, disclose a marked improvement in the five-year period. Room for improvement is much greater in some states than in others. As Table 6-12 shows, the median area coefficients of dispersion in 1961 for four states were over 35 percent. But again a hopeful trend appears, because the number of states with a good record increased strongly between 1956 and 1961.

The Role of the States in Reform

What part should state governments play in improving assessment procedures, and, indeed, in reforming the property tax?

administrative decision. Tax liability for retail sales tax or individual income tax is determined by the taxpayer, subject to the possibility of audit by administrators. Figures showing the results of state audits are rare and, for this reason, coefficients of dispersion for state retail sales and individual income tax cannot be computed as they have been by the Bureau of the Census for assessments of nonfarm houses. Whether or not such coefficients, if computed, would be larger or smaller than those presented above for nonfarm houses must be uncertain.

Separation of State and Local Revenue Sources

Three or four decades ago the theory in vogue was that separation of state and local sources of revenue would bring about the reform of the property tax, especially of assessment. State governments would withdraw from property tax, leaving it wholly in the hands of local governments, and thereby remove the incentive for competitive undervaluation. E. R. A. Seligman argued also that real estate, the backbone of the tax, could be "far better valued by officials of the neighborhood who are cognizant of local conditions."[21]

Some economists argued against separation. T. S. Adams declared that local desire to evade the state tax was a minor factor in inefficient assessment. Discontinuance of the state tax would, therefore, bring no improvement. Adams went on to predict that if state governments withdrew from use of property tax, state supervision and guidance of local governments in assessment would diminish. It was, he believed, "idle and academic—in the worse sense—to say that we can have general or central supervision over local taxes without the central jurisdiction making active use of the same basis of taxation."[22]

The argument in favor of state withdrawal was strongly reinforced by the desire of local governments to gain full control of property tax revenue and, in the 1930's and 1940's, state withdrawal became a fact. The evidence is strong that harm resulted. Local governments, in sole possession of general property taxation, did not improve administration; instead, standards of equity and assessment deteriorated. Moreover, the property available to local units as a tax base did not match particular local needs for expenditure. State governments were persuaded to provide financial assistance to poor localities. But sometimes this aid was misdirected: it went to units with no rational basis for existence, or to units whose fiscal ability, measured by property valuation, was misjudged.

[21] *Essays in Taxation* (9th edition, 1921), p. 353.
[22] "Separation of State and Local Revenues," *Annals of the American Academy of Political and Social Science* (March 1915), p. 134.

State Intervention

Recently a reform movement has developed that aims at rehabilitating the property tax; it assumes that state governments will be the prime movers. State governments are not to secure any revenues from the tax; their interest in reform is to be motivated by their interest in obtaining efficient and effective local government.

In what ways might greater state responsibility be displayed? One extreme is presently illustrated by Hawaii where a state agency assesses all real property, collects the revenues, and turns over the collections to the local governments. The four local units (counties) determine their tax *rate*. The record shows relative uniformity of assessments with a low degree of dispersion within and among the four counties.[23] The governmental organization of Hawaii, as well as its taxes, is highly centralized: public education, public health, and welfare functions are carried on and financed by the state government. This centralization, which differentiates Hawaii from the other states, makes centralization of assessment a natural phenomenon. Without such centralization, imitation of Hawaii is unlikely.

State governments may, perhaps, press for reforms in three other directions:[24]

(1) *Local assessment districts should be reorganized.* Each district should have adequate resources to provide professional assessment. Just how this could be done would depend on the situation: in some states the county could be the appropriate unit, but in states with many small counties the creation of regional assessment districts or assessment by state officers would be necessary.

(2) *Administration of assessment must be professionalized.* In a good many cities and large counties this step has already been taken. But over the nation the majority of assessors are elected, often for short terms, and often for part-time work.[25] Professionali-

[23] Y. S. Leong and R. M. Kamins, "Property Taxation in the 50th State," *National Tax Journal* (March 1961), pp. 59-69.

[24] *The Role of the States in Strengthening the Property Tax* spells out what state governments should do. This report was prepared for the ACIR by Frederick L. and Edna T. Bird.

[25] "Local governments are accustomed to employing trained accountants, engineers, health officers, social workers, and school teachers, but they seem willing

zation and the reorganization of assessment districts are obviously interrelated steps. Assessors qualified to do the difficult task of property valuation can only be secured when properly paid, and this, in turn, requires that each assessing unit have resources to support qualified officials.

(3) *A state agency devoted to supervising the administration of local property taxation must be established.* This agency will also engage in assessing some classes of property. Over the decades state governments have provided or offered help to local governments. Most commonly state supervisors of local assessors have given technical instruction, kept an eye on local performance, heard complaints, ordered reassessment, and so on. But strong supervision has seldom been authorized or exercised. And unless steps (1) and (2) are taken, supervision cannot be effective. The ablest and most determined supervisor cannot operate through part-time, badly paid, and unprofessional local assessors; strong supervision can, however, promote professionalization of assessors and district reorganization.

An important technique in the exercise of supervision would be collection and analysis of assessment ratios, with public announcement of the results. Individual assessing areas would thereby become aware of their own performance; taxpayers would secure information by which the equity of their assessments might be judged; state legislatures would have at hand more accurate measures of local fiscal ability.

Erosion of the Base

Reform of the property tax, so that it may become a more powerful source of local revenue, will require that erosion of the base of the property tax be halted and even reversed. This also is mainly a task for state governments. Some of the erosion is so long-established and so widespread as to be "impervious to question."[26] Exemption of the property of nonprofit religious, charitable, and edu-

---

to elect as assessor any resident citizen who is old enough to vote and does not have a criminal record, and pay him less than the school janitor. Very fortunately this is not the universal procedure, but it is sufficiently widespread to explain in part why assessing is mediocre to poor in many areas." *Ibid.*, p. 104.

[26] *Ibid.*, p. 83.

TABLE 6-13. Homestead Exemptions, 1961

(Money amounts in millions of dollars)

State	Amount of Homestead Exemptions	Percentage of Assessed Value
Florida	$4,213	32.0
Georgia	858	33.7
Hawaii	181	8.4
Louisiana	765	34.7
Mississippi	370	44.5
Oklahoma	418	23.1

Source: *1962 Census of Governments*, Vol. II, p. 6.

cational institutions rests upon the opinion that they render semigovernmental services and promote the public welfare. But local governments can fairly ask that the exemption not be broadened. Exemption of major classes of property—intangible and some types of tangible personal property—has often been undertaken as a step in the reform of the general property tax; this erosion also is justifiable. But erosion by state legislation to provide hidden subsidies to private persons or firms is highly questionable. The property tax is paid directly only by owners, and property tax concessions cannot, therefore, be assured for a veteran or an aged person who is not an owner-occupant of real property. A tax concession to a class of persons—the aged—assumes that all of them are in need, and this is not so.

Some of the major exemptions are described below:

Homestead Exemptions

Six states allow some exemption from the local property tax to owner-occupied homes or farms, the exemption ranging from $1,000 in Oklahoma to $5,000 in Florida and Mississippi. Table 6-13 shows the total dollar amount of this exemption by states, as well as the total as a percentage of gross assessed value. In two of the six states—Louisiana and Mississippi—the state governments reimburse localities for loss of property taxes.[27] In the other four states

[27] Iowa provides a homestead exemption by way of a tax credit paid from state funds, and four other states provide the exemption only against *state* taxes.

TABLE 6-14. Veterans' Exemptions, 1961

(In millions of dollars)

State	Amount of Veterans' Exemptions
California	$ 972
New York	634
Connecticut	263
New Jersey	217
Iowa	122
Other[a]	378
	$2,586

Source: Same as Table 6-13.
[a] Arizona, Idaho, Indiana, Maine, New Hampshire, New Mexico, Oregon, Rhode Island, and Wyoming.

the exemption narrows the tax base of local governments. The narrowing is quite uneven—severe in a residential locality and light in an industrial one. The homestead exemption is, of course, useless to persons living in rented quarters.

Veterans' Exemptions

While thirty-two states grant some kind of property tax exemption to veterans, the 1962 Census gives figures only for fourteen, and in only five does the exemption total in excess of $100 million for 1961 (Table 6-14). Benefits to veterans should not depend upon property ownership, and the cost of the benefits should not fall chiefly upon nonexempt property. State benefit programs should rest upon the need and the merit of veterans and be financed from the general revenues of the state.

Exemptions for the Aged

Four states—Massachusetts, Maine, Indiana, and New Jersey —give a property tax exemption to the aged, and in many other states such a step is under discussion. The defects of the homestead and the veterans' exemptions apply also to this program.

Business Exemptions

Exemption from the local property tax for a specified period has, intermittently, been tried in many states. At present eight states

(Alabama, Louisiana, Kentucky, Maryland, Mississippi, Rhode Island, South Carolina, and Vermont) allow local units to exempt certain types of industrial property. The aim is to induce investment in the locality by new firms, and three of the eight states permit existing firms to share in the subsidy by exempting *additions* to plant and equipment. Quantitative evidence concerning the effects of the exemption is scanty and unsatisfactory, partly because administration is usually by local governments with no central recording of the relevant data, and partly because data concerning investment and locational decisions by firms are often unreliable. Even if positive advantages are secured by a particular locality, these are offset by the injury to competitors elsewhere and to taxpayers in the locality. In a national sense, the exemption is bound to be injurious.

The States' Responsibility

Most of the erosion of the local property tax base is a matter of state decision; state legislatures have thereby subsidized worthy purposes or groups at the indirect expense of local governments. This form of subsidy fails to provide equitable benefits since provision is denied to members of the group who do not own real property and quite often given to those who do, regardless of their need; it fails also in the equitable distribution of costs, since the amount of property removed from the tax base of a locality is unrelated to its total financial situation. How, then, can one explain the use of property tax exemptions? State legislatures, responsive to organized pressure, use property tax exemption as a way to act without placing an expenditure in state (or local) budgets. But a slice is taken from the tax base of local governments. The indicated conclusion is that, if a state subsidy is to be offered, its weight should be on state rather than on local resources. An obvious step, when the subsidy takes the form of a property tax exemption, is reimbursement to local governments for the shrinkage in their tax base.

State Assessment of Types of Property

Some kinds of property are quite unsuitable for local assessment. Such an instance emerged a century ago with the railroads. Valuation of the operating property of a railway, piece by piece, made no sense; the valuation had to be of the whole system, or at least of the part lying within a state. As a result, most states decided to make a central assessment of railway property, the property of most public utilities, and sometimes other classes of property. Local governments, however, often are allowed to assess nonoperative property, that is, property with a local situs which, while owned by the utility, is not part of its business operations. In 1961, state-assessed property amounted to $27,843 million out of a total of $355,716 million of taxable property. The state-assessed property was classified as follows: [28]

Property	Millions of Dollars
Railroads	$ 5,939
Other public utilities	18,754
Other (mostly mining property)	3,150
Total	$27,843

The shift to state assessment was not easily achieved; it had to overcome "both the hostile presumption against any state agency and the natural inertia supporting the local assessor."[29] And the shift did not follow any simple pattern. Sometimes states not only valued but taxed the property for their own use; sometimes they apportioned the centrally assessed valuation for taxation by local units. The methods that states used to apply the property tax to centrally

[28] *1962 Census of Governments,* Vol. II, p. 29. States show great variation in the percentage of total local taxable assessed value which is represented by state-assessed property, as may be seen in the following tabulation based on figures for 1961:

Percentage of Total	Number of States
None	11*
Under 9.9	11
10.0–19.9	14
20.0–29.9	10
30.0–39.9	1
40.0–49.9	2
50.0–59.9	1
Over 60.0	1 (Hawaii, 100%)
Total	51

* Including the District of Columbia.

[29] Jens P. Jensen, *Property Taxation in the United States* (1931), p. 420.

assessed property were also very diverse.[30] The wisest step would be to abolish the congeries and replace them by some reasonable single substitute. But this seems unlikely to happen. Each state can and should, however, equate its taxation, *intrastate,* with the taxation of locally assessed property. The evidence seems to be that utility property is assessed in many states at values relatively higher than locally assessed property.

Interstate allocation of centrally assessed property is plagued by state over-reaching. The ACIR has commented that "a tendency exists for the states to allocate to themselves fractions of value that add to more than 100 percent of total value."[31] Fair allocation formulas have been framed (notably by the Western States Association of Tax Administrators), but progress toward adoption has been very slight.

Conclusion

The recent trend toward rehabilitation of the property tax should be strengthened and accelerated. This will require vigorous support from state governments. Is effective support likely to be forthcoming unless it is accompanied by restoration of the tax as a source of state revenue? State withdrawal from the use of the property tax in the past three decades has been widely approved—not, indeed, because of the inherent merit of "separation" of state and local revenues, or because of inequities in property taxation. The economic and distributional faults of this tax are no greater than those of state sales and business taxes. Moreover, the faults, whatever they may be, are not altered when manifested at the local, rather than at the state level. Withdrawal by state governments is applauded because, thereby, local governments are provided with the only major tax from which they can safely secure a large and dependable revenue.

[30] *1962 Census of Governments,* Vol. II, pp. 3–4, describes the property tax bases used by the states for railway and other utilities. These are too detailed for presentation here. Moreover, no general description by states of what utility property is centrally assessed would be accurate. A state will follow different policies toward different utilities; states will differ among themselves concerning the scope of central assessment, and concerning the extent of its application even to a given type of utility.

[31] *The Role of the States in Strengthening the Property Tax,* Vol. 1, p. 147.

Exercise of state supervision over local performance of many governmental functions—education, health, welfare—is extensive. It rests simply upon a concept of state responsibility, unassociated with a concept of state financial gain. A state government is concerned with efficient performance of all duties by all its governmental units. State interest in establishing and maintaining reasonable standards of property tax administration should be as vital as its interest in public education. Moreover, efficient local use of property tax will simplify for state governments the problems of financial transfers to localities.

A political philosophy widespread in the United States is that strong local governments are vital to successful democracy, and that their strength can be maintained only by possession of appreciable financial independence. These generalizations or beliefs must, however, be given a reasonable interpretation. Strong local government does not mean anarchic autonomy; appreciable financial independence does not mean nonreceipt of state grants-in-aid. State governments should formulate a pattern of financial rules appropriate to the different types of local units; they should see that the rules are observed; they should supply needy units with grants which, when added to local revenues, will enable governmental services to be provided at an acceptable level. Local autonomy has meaning only within this framework.

Are state governments efficient enough to do their part in reforming the property tax? Do not many state governments themselves need reform which should, perhaps, precede reform of local taxation? Sometimes the answer should be affirmative. It would be retrograde if an inept and unrepresentative state legislature tried to reform administration of property tax in localities which, through professional assessors, had already secured uniformity in assessment of property. In most states, however, the glaring weakness of property taxation is displayed in governmental units too poor or too small. If attention is centered on them, state action can bring improvement nearly everywhere. Moreover, the framework indicated above for reforming the property tax does not, in any event, indicate state intrusion upon local units that already perform well.

Some critics allege that rehabilitation of the property tax is inspired by a desire to restrain the growth of government. Talk of vigorous local governments financing important functions from their own revenues is subterfuge; the covert and real purpose is to hinder a shift of functions to a higher governmental level—state or federal—where paucity of financial resources would be a less serious obstacle to performance. The allegation is not without substance; some proponents of strong local government are concerned merely to secure less government. But such a manifestation of deceit should not obscure the merit of the traditional position. Strong local government has been the bulwark of democracy; strength and vitality in local government have been nourished by local decisions concerning the levy of taxes; the property tax is the only major tax that is suitable for local administration. And the admission should be made that even perfect rehabilitation would not provide many local governments with financial means adequate to their needs. It is the duty of each state government to see that the level of performance of governmental services is adequate everywhere within its boundaries, and this will require extensive use of intergovernmental transfers. Efficient use of the property tax will help rather than hinder this process. Besides supplying localities with a substantial portion of the revenue that they need, it will establish a fair base from which additional financial needs can be measured.

CHAPTER VII

Nonproperty Taxes and Nontax Revenue

> "After all the proper subjects of taxation have been exhausted, if the exigencies of the state still continue to require new taxes, they must be imposed upon improper ones." *The Wealth of Nations,* Book V, Chapter 2.

THE DOMINANCE OF THE PROPERTY TAX as a source of tax revenue for local governments rests chiefly on the scarcity of alternatives. A local government has a limited and artificial territorial jurisdiction; movement of persons and of some types of property beyond its boundaries is easy, and this movement may be induced by differential local tax rates. But real property, and especially real estate, is immobile, and it can therefore be taxed by local governments with a less acute fear of consequences.

These simple generalizations are, however, less forceful and applicable for some types of local governments than others. A *large city* may have advantages as a center for distribution or manufacturing that are not greatly impaired by a city sales or income tax. A large city, will, moreover, have administrative resources that may enable it to handle taxes quite beyond the capacity of a small city.

Local Nonproperty Taxes

It is, therefore, not surprising that the first major employment of local nonproperty taxes was made by large cities. In 1934 New

York City adopted a retail sales tax, and in 1938 New Orleans followed suit. Philadelphia in 1938 varied the pattern by adopting an earnings tax. The urgent and decisive force behind these experiments was the impact of severe depression. New York City was spending heavily for relief, and opposition to a sales tax was appeased by declaring the tax revenue to be "a contribution to relief." In Philadelphia similar financial pressures led, in 1938, to enactment of a sales tax which was, however, repealed after ten months because of the belief that trade was being diverted from the city. A flat-rate (1½ percent) tax on income earned in Philadelphia by individuals and unincorporated businesses was accepted as a substitute. Dividends, interest, and corporate profits were not taxable.

These examples awakened the interest of city governments over the nation, an interest which was revivified in postwar years by the accumulation of a large backlog of desired public services. In two states, Ohio and California, "home rule" statutes allowed extensive tax powers to local governments, that is, specific enabling legislation for particular localities was not necessary. Accordingly, in 1945-46 five California cities enacted sales taxes, and other California cities soon followed. Before long these cities were imposing *use* taxes in attempts to protect the trade of their own merchants. Businesses that sold in many municipalities found it nearly impossible to comply with the numerous and dissimilar local requirements. The confusion was resolved in 1955 by converting local taxes to a 1 percent tax supplement to the state sales tax. A local income tax was adopted by Toledo, Ohio, in 1946, and other Ohio cities followed.

The experience of Pennsylvania was somewhat different. In 1947 the state government authorized local governments to utilize any tax not used by the state. The response was so exuberant that the state legislature was forced to draw up ground rules for the local use of taxing powers. No adequate appraisal of the Pennsylvania experience is available, but it seems likely that the "tax anything" law was not one that should be copied in other states.

Geographic Distribution

The use of local sales and income taxes has become quite extensive. *Local income taxes* are levied in six states, although in Alabama only one city and in Missouri and Michigan only two and three cities, are involved. Table 7-1 shows the number of municipalities, by states, levying an income tax in 1963.

TABLE 7-1. Municipal Income Taxes, 1963

State	Municipal Units Levying Income Tax	Rates
Pennsylvania	44 cities 350 boroughs 145 townships 1,265 school districts	1% or less except for Philadelphia (1.625%)
Ohio	83 cities and villages	.5% to 1%
Kentucky	13 cities 1 county	1% to 2%
Michigan	3 cities	1%
Missouri	2 cities	.5% and 1%
Alabama	1 city	2%

Source: Advisory Commission on Intergovernmental Relations, *Tax Overlapping in the United States, 1964* (1964), Table 59.

Local general sales taxes, now used in thirteen states by over 2,000 local governments, are most numerous in Illinois, California, and Mississippi. Table 7-2 shows the pattern.

Relative Importance of Types of Taxes

The *general* sales tax was by far the most productive of local nonproperty taxes in 1963, yielding over 38 percent of total non-property tax revenue. This tax was levied by approximately 2,000 local governments. As Table 7-3 shows, *selective* sales taxes produced $518 million—19 percent of the total. The most important of these taxes was that on public utility gross receipts, levied in most states by local governments under their regulatory power. Income taxes yielded 11 percent of nonproperty tax revenue.

Because of the spotty distribution of nonproperty taxes, aggregate figures of collections for all local governments, or even for all cities, obscure their importance for some local governments. Table

TABLE 7-2. Local General Sales Tax Rates, January 1, 1964

State	State Tax Rate	Units Levying Local Sales Tax				
		½%	1%	2%	3%	4%
Alabama	4%					
77 municipalities		—	72	5	—	—
18 counties		2	15	1	—	—
Alaska	—					
32 municipalities		—	2	20	10	—
4 school districts		—	2	2	—	—
Arizona	3					
9 municipalities		3	6	—	—	—
California	3					
385 municipalities		—	385	—	—	—
58 counties		—	58	—	—	—
Colorado	2					
6 municipalities		—	5	1	—	—
Illinois	3½					
1,170 (approx.) municipalities		1,170	—	—	—	—
68 counties		68	—	—	—	—
Louisiana	2					
14 municipalities		—	14	—	—	—
4 parishes		—	4	—	—	—
1 school district		—	1	—	—	—
Mississippi	3					
151 municipalities		39	112	—	—	—
New Mexico	3					
23 municipalities		—	23	—	—	—
New York	—					
8 municipalities		—	2	5	—	1
5 counties		—	1	3	1	—
1 school district		1	—	—	—	—
Tennessee	3					
2 counties		—	2	—	—	—
Utah	3					
133 municipalities		133	—	—	—	—
24 counties		24	—	—	—	—
Virginia	—					
1 municipality (Bristol)		—	—	—	1	—

Source: *Tax Overlapping*, Table 45. Footnotes concerning details are omitted.

TABLE 7-3. Local Nonproperty Tax Revenue by Type of Tax, 1963

(Money amounts in millions of dollars)

Type of Tax	Amount	Percentage of Total
General sales	$1,065	38.5
Selective sales	518	18.7
Motor fuel	32	
Alcoholic beverages	33	
Tobacco products	64	
Public utilities	332	
Other	57	
Income	313	11.3
License and other	867	31.5
Total	$2,763	100.0

Source: U. S. Census Bureau, *Governmental Finances in 1963* (1964), p. 22.

7-4 lists the twenty-two cities for which, in 1962, nonproperty taxes amounted to more than 30 percent of all their tax collections. For these cities, dependence on the property tax has weakened.

Development of new sources of revenue has, then, been mostly an urban phenomenon confined to a *limited number of states*. In these states—whether from a strong and positive home rule senti-

TABLE 7-4. Local Nonproperty Taxes as a Percentage of Total Local Tax Collections, Selected Cities, 1962

City	Percentage of Local Tax Collections	City	Percentage of Local Tax Collections	City	Percentage of Local Tax Collections
Columbus	74.1	Long Beach	49.3	San Diego	37.4
Toledo	60.8	Cincinnati	47.8	Norfolk	37.1
St. Louis	59.5	Birmingham	46.4	New York	36.6
Louisville	55.1	Tampa	45.6	Oakland	32.3
Philadelphia	53.6	Seattle	44.5	Honolulu	31.2
New Orleans	51.7	Los Angeles	41.8	Miami	30.5
Kansas City, Mo.	50.0	Chicago	39.3		
Dayton	49.3	Phoenix	37.6		

Source: Derived from *Tax Overlapping*, Table 24.

ment, or from a disinclination of legislatures to lift local problems to the state level—local governments have been allowed to experiment with taxes. But in most states this sort of experimentation has been unacceptable.

Local nonproperty tax revenue was less than 15 percent of total tax collections in 36 states in 1962. Fourteen states collecting more than 15 percent are given below:[1]

Alabama	44.2%	Louisiana	22.1%
Hawaii	33.0	Virginia	20.7
Alaska	26.0	Kentucky	20.5
Nevada	25.4	Mississippi	19.4
New Mexico	24.9	Missouri	18.7
Pennsylvania	23.8	Florida	16.5
New York	23.0	Washington	16.0

Defects of the Taxes

The defects of these local nonproperty taxes are plain. Because of the limited geographic jurisdiction of the governmental units, the distribution of employment and of purchasing is distorted. Decisions of workers, firms, and consumers are altered, impairing efficiency. Compliance costs are high, especially for firms that do business in many taxing jurisdictions. The injurious effects of the taxes may not be confined to the local areas that levy them; they may affect the economic development of the state, and, more obviously, state governments may find their future freedom to use taxes hindered by the prior occupancy of their local units. The types of nonproperty taxes in common use do not, moreover, rate highly on grounds of equity even when levied by a large geographic jurisdiction. Local levy aggravates and adds to the inequities, since incidence depends upon residence inside or outside the boundaries of a city. Proponents of the local nonproperty taxes have, nonetheless, one effective retort to complaints: admitting all of the above defects, what of the faults of alternative local taxes? Are they greater or smaller?

State Intervention

State governments, if fearful of excesses of local autonomy, may intervene with restraint or with vigor. A modest step by a state gov-

[1] *Tax Overlapping,* Table 21.

ernment might be, for example, to provide local governments with information, training facilities, and technical advice. State legislation might, furthermore, enable localities to act in concert in framing and administering a revenue measure. More vigorous intervention might take the form of authorizing localities to levy a supplement to a state tax, or of permitting a tax credit. Both of these devices require the prior adoption of a tax by a state government, and both may be suspect or unwelcome to localities because they bring state control.

The *tax supplement* means that local governments are allowed to add a local tax rate to the state rate. Each local government has the responsibility of imposing the tax and of specifying its rate (within limits). The state administers the total tax, sharing an appropriate amount of collections with the local governments. In six states—Mississippi, California, Illinois, New Mexico, Tennessee, and Utah—local sales tax supplements are in use. The tax supplement could not be employed where segments of the base of a tax are not plainly definable as within a local jurisdiction. Local supplements to a state income tax, for example, would raise questions concerning the location of income which could be solved only by arbitrary decision.

The *tax credit* allows taxpayers to offset (credit) an amount paid as a specified local tax against their tax liability for a similar state tax. While complete state collection and administration of the local tax is not a necessary feature of crediting (or even identical state and local definitions of tax base, and so on), such steps seem likely to be the rule. At present state-local credits have little application. One clear instance is the Florida cigarette tax. The state levies and collects a tax of eight cents per package, but if local units impose a tax, it is creditable against the state tax. The local units have taken maximum advantage of this arrangement, reducing the net state tax to zero. (The state retains 3 percent of collections to cover its administrative expenses.) The credit, therefore, operates as a state-collected, locally-shared tax.

Tax sharing has long been extensively used at the state-local level. As indicated in Chapter II, when state governments sliced off types of property from the base of the general property tax, they usually agreed to share with localities the proceeds of the state taxes levied as substitutes. Centralization at the state level, for the sake of efficient collection, led to sharing the proceeds with local units on some agreed basis. Frequently the basis was changed later when the formula—based upon origin of collections—provided too much revenue for rich localities and too little for poor ones. The shared taxes, in such cases, have lost their distinctive feature; they resemble grants-in-aid except that, unlike grants, their annual amount depends on annual yield.

The theoretical similarity between the tax supplement, the tax credit, and tax sharing at the state-local level is obvious. The different names reflect a different historical origin rather than a difference in substance. All the devices bring centralization; all reflect the ineluctable fact that local governments are narrowly circumscribed in their capacity to tax.

Nontax Revenue

State governments first ventured extensively into commercial enterprises in the 1820's. By this time a population of over two and a half million had poured into the West, and streams of internal commerce had begun to take shape. Internal improvements would swell this commerce; they would, moreover, enhance the economic growth of states served by them. But the improvements were too risky and required too much capital for private enterprise to handle.[2] Why might not large-scale improvements be federal? Because "a defect of constitutional authority"—to use President Madison's phrase—barred such action. The Constitution had made no provision for federal expenditure of this sort. To use the welfare clause as justification for federal action might endanger the Union because it would obliterate the functional boundaries between federal and state responsibility.

Since federal intervention was debarred, use of direct state enterprise or state guarantees seemed indicated. It happened that, at this very time, state governments could borrow with unprecedented ease. The nation was prosperous, and foreign capital (especially British capital) was flowing into the United States. The safest use of

[2] At this time no industrial enterprise in the nation had a capital of as much as a million dollars.

this capital was in federal securities, but in the 1820's they were being retired out of federal surpluses at a remarkable rate. What was more natural than that foreign investors, unacquainted with the intricacies of federalism, should regard state securities as a close substitute for federal? Accordingly, the issuance of state debt for internal improvements found a ready market.

Almost all of the state enterprises proved unprofitable. And when, after 1837, the nation suffered first a severe economic crisis and then a prolonged depression, states that had borrowed for internal improvements suffered acute financial difficulties. Some defaulted, and in all of them a revulsion of opinion led citizens to amend state constitutions to prohibit the use of state credit for business undertakings.

Public Service Enterprises

When the next great revival of interest in public ownership developed, local rather than state governments were to be the instruments. A keen debate developed late in the nineteenth century over public versus private ownership of public service industries—the supply of water, gas, electricity, transportation, and so on. These enterprises were "natural" monopolies. Competition in the supply of such services was not sensible. The choice was either to make the activity a public function, or to assign it to a private company subject to public regulation. More than a century ago, John Stuart Mill stated the alternatives clearly:

When, therefore, a business of real public importance can only be carried on advantageously upon so large a scale as to render the liberty of competition almost illusory, it is an unthrifty dispensation of the public resources that several costly sets of arrangements should be kept up for the purpose of rendering to the community this one service. It is much better to treat it at once as a public function; and if it be not such as the government itself could beneficially undertake, it should be made over entire to the company or association which will perform it on the best terms for the public.[3]

On what grounds might a choice be made between (a) public ownership and operation, and (b) private ownership and operation

[3] *Principles of Political Economy* (Ashley Edition, London, 1920), pp. 143–44.

with public regulation? Here a split in opinion developed which continued into the twentieth century. D. F. Wilcox, long a leading advocate of municipal ownership, believed that "the complexity and difficulty of public control, either by franchise contract or by police regulation," were so great that public ownership and operation were indicated.[4] The public service corporations required a franchise in order to get under way; they had to secure government permission to use the streets, or to acquire land by the right of eminent domain. Government, and especially local government, had to grant special privileges to public service enterprises. On grounds of efficiency alone, Wilcox favored public ownership and operation.

Professor F. W. Taussig, while much less certain, still believed that "the experiment of public ownership and operation should be tried, and every effort made to bring it to a successful issue. The most promising field would seem to be the municipality of moderate size."[5]

It was important, however, to select for the experiment those ventures that might, on economic grounds, be most likely to be successful as government enterprises, and here a number of general tests were offered: (1) Did the business have a small capital account? (2) Were its operations routine in nature? (3) Was the flow of revenue certain and steady?[6] A small capital account was desirable because government, at least at the local level, often seemed unable to establish and maintain an accurate system of accounting for depreciation. The Census Bureau has regularly complained that such statistics of municipal public service enterprises are defective. When, in 1952, Professors Robert M. Haig and Carl S. Shoup examined the financial problems of New York City, they found that "the best data available on the financial significance of the various public enterprises to the city are those published by the Census Bureau."[7] The desirability of routine operations arose because government enterprises seemed not to be energetic in introducing tech-

[4] *Municipal Franchises* (1910), p. 803.
[5] *Principles of Economics* (1921), Vol. II, p. 433.
[6] Adam Smith explained the success of the post office as a government enterprise as follows: "The capital to be advanced is not very considerable. There is no mystery in the business. The returns are not only certain, but immediate." *The Wealth of Nations* (Everyman's Library), Vol. II, p. 300.
[7] *The Financial Problem of the City of New York: A Report to the Mayor's Committee on Management Survey* (1952), p. 319.

nological changes. If, moreover, the operations were subject to easy scrutiny by users of the services, performance could be kept up to the mark. The advantage of a certain and steady flow of income was that the government enterprise could operate on a semi-cash basis, avoiding the accumulation of debts and reserves.

For the first four decades of this century, municipal ownership and operation of public service companies progressed, and great expectations were entertained by proponents. But in the last two decades municipal ownership has lost its appeal. The reasons are twofold: public regulation has become more effective, and the actual results of municipal ownership and operation have been disappointing. A brief examination of recent financial results is offered below.

WATER SUPPLY. Perhaps three-quarters of the localities with a water supply system are operating them under public ownership, making this the most extensive example of municipal utility enterprise. Here the welfare consideration of public health has been decisive. Private enterprise cannot be expected to give adequate weight to the health benefits accruing to the whole community through a pure supply of water. Similar considerations arise out of the need for adequate fire protection. Moreover, municipalities—especially the large ones—have had to reach out to distant areas in order to secure a water supply, and this often requires the use of extraordinary powers not readily delegated to a private concern.

During the past decade the ratio of operating expenditure to revenue for water supply systems has held steady at about 68 percent; annual revenues have exceeded operating expenses plus interest by approximately 45 percent (see Table 7-5). It should, however, be noted that the companies pay no taxes, that they borrow at

TABLE 7-5. Operating Revenue and Expenditure, Local Water Supply Systems, 1953 and 1963

(Money amounts in millions of dollars)

Year	Revenue	Expenditure	Ratio of Expenditure to Revenue
1953	$ 939	$ 631	67.2%
1963	1,865	1,273	68.3

Source: Appendix Table A-18 where figures are shown for the decade.

a low rate because they issue tax-exempt bonds,[8] and that adequate amortization charges are not included as costs. But no attempt can be made to adjust the figures.

OTHER PUBLIC SYSTEMS. Public ownership of *electric power* is much less usual, and, at the local level, is usually confined to distribution systems. Some aggregate figures of revenue and expenditure appear in Appendix Table A-18. Public systems of *gas supply* have recently been growing in the South, and are financially self-supporting. Public *transit systems,* however, do not manage to cover operating expenses. In the near future the deficits seem likely to mount rather than diminish, since the recent modest additions to public transit have been rescue operations by which unprofitable privately-owned systems have been bought out. No simple explanation of transit deficits is plausible, and no simple remedy can be offered. An increase in fare would cause some riders to use their private automobiles instead, leaving some transit capacity unutilized and adding to the congestion of city streets. In metropolitan areas attempts to change from a flat charge to differential fares based on distance or the time at which a ride is taken have met with strong and effective resistance. The New York subway system, for example, has had a flat-rate fare for decades. The fare was increased from 5 to 10 cents in 1948, and from 10 to 15 cents in 1953. Despite large operating deficits (exclusive of debt charges), the fare remains at 15 cents. The system pays no taxes, either federal, state or local; costs of construction, new equipment, and debt service are borne by the city.

SELF-SUPPORT OR DEFICIT. A common generalization is that public service enterprises should be self-supporting. As must now be apparent, this generalization hides ambiguities. Sometimes it means merely that the enterprises should cover operating costs, or operating costs plus depreciation and interest. But since the enterprises do not pay taxes, a sum equivalent to the taxes that would be paid by a private concern should also be included as a cost. Unless this is done, consumers of the services are subsidized in kind, the amount of the subsidy depending on the amount of their consumption. And even if a decision is made to include as costs all expenses that would be borne by a similar private enterprise, debate will arise

[8] See Chapter VIII for a discussion of these and other aspects of local debt.

concerning equivalents. What *are* the appropriate amounts to include in lieu of taxes? What amount of subsidy is provided by the right to issue bonds with provisions exempting the income from federal income tax? Answers to these questions are hard to come by, and yet without standard municipal accounting no factual basis exists for determining or evaluating pricing policies.

A local government may make a deliberate decision to operate a public enterprise at a deficit. Such a plan may be thought desirable if it promotes some *collective* goal, or if it brings about a *redistribution of income* from richer to poorer persons. Thus a deficit in a water supply enterprise may be thought desirable on the ground that some portion of the benefits from water consumption accrues to citizens collectively rather than to them as individuals. Similarly a deficit in a public transit system may be accepted on the ground that consumption is largely by low-income users, and that the amount of consumption varies inversely with income.

The situation where benefits from the enterprise accrue, in some degree, to nonconsumers of its services is difficult to make precise. Spillovers occur from actions by *private* enterprise. A firm, by its location and existence in an area, may bring increases in property values; it may bring other collective benefits of which no account can be taken in its pricing policy. One might argue, therefore, that unless the external benefits resulting from a public enterprise are both widespread and of obvious significance, pricing below cost requires some other justification—perhaps a welfare one.

The question relevant to this case is: Who are the *recipients* of the subsidy when pricing is less than cost? Obviously the users, and they receive a subsidy in kind rather than in money. If all users are low-income, or indeed if the amount of consumption is inverse to income, the subsidy would seem to be properly directed. Actual measurement of use in relation to income status is difficult. But the common situation is that some users of the services of a transit system have low incomes, and some do not; some low-income users are large users, some are small, and some are nonusers. Subsidization in kind (through a deficit) has the built-in defect that it is specific rather than general. A low-income person who is a nonuser gains no subsidy. Therefore government, when subsidizing for welfare reasons, should be wary of subsidization through pricing of commercial services below unit cost.

Still another awkward question arises when the *incidence of the deficit* is examined. The annual deficit of, for example, a transit system, has to be met by taxes. The taxes may offset—wipe out—the subsidy. If the incidence of these taxes is regressive, their burden, as a percentage of income, falls more heavily on low- than on high-income persons. The likelihood—almost the certainty—is, however, that individual low-income persons who are steady users of the transit system will retain a substantial subsidy. Local tax systems, while regressive, do collect much larger *absolute* amounts from persons as their income rises. Thus, a sales tax with an effective rate of 4 percent for a person with an income of $2,000, and 2 percent for a person with an income of $10,000, collects $80 and $200 from each, respectively. A flat subsidy via a low transit fare of $100 yearly per steady user would, therefore, be cut into but not wiped out for a low-income user by a regressive tax; it would be for a high-income user.

In view of the imperfections of subsidization through public enterprises, one may wonder why it is so extensive. Part of the explanation seems to be inflexibility in the face of changing circumstances, and part the familiar intrusion of "political" decisions. Rising money costs, coupled with a rising price level, have prevailed for three decades; increases of prices of the products of public enterprises have lagged. The visibility of unit increases in transit fares is great; the effectiveness of protest in checking action has been demonstrated; the certainty that repeated deficits will not bring a decrease in supply of the service—all these factors encourage irrational pricing by municipal enterprises despite the desperate need of local governments for additional revenue.[9]

Highways

Except for streets and toll roads, the highway system is financed mainly through user taxes, especially on motor fuel. This is a form

[9] J. A. Stockfisch estimated that in 1957 Los Angeles could have raised $35.0-$37.6 million if a more rational method of pricing had been followed by its enterprises (the Harbor Department, the Airport Department, the Power System, and the Water System). This revenue could have been used either for tax relief or for financing additional activities. "Fees and Service Charges as a Source of City Revenues: A Case Study of Los Angeles," *National Tax Journal* (June 1960), pp. 111-21.

of indirect pricing. Almost all of the revenue of governments from taxation of motor fuel and motor vehicles is earmarked for highway purposes. It is, therefore, plausible to describe the highway system as a sort of public utility, operated by government. The analogy is, however, imperfect since the linkage between individual payment and benefit is imprecise. In particular, most highway users in thinly settled areas secure benefits in the form of good roads for which they do not make equivalent payments in the form of highway user taxes; highway users in urban areas are in the opposite situation.

Streets are financed mainly from general taxes; in addition, a limited mileage is financed by *tolls*—direct pricing—which link cost with benefit to the user. A major factor in the decision to utilize one or the other method is cost of administration. Toll highways have limited entry and egress points, and this feature implies and requires a heavy traffic density in order to meet administrative costs.

TOLL ROADS. Toll roads in the modern sense are a phenomenon of the 1930's and the postwar years. Interest in them was stimulated because too much of the revenues from users of motor vehicles had gone to lightly travelled roads, and too little to roads with heavy traffic. When people became convinced that more resources should be devoted to the latter, several obstacles stood in the way. Formulas for allocation of revenues from user charges were often firmly embedded in state legislation, and proposals for alteration raised objections. Increase of user charges was unpalatable, and, besides, would not meet the problem unless a new allocation of expenditure could be secured. Toll roads *did* seem to be a feasible solution. In areas of heavy traffic they could be financed on the benefit principle so that users would pay tolls covering the costs of construction and maintenance. The toll method of finance, moreover, allowed borrowing for construction through revenue bonds, thus avoiding constitutional or statutory restrictions applicable to regular borrowing.

For a number of years toll road mileage grew very rapidly, and continued growth seemed likely in areas of heavy traffic. But the Federal Highway Act of 1956 put a damper on new toll road construction which seems likely to be effective for several decades. The act provided (among other things) for construction of a National System of Interstate and Defense Highways of 41,000 miles. Ninety percent of the cost is paid for by federal grants from a new Highway Trust Fund into which revenue from federal excises on gasoline, tires, and so forth, is deposited. Although the roads have limited access, with existing toll roads incorporated into the system, federal money cannot be used to construct toll roads. Since much of the mileage suitable for toll roads is now part of the interstate system, future toll road construction seems likely to be modest.[10] Nonetheless, for many years ahead, a modest highway mileage will be financed by the levy of tolls on users—a direct pricing system. Expenditure for operation and construction of the toll road system in 1963 was $433.7 million, while revenue was $440.4 million.

OTHER HIGHWAYS. On all other highways, some $11,301 million was spent by all levels of government in 1963. (See Table 7-6). Most federal expenditure—95 percent—was intergovernmental, that is, in the form of grants; 16 percent of state expenditure was intergovernmental.

TABLE 7-6. Highway Expenditure by All Levels of Government, 1963

(In millions of dollars)

Level of Government	Highway Expenditure		
	Direct	Intergovernmental	Total
All levels	$11,301		$11,301[a]
Federal	165	2,981	3,146
State	7,425	1,416	8,841
Local	3,710	29	3,739

Source: *Governmental Finances in 1963*, p. 24.
[a] Duplicative transactions between levels of government excluded.

[10] The publicly owned toll road mileage, according to the year of construction, is as follows:

1924–40	266 miles	1953	88 miles	1959	133 miles
1947	47	1954	123	1960	22
1949	30	1955	471	1961	—
1950	130	1956	900	1962	—
1951	85	1957	611	1963	398
1952	118	1958	253		
				Total	3,674

Source: U.S. Bureau of Public Roads, National Highway Planning Division.

Revenue from highway users in 1963 was $8,802 million. Table 7-7 shows, by level of government, the sources from which this was obtained.

TABLE 7-7. Revenue from Highway Users Collected by All Levels of Government, 1963

(In millions of dollars)

Level of Government	Source of Revenue			Total Revenue
	Motor Fuel	Motor Vehicles	Current Charges	
All levels	$6,441	1,900	461	8,802
Federal	2,558	—	n.a.	2,558
State	3,851	1,780	461	6,092
Local	32	120	n.a.	152

n.a.=not available.
Source: *Governmental Finances in 1963*, p. 22; *Compendium of State Government Finances in 1963* (1964), p. 17

User Charges for Noncommercial Activities

Besides the commercial enterprises outlined above, state and local governments carry on noncommercial activities for which they collect *user charges*. While all of these activities yield collective benefits, they also yield to individuals some direct and measurable benefits that justify a user charge. At one end of the spectrum are charges which are barely distinguishable from those made for business-type services, for example, housing. At the other end are charges, usually called fees or license charges, which are primarily for regulatory purposes, for example, court fees, licenses for restaurants, and so on.

The basis upon which the level of charges for a particular service is set will often be either some rough estimate of the value of a particular benefit, or of the cost of rendering the service. But the charge will usually *fall short* of the benefit value or unit cost, and this shortfall may be justified either because of (a) equity, that is, welfare or redistributional reasons, or (b) spillovers of benefits or costs. For example, the provision of elementary and secondary education yields benefits to people generally that spill over to such an extent that taxes, rather than fees, are used as the means of finance. Moreover, the amount of education provided becomes a public decision and parents are compelled to send their school-age children to school.

Considerations of equity may be advanced even when the benefits from a governmental service are direct and divisible, and when spillovers are unimportant. When some of the recipients are indigent, the fact of direct benefit is irrelevant since, by definition, such persons cannot pay the charge. When some of the recipients are low income, equity may indicate that the user charge be reduced for them if a progressively graduated charge is feasible to take account of the varied income status of users.

Should *local* governments give weight to equity considerations in determining user charges? A negative answer can be, and has been, offered. Equity, when interpreted to mean redistribution of income, can only be handled fairly and efficiently at the *national* level. Action at the local level is bound to be uncoordinated and discordant. When particular governmental services are furnished free, or at less than cost, the incidence of redistribution to individual users is unlikely to be equitable. Benefits will accrue to users in proportion to their consumption *of these services*. Moreover, redistributional benefits should, ideally, be in money form (generalized purchasing power), and not in the form of particular services. Otherwise, those recipients will benefit who have high preferences for the particular services, while other low-income persons with low preferences will not benefit. Again, redistribution that applies only to persons in a small geographic area will either be so trivial that it has a small effect, or so strong that it endangers the economic position of an area.

The abstract cogency of these arguments is undeniable, and yet they are often irrelevant to actual situations. For example, besides absorbing the hospital charges of indigent persons, most local governments levy user charges on low-income persons which are less than cost. Any other course of action would be politically unattractive and repugnant to humanitarian sentiment.

For many services, however, the justification of uniform user charges that fail to cover cost is not apparent. If water is unmetered and is supplied at low charges, its use is often wasteful and frivolous; if on-street parking is free, or if, when metered, the charge is low and enforcement is lax, downtown shopping areas are injured and driving is impeded. Activities of individuals and groups which require special governmental regulation (for example, elevators, boilers, ownership of animals, operation of restaurants, and sale of milk) should be charged adequate fees. Numerous instances exist where user charges, based on cost, would serve as a crude rationing or control device to limit expansion of consumption of services for which, when the charge is low, the demand is elastic. This elasticity is enhanced when individual consumption is gradual and represents a small part of total consumption. Administrative problems are, however, sometimes an impediment to collection of any charge.

RECENT TRENDS. In postwar years, state and local collection of user charges has been growing relatively as well as absolutely. Such charges provided 12.9 percent of general revenues collected by local governments from their own sources in 1953; they provided 16.3 percent in 1963 (Table 7-8). For state governments the corresponding figures were 6.7 percent and 9.6 percent.[11] Behind this growth has been the search of state and local governments for revenue to finance expanding governmental needs, and the resistance, especially at the local level, to higher tax rates. In the future the force of these trends seems likely to strengthen, and therefore the growth of user charges will accelerate. To a large extent local governments (and, to a smaller extent, state governments) do provide many services that yield direct and measurable benefits to individuals for which collection of user charges based on cost would seem justified. The charges would bring a desirable linkage between individual payment and benefit; they would not result in significant

TABLE 7-8. Ratio of Local and State Government User Charges to General Revenues, Selected Years, 1953-63

(*In percent*)

Year	Local	State
1953	12.9	6.7
1962	15.3	9.3
1963	16.3	9.6

Sources: Appendix Tables A-19 and A-20.

[11] Until 1952 figures for user charges were merged with miscellaneous revenues.

TABLE 7-9. Local and State User Charges for Governmental Services, 1963

(Money amounts in millions of dollars)

Governmental Service	User Charge		Percentage of Total Charges	
	Local	State	Local	State
Nonhighway transportation	$ 335	$ 56	7.2	2.3
Natural resources	238	118	5.1	4.8
Hospitals	815	333	17.6	13.5
Housing	446	8	9.6	0.3
Sanitation	633	—	13.6	—
Education	1,240	1,260	26.7	51.1
Highways	n.a.	461	n.a.	18.7
Other	932	226	20.1	9.2
Total	$4,639	$2,462	100.0	100.0

n.a.= not available.
Sources: Appendix Tables A-19 and 20.

shrinkage of collective benefits; they would provide needed revenue.

LOCAL SERVICE REVENUES. Table 7-9 shows the principal services for which local governments levied user charges in 1963, and Table 7-10 shows the ratios of charges to expenditure on these services in

TABLE 7-10. Ratio of Local and State User Charges to Expenditures for Governmental Services, 1953 and 1963

(In percent)

Governmental Service	Local		State	
	1953	1963	1953	1963
Nonhighway transportation	56.0	59.7	47.8	49.5
Natural resources	16.6	16.2	15.3	10.8
Hospitals	27.1	41.5	10.9	16.6
Housing	35.8	36.1	—	66.7
Sanitation	17.0	28.9	—	—
Education	4.7	6.5	27.6	26.6
Highways	4.3	n.a.	3.2	6.2
Total	8.7	11.0	8.7	10.9

n.a.= not available.
Sources: Appendix Tables A-19 and 20.

1953 and 1963. Most of the ratios have been rising. For a few categories—public hospitals, nonhighway transportation, housing, and sanitation—the charges comprise from 25 to 50 percent of expenditure; for education and highways the ratios are low. Education is viewed as a collective function and the chief user charges are for school lunch sales ($862 million of the $1,240 million collected in 1963); highways, at the local level, are also viewed as collective, and collection of charges (except for parking) raises severe administrative difficulties.

STATE SERVICE REVENUES. The purposes for which state governments collect user charges are more concentrated (Table 7-9). Education is the largest item; user charges amount to half of total state user charges. They furnish, however, only one-quarter of state expenditures on education (exclusive of local school costs). Nine-tenths of this state expenditure (again exclusive of local school costs) is for state institutions of higher education. A controversy of long standing over the financing of these institutions has, in recent years, become much more acute. This controversy relates to the low level of charges (fees) of state, compared to private, institutions. Private institutions complain of "unfair" competition, and certainly the subsidy here has a peculiar bias, since it goes to *some* institutions in a state and not to others that nonetheless are providing similar or identical services.

Of the other types of state user charges, the steady rise of highway charges stems from toll facilities (Table 7-10). State user charges from hospitals come largely from mental institutions, which account for over 60 percent of state hospital expenditure. The two classes of state user charges that approach the category of commercial charges are housing and nonhighway transportation. The latter breaks into two parts, (a) air transport, and (b) water transport and terminals. Subsidization of both raises again familiar questions.

Summary

The notable result of the search of local governments for non-property taxes has been that local sales and income taxes have become important sources of revenue to some *large* cities. In smaller localities freedom to levy miscellaneous taxes has been of questionable value. Indeed, it may be that the use of sales and income taxes by local governments is fiscal perversion. State intervention, sooner or later, seems likely to come.

Development of nontax revenues seems to have promise. In the past, considerations of equity and of redistribution have led public enterprises to price their services far below cost, and have persuaded local governments to levy user charges for noncommercial activities that do not reflect particular benefits. The probability is that, in these respects, the pursuit of equity has been misdirected; the inefficiencies of applying an equity test at the state and local level have been forgotten. Subsidization in kind has, moreover, serious built-in defects, and these are exaggerated when action is confined to a small geographic area. It would seem, therefore, that if public service enterprises would follow a rational system of pricing, they could provide local governments with much needed new revenue. Increased user charges also should be cultivated.

CHAPTER VIII

State and Local Debt

"So foul a sky clears not without a storm." *King John,* Act IV, scene 2.

HISTORICALLY, THE VOLUME of state and local borrowing has proceeded in waves, usually in an inverse direction to the volume of federal borrowing. The first wave of state borrowing developed in the 1820's and 1830's when many states engaged in "internal improvements"—canals, highways, railways, and so on. This effort was feasible not only because the nation was prosperous and had begun to accumulate savings, but also because the federal debt was being retired with great celerity. Holders of this debt, forced to seek new outlets for their capital, were attracted to state issues. Unfortunately, many of the internal improvements turned out to be unprofitable; the debt issued for them proved to be deadweight. When, in 1837, severe depression struck and continued for several years, the burden of this deadweight debt was aggravated. Nine states and one territory defaulted.[1] All state credit was impaired, and borrowing by state governments came to an abrupt halt. Most of the states resumed interest payments before 1850, although four states repudiated some debt.[2] In a spirit of reaction against the mistakes that had

[1] Default is a broad term, meaning that a government, for whatever reasons, is failing to pay interest, or installments of principal, when due. The default may be temporary or long-continued. No satisfactory method of weighting the seriousness of a default is available.

[2] B. U. Ratchford, *American State Debts* (1941), pp. 98-99 and 134.

179

been made, many state constitutions were framed to restrict future state borrowing.

The Civil War brought a new wave of state borrowing. Defense had not, at this time, become wholly a federal function, and the state governments borrowed to finance military operations. But at the close of the war the debts of the northern states were retired, usually through federal financial assistance. In the Reconstruction period, after 1865, carpetbag governments in the southern states issued considerable amounts of bonds, the proceeds of which were often wasted. After ejection of the carpetbaggers, nine southern states made extensive adjustments. Most of the debt was repudiated; the remainder was scaled down and, in the process, a few states reduced pre-Civil War debts.[3]

In the last two decades of the nineteenth century, borrowing by state governments declined sharply. State debt, less sinking funds, was $9.15 per capita in 1870 and only $3.15 in 1900. Bitter experience, coupled with a conservative philosophy, had led voters in most states to endorse severe constitutional or statutory limitations upon state borrowing.[4]

It turned out, however, that some *local* governments in the 1870's had become creditworthy; they stepped into the vacuum and began to borrow extensively to finance internal improvements, notably railways. Their experience paralleled the earlier experience of the states. Borrowing was overdone; much of the capital was wasted; the annual carrying charges were beyond what local governments were prepared to finance. After 1873 defaults were widespread—perhaps 20 percent of the total.[5] State governments nearly everywhere imposed limitations on local borrowing, usually in the form of a debt-to-property ratio.

For two decades these limitations were restrictive, but in the twentieth century they proved to be elastic. Local governments, especially large cities, borrowed at an accelerating pace for the construction of schools and streets. In 1902, as Table 8-1 shows, local

[3] *Ibid.*, pp. 191-96.

[4] A. James Heins, *Constitutional Restrictions Against State Debt* (1963), pp. 7-10, gives a brief history of state action.

[5] A. M. Hillhouse, *Municipal Bonds* (1936), pp. 15-17. Defaults amounted to about $100 to $150 million out of a total of $750 million.

TABLE 8-1. State and Local Debt Outstanding, Selected Years, 1902–63

(In millions of dollars)

Year	Local Debt	State Debt	Total
1902	$ 1,877	$ 230	$ 2,107
1913	4,035	379	4,414
1927	12,910	1,971	14,881
1932	16,373	2,832	19,205
1938	16,093	3,343	19,436
1946	13,564	2,353	15,917
1948	14,980	3,676	18,656
1960	51,412	18,543	69,955
1962	59,077	21,971	81,048
1963	64,276	23,176	87,452

Sources: U. S. Census Bureau, *Historical Statistics of the United States: Colonial Times to 1957* (1960), pp. 728 and 730 (henceforth cited as *Historical Statistics*); *Governmental Finances in 1960* (1961), p. 22; *Governmental Finances in 1962* (1963), p. 26; *Governmental Finances in 1963*, (1964), p. 29. Years are fiscal unless otherwise noted.

debt was eight times larger than state debt. And, despite the new interest of state governments in highway construction during the 1920's, the size of local debt outstanding in 1932 was nearly six times that of state debt.

The onset of depression in the 1930's did not at first slacken state and local borrowing. But as the depression continued and deepened, the reaction was very severe, and after 1932 net borrowing—that is, borrowing minus repayments—was negative for more than a decade. The rate of interest paid by state and local governments rose sharply, despite a marked drop in flotations (in 1932, 52.5 percent of the issues bore a rate of 5 percent or more, and many offerings could not be marketed at all); interest remained high, compared with the rate on federal debt. Table 8-2 shows state and local interest payments per $1,000 of personal income for selected years from 1902 to 1963. As income fell after 1929, the rise in these figures was startling.

Equally startling was the rise in defaults. By the mid-1930's perhaps 10 percent of municipal bonds—$1.5 billion out of more than $15.0 billion—was in default. Some rough indication of the impact of the depression is provided by the growth in the number of defaults. For the five years prior to March 1932 about 226 defaults took place—an average of 45 yearly. On November 1, 1932,

TABLE 8-2. Interest Expenditure of State and Local Governments Per $1,000 of Personal Income, Selected Years, 1902–63

	Interest	
Year	In Millions of Dollars	In Dollars Per $1,000 of Personal Income
1902	$ 68	$ 3.37
1913	147	4.36
1927	584	7.34
1932	741	14.79
1934	739	13.79
1948	399	1.89
1957	1,106	3.18
1960	1,670	4.17
1962	2,008	4.57
1963	2,199	4.77

Sources: Derived from *Historical Statistics*, pp. 139,728, and 730; *Governmental Finances in 1960*, p. 18; *1962*, pp. 22 and 47; *1963*, pp. 35 and 52.

678 local units were listed; two years later the figure was 2,654, and on November 1, 1935 it was 3,251.[6] Default was not confined to bonds of inferior quality, since 90 percent were, in 1929, rated as Aa or higher.[7]

What lay behind the traumatic record? State and local debt had doubled in the 1920's, while GNP had risen by only 40 percent. Much more significant in impact was the fall in the price level, incomes, and employment, each of which added to the burden of debt. Despite increases in rates, local tax revenues declined by 17 percent in the years from 1930 to 1934. Tax delinquency in 1934 was more than 23 percent in 150 cities with populations over 50,000.

During World War II state and local net borrowing remained low. Public construction for civilian purposes was at a standstill, and, as revenues picked up with full employment, state and local

[6] Hillhouse, *op. cit.*, pp. 18-19. Over one-quarter of the defaulting governmental units were reclamation, irrigation, and special assessment districts. Only one state, Arkansas, defaulted on its debt. During the 1920's Arkansas borrowed heavily for highways and confederate pensions. Spending of the borrowed money was both wasteful and corrupt. Default came in 1932-33, followed by a bitter struggle over refunding. See Ratchford, *op. cit.*, Chap. XV.

[7] The quality ratings range from Aaa (the best rating) down to Caa.

governments had large surpluses which they used to retire debt. At the end of 1946 their gross debt was 15 percent less than in 1938. And this was not the only favorable financial circumstance. Yields on state and local bonds were low beyond all precedent, with the result that new borrowing cost less and old debt could be refunded on a favorable basis.

The contrast between the market reception of state and local bonds in 1946 and the middle 1930's was marked. In 1937 the average yield of high-grade long-term state and local bonds was 2.52 percent, compared to a yield of 3.06 percent for Aaa corporation bonds, that is, the differential as a percentage of the corporate yield was 18 percent; in 1946 this differential was 57 percent (yields of 1.10 percent on state and local bonds and 2.53 percent on corporation bonds). The main force behind this surprising performance was the exemption of interest on state and local bonds from federal income tax. The value of this exemption had risen because of the marked wartime increase in the level and progression of federal income tax rates, coupled with the decrease in the volume of exempts and pessimistic market expectations concerning future increase in their volume.

This overview of state and local debt should call attention to *differences* between the growth of state debt and local debt in recent decades. Beginning in the 1930's, state debt grew at a faster rate than did local debt (Table 8-3). The severity of the depression forced states to assume governmental tasks which, in ordinary circumstances, were local. But it also led them to assume new govern-

TABLE 8-3. Relative Growth of State and Local Debt, Selected Years, 1938–63

(Base year 1938=100.0)

Year	Local	State	Total
1938	100.0	100.0	100.0
1948	93.1	109.9	96.0
1960	319.5	554.7	360.0
1962	367.1	657.2	417.0
1963	399.4	693.4	449.9

Source: Table 8-1.

mental responsibilities, a factor that has, since World War II, grown in importance. Nonetheless, the actual amount of local debt in 1963 was nearly three times as large as state debt (Table 8-1).

While Table 8-3 shows the remarkable overall increase in state and local debt during postwar years, the increase has not been uniform among the governmental units. The net per capita long-term debt of *state* governments grew from $19.83 in 1948 to $103.76 in 1963, that is, by $83.93, but, as Table 8-4 indicates, in two states (South Dakota and Arkansas), a *decrease* occurred, and in many states the increase was less than the average. Similarly, Table 8-4 shows an uneven increase in the debt of forty large cities, and a decrease in one.

In postwar years the default record has been excellent. Only six defaults of large issues, and forty or fifty of small, are recorded. Of the large defaults two created some alarm and evoked memories of the 1930's: the West Virginia Turnpike Commission ($133 million of revenue bonds) in 1958, and the Calumet Skyway Toll Bridge ($101 million of revenue bonds) in 1963. But reassuring features were apparent. Debt management had improved, notably through

TABLE 8-4. Change in Per Capita Net Long-Term Debt[a] of State Governments and 41 Large Cities, 1948–63

Per Capita Change	Number of State Governments	Number of Large City Governments
Decrease		
0–$49	2[b]	1[c]
Increase		
0–$49	20	4
50–99	12	5
100–149	9	7
150–199	2	6
200–249	1	9
250–299	1	4
300–349	0	1
350 and over	1[b]	4[c]

Sources: U. S. Census Bureau, *Compendium of State Government Finances in 1948* (1949), *in 1963* (1964); *Compendium of City Government Finances in 1948* (1950), *in 1963* (1964).

[a] The net debt is the debt outstanding minus offsets in the form of cash and investment assets specifically held for debt redemption.

[b] Arkansas, — $12.10; South Dakota, — $8.00; Delaware, +$481.55.

[c] Minneapolis, — $20.87; Cincinnati, +$411; Oklahoma City, +$511; New York City, +$593; Memphis, +$886.

prudent retirement practices; interest rates were low, and therefore annual interest charges as a percentage of general revenues were less in 1963 than in 1936 (4.1 percent compared to 9.9 percent). Most important was the *stable* growth of GNP, incomes, consumption, and property values in postwar years. Recessions have been both mild and brief; the trend of prices has been upward. The financial structures of state and local governments have not, therefore, faced shocks which increased the burden of old debt charges and put a curb on new borrowing.

Characteristics of State and Local Debt

State and local borrowing may be described in terms of its form, purpose, duration, and tax exemption.

Forms of Debt

State and local debt nowadays is almost always in *serial form,* that is, when the debt is incurred, provision is made for annual retirement of the principal, so that the annual carrying charge for a twenty-year issue includes a sum sufficient to redeem, say, one-twentieth of the principal, as well as a sum for interest. This method is much superior to the older device of sinking funds which required the accumulation of large sums for redemption of an issue. The temptation to raid such funds, or to alter the terms, was often irresistible to hard-pressed state and local governments.

Purposes of Borrowing

Most state and local borrowing is for capital expenditure—roads, buildings, public service enterprises, and so forth—although only one-half to three-quarters of all capital expenditure is financed by borrowing. Table 8-5 shows the purposes for which state long-term debt had been incurred in 1941 and 1963. Besides a sevenfold increase in the total amount, there were significant shifts in particular items. While highway debt was dominant in both years, borrowing for toll roads—negligible in 1941—was 60 percent of the highway debt in 1963. Debt for educational purposes rose from 4 percent in 1941 to 19 percent in 1963, while debt for public welfare—important in 1941—was negligible in 1963.

Table 8-6 shows the purposes of the long-term debt of the forty-

TABLE 8-5. Functional Distribution of State Long-Term Debt, 1941 and 1963

(Money amounts in millions of dollars)

Function	Amount		Percentage of Total		
	1941	1963	1941	1963	Change
Highways	$1,373	$ 9,893[a]	45.8	43.5	− 2.3
Education	122	4,407	4.1	19.4	+15.3
Hospitals	50	255	1.7	1.1	− 0.6
Water transportation and terminals	151	342	5.0	1.5	− 3.5
Public welfare	449	n.a.	15.0	n.a.	
Other[b]	855	7,855	28.5	34.5	+ 6.0
Total	$3,001	$22,752	100.0	100.0	

n.a. = not available.

Sources: U. S. Census Bureau, *Financial Statistics of States, 1941,* Vol. 3, "Statistical Compendium" (1943), p. 66; *State Government Finances in 1963,* p. 39.

[a] Includes $6.0 billion for toll facilities.

[b] Includes general control, natural resources, public welfare, parks and recreation, veterans' aid, and housing and community development.

three largest *cities* in 1941 and 1961 (figures for *all* local debt are not available). General debt had risen, relative to utility debt, from 50.6 percent to 64.1 percent of the total. One new function, housing and urban renewal, had emerged and, in 1961, accounted for 11.8 percent of total debt.

Life of Debt

The life of most state and local debt is geared to the expected life of the asset provided by the debt, or to an estimate of the revenue to be derived from the asset—but the gearing is loose. The life of water and sewer issues is usually thirty years, a maturity that readily assures receipts covering interest and annual maturities.[8]

In recent years the volume of borrowing by state and local governments has been contracyclical. The peak rate of bond sales during the years from 1952 to 1960 was reached in recession troughs. Not all types of projects are affected. Schools, water, and sewer projects are carried forward without regard to the condition of the

[8] Roland I. Robinson, *Postwar Market for State and Local Government Securities* (1960), pp. 46-47.

TABLE 8-6. Functional Distribution of Long-Term Debt of 43 Largest Cities, 1941 and 1961

(Money amounts in millions of dollars)

Function	Amount		Percentage of Total		
	1941	1961	1941	1961	Change
General Debt[a]	$3,208	$ 8,244	50.6	64.1	+13.5
Education	586	1,039	9.2	8.1	
Highways	653	1,479	10.3	11.5	
Sewerage	374	1,090	5.9	8.5	
Housing and urban	n.a.	1,514	n.a.	11.8	
Other and unallocable	1,595	3,121	25.1	24.3	— 0.8
Utility Debt	3,136	4,622	49.4	35.9	—13.5
Water supply systems	1,148	2,249	18.1	17.5	
Other utilities	1,988	2,373	31.3	18.4	
Total Long-Term Debt	$6,344	$12,866	100.0	100.0	

n.a.= not available.

Sources: *Financial Statistics of Cities Having Populations over 100,000, 1941*, Vol. 3, "Statistical Compendium," (1943), pp. 101–02; *Compendium of City Government Finances in 1961* (1962), p. 83.

[a] The Bureau of the Census cautions that the scope of municipal government operations differs. In particular, public schools may be operated by the municipal corporation or by an independent school district. Such differences mean that the debt figures do not include all debt of the cities as geographic units.

money market, but other types of state and local capital projects "have shown a very pronounced contracyclical movement."[9] This results even though officials responsible for the technical details of issuance may commit themselves not when interest rates are lowest, but when the market will provide a rate within the ceiling specified by the legislative body in authorizing the issue; and even though voters, as well as state and local officials, are more disposed to endorse borrowing for capital purposes in good years, that is, in years when interest rates are high.

In 1963, 95 percent of state and local debt was *long-term* (Table 8-7). This is in distinct contrast to federal practice, since 45 percent of federal marketable interest-bearing debt matures within one year. The federal Treasury also issues a variety of intermediate-term debt that has no parallel in state and local practice. State and

[9] Frank E. Morris, "Impact of Monetary Policy on State and Local Governments: An Empirical Study," *Journal of Finance* (May 1960), p. 234.

TABLE 8-7. Outstanding Long-Term and Short-Term[a] State and Local Debt, 1963[b]

(Money amounts in billions of dollars)

Period of Debt	Debt			Percentage of Total
	State	Local	Total	
Total	$23.2	$64.3	$87.5	100.0
Long-term	22.8	60.4	83.2	95.0
Short-term	0.4	3.9	4.3	5.0

Source: *Governmental Finances in 1963*, p. 29.
[a] Repayable within one year.
[b] End of fiscal year.

local governments use short-term debt mostly in anticipation of tax receipts; they seldom use it to finance the start of capital projects. State and local officials are less close to, and less versed in the behavior of, money markets; they are unwilling to issue short-term debt in the expectation that a more favorable long-term market will develop. They have, in any case, less flexibility and discretion, since refunding of short-term credit is subject to constitutional or statutory limitations, and is, moreover, frowned upon by local banks.

Tax Exemption

The most important and distinctive characteristic of state and local issues is that interest on them is almost the only form of income exempt from federal income tax. The federal government does not tax the interest on state and local securities through income tax, and state and local governments cannot tax federal securities. The federal government does tax the interest on its own securities. State and local governments may tax their own securities, although most do not exercise this right; they may, and generally do, tax each other's securities.

The failure of the federal government to tax the income of state and local securities rests, since 1913, upon the *specific statutory exclusion* of such income by Congress. The late Justice Holmes once declared that "most people not lawyers" would assume that the Sixteenth Amendment to the Constitution gave the federal government the right to tax all income. But when the amendment was in process, assurance was given to some state governors that the amendment merely was to remove the constitutional requirement that a federal income tax, as a "direct" tax, be apportioned among the states according to population. And when Congress passed the individual income tax of 1913, it implicitly accepted this position by providing that interest on state and local securities be excluded from income. This statutory exclusion has been retained to the present.

The Supreme Court has never been able to pass on the question of the constitutional right of Congress to delete the exclusion and to tax interest on state and local securities as income. For some years after 1913, the inference of many decisions seemed to be that the Amendment had not altered the taxable status of state and local securities. But in the late 1930's several decisions that curtailed the immunity of governmental instrumentalities raised doubts anew.

These decisions seemed to depend on the theory that *nondiscriminatory* taxation, federal or state, was permissible and tolerable. The epigram of Chief Justice Marshall in *McCulloch v. Maryland,* that "the power to tax involves the power to destroy," had been capped by the epigram of Justice Holmes that "the power to tax is not the power to destroy while this Court sits." The courts, as the referees of a federal system with a dual sovereignty, would protect the states even if, as Justice Butler believed, the doctrine of reciprocal immunity was "presently marked for destruction."

So far this has not happened, but if it should happen and if, by statutory provision, the state and local governments were given the right to tax federal securities and the federal government the right to tax state and local securities, the position of the state and local governments would legally be much more insecure. A statutory right of the states to tax the income on federal bonds could be repealed by any subsequent Congress. The *federal* right to tax state and local securities would, presumably, be a constitutional right; it would continue even if the state right were repealed. One can argue, of course, that a future Congress would not take the unjust action of taxing state and local securities without permitting state and local taxation of federal securities. State and local interests are adequately represented in the Congress, and this is protection against mistreatment. But the states and localities have been unwilling to trust this assurance. They maintain that their present position should be altered only by *constitutional amendment*. If Congress itself simply removed the exclusion, this would indicate congressional opinion that the exclusion was undesirable. The Supreme Court then, in the event of a state-local appeal against the exclusion, would be forced to make a decision that should rest with the people of the nation.

For more than forty years the federal Treasury has made intermittent efforts to abolish the exemption, at first only for *future* issues, but in 1942 for *outstanding* issues as well. All efforts have failed, in the face of sharp resistance by state and local governments and the unwillingness of Congress to impair the financial powers of these governments at a time when their financial responsibilities were large and expanding.

YIELD DIFFERENTIALS. Tax-exempt bonds have always sold at a lower yield than taxable bonds of similar quality and maturity. The yield differential depends chiefly upon the relative expected supply of the two kinds of bonds and upon the anticipated amount of tax that can be avoided. Let it be assumed that the holder of exempts does not pay income tax on the interest. If all income were taxed proportionally, and all bondholders were subject to the tax, then the provision for tax-free interest on certain bonds would bring about an increase in their price equal to the value of the exemption to every buyer. An issuing government would not be the loser since the lower yield at which it issued the tax exempts would be equivalent to the taxes it agreed to forego. But when income is taxed progressively, the value of the exemption becomes worth more to buyers according to the size of their taxable income, and this graduated value will not be fully reflected in the price of an issue.

Why the exemption is worth more (or less) to some buyers is illustrated by the following example, based on the following taxable income brackets and rates:

Taxable Income	Tax Rate
0 to $20,000	20%
$20,000 to $40,000	60
$40,000 to $60,000	80
Over $60,000	90

A taxpayer in the top (90 percent) bracket who buys a taxable bond yielding $40 annually, can keep only $4. To him, the exemption from income tax is worth thirty-six/fortieths of the yield. He would be as well off to purchase at par a tax-exempt yielding 0.4 percent as a taxable one yielding 4 percent. A taxpayer in the 80 percent bracket keeps $8 out of $40, and to him the exemption is worth thirty-two/fortieths of the yield. An equivalent exempt to him must yield 0.8 percent. A taxpayer in the lowest (20 percent) bracket keeps $32 out of $40, and to him exemption is worth only eight/fortieths of the yield. An exempt yield of 3.2 percent is equivalent to 4 percent from a taxable bond.

If it is assumed that the actual supply of exempts is relatively small, then all could profitably be bought by persons in the top bracket and the yield would be 0.4 percent. But if the supply increases, the demand of buyers in the lower brackets has to be tapped. If buyers in the lowest bracket have to be attracted, the yield would rise to 3.2 percent. In this instance, they are the marginal buyers, those whose income after taxes is the same whether they buy exempts or taxables. Since this is an undifferentiated market, all buyers get the same yield as the marginal buyers and the high-income buyers secure a sort of surplus or tax saving.

Over the decades the *differential* between the yield of taxable and exempt securities has widened or narrowed in response to pressure from various forces. In the 1920's, when the rates and progression of the federal tax were sharply decreased and when many expected that these trends would continue, the differential narrowed (see Table 8-8).

TABLE 8-8. Comparative Yields on High-Grade Long-Term Municipal and Corporate Bonds,[a] Selected Years, 1928–63

(In percent)

Year	Average Yield		Differential	Differential as a Percentage of Corporate Yield
	Municipal Bonds	Corporate Bonds		
1928	3.92	4.50	0.58	13
1938	2.25	2.85	0.60	21
1946	1.10	2.53	1.43	57
1962	3.03	4.33	1.30	30
1963	3.06	4.26	1.20	28

[a] Moody's Investors Service, Aaa municipal bonds and Aaa industrial bonds.

In such circumstances, the advantage to high-income persons from holding exempts was modest, and so was the loss to the federal Treasury from its inability to tax the income from exempts. During the 1930's the differential widened, and during World War II widened further; by 1946 the yield of high quality exempts was less than half that of similar taxable bonds. Behind this lay the marked increase in the level and progression of federal income taxes, as well as the decrease in the volume of exempts. In postwar years, the differential has narrowed, partly because of a modest decrease in federal income tax rates but mostly because of the great rise in the volume of exempts. The gross proceeds from issues of state and local securities which, in 1946, amounted to 6.2 percent of all new security issues, has recently been over 20 percent. State and local securities must now be sold to buyers with a low marginal rate of federal income tax. As a result, the advantage to state and local governments from the exemption privilege has diminished; the advantage to high-income buyers has increased.

HOLDERS OF EXEMPTS. Table 8-9 shows the estimated ownership of state and local interest-bearing securities on June 30, 1963. While a modest portion (7.5 percent) was held in investment funds of state and local governments themselves, most was privately held by investors exposed to federal income taxation. Three groups are conspicuous: high-income persons, commercial banks, and casualty insurance companies.

TABLE 8-9. Estimated Ownership of State and Local Securities Outstanding as of June 30, 1963

(*Money amounts in billions of dollars*)

Owner	Securities Outstanding	Percentage of Total Ownership
Individuals	$31.7	36.9
Commercial banks	27.9	32.5
Insurance companies	14.1	16.4
State and local governments	6.4	7.5
Other	5.8	6.7
Total	$85.9	100.0

Source: *Annual Report of the Secretary of the Treasury*, Fiscal Year 1963, p. 626.

The attraction of exempts for *high-income persons* has been examined. The volume of exempts held by this group has always been less than an inspection of the tax advantages might suggest. The explanation is that many high-income persons prefer to be active rather than passive investors; they prefer an investment that may bring either appreciable capital gains, or, as with ownership of equities, involves participation in the operation of a business. To them the tax advantages of exempts are not decisive. They are erratic buyers, shifting into and out of exempts inversely to the attractiveness of other investments. Holdings of exempts by *commercial banks* are also quite variable. When the demand for loans by business is large and growing, the banks will not buy, and may sell, exempts; when business demand declines, they buy exempts. *Casualty insurance companies* have variable earnings because of unpredictable losses from year to year. Exempts provide them with fair liquidity, as well as with a secure and tax-free income.

As a consequence of the variability in the holdings of these important groups, fluctuations in interest rates of exempts are greater than those of other comparable long-term rates.[10]

PROPOSALS FOR ABOLITION. Most proposals for abolishing tax-exempts have assumed that mere reciprocal abolition—permitting state and local governments to tax income from federal securities, and the federal government to tax the income from state and local securities—would not be attractive to state and local governments. Such a move would, it seems, bring a net financial gain to the federal Treasury which could tax this addition to the income tax base at high and progressive rates. But state and local governments would suffer a net financial loss, since the interest rates payable on their bonds would rise, while the additional revenue that they might secure from taxation of interest on federal debt would be modest. Some *extra* inducement would, therefore, be needed to secure state-local consent.

The benefits derived by state and local governments from the issuance of exempts accrue more to governmental units in high-income areas than in low simply because the former units issue more debt. High-income states have a high state-local debt per capita;

[10] Roland I. Robinson, *op. cit.,* pp. 89-90.

low-income states a low debt (see Appendix Table A-21). Regarded as a subsidy, therefore, exemption is inefficient. And even though the exemption may not be more valuable to governmental units with high credit ratings than it is to those with low, the exemption is not distributed according to need.

In January 1962 the Brookings Institution sponsored a conference of experts on taxation of state and local securities.[11] Discussion appeared to indicate that even if a satisfactory financial compensation to state and local governments could be devised, some state and local governments would remain fearful on political grounds. An arrangement would rest on legislation by Congress which, conceivably, future Congresses could alter. Even if at some future time Congress did not alter the money value of the compensation, it might assert federal control over how the money was used. A key problem to removal of the exemption is, therefore, devising a plan to allay this fear.

Debt Limitations

Most of the states impose limitations on the authority of the state legislature to borrow. In origin, the limitations reflect impulsive reactions to periods of misdirected overborrowing; their objective is to protect taxpayers, and the credit of the governments, against recurrence of similar mistakes. Professor B. U. Ratchford, the leading student of state debt limitations, has classified three groups of states by their borrowing practices: in Group I the constitution prohibits state borrowing except as authorized by a *constitutional amendment;* in Group II borrowing proposals must be (a) *enacted* by the legislature and then (b) *approved* by a popular referendum; in Group III *legislatures* make the borrowing decisions. The number of states falling in the three groups is shown in Table 8-10. As will appear hereafter, devices exist, and have been used, to escape from these limitations. But evidence that limitations have actually limited state government borrowing is offered in Table 8-11. In every one of three years analyzed—1938, 1957, and 1959—per

---

[11] As background material David J. Ott and Allan H. Meltzer prepared a study, *Federal Tax Treatment of State and Local Securities* (1963), in which all the economic issues are explored in detail. The study also summarizes the conference discussion.

TABLE 8-10. States Classified by Limitations on Borrowing Authority, 1938 and 1958

Group[a]	Number of States	
	1938	1958[b]
Group I	18	21
Group II	17	21
Group III	13	8
	48	50

Sources: *American State Debts*, p. 441; Ratchford, "State and Local Debt Limitations," *National Tax Association 1958 Proceedings* (1959), p. 225; O. F. Gwinn, *State Government Debt Financing, 1946-59* (1962), pp. 17-18.
[a] See text for characteristics of each group.
[b] See Appendix Table A-22 for a listing of states in each group in 1958.

TABLE 8-11. Long-Term State Debt Per Capita by Limitations on Borrowing Authority, 1938, 1957, and 1959

Group	1938	1957	1959
Group I	$13.03	$ 63.11	$ 62.89
Group II	22.89	82.86	96.96
Group III	33.79	137.29	195.30
Total	$19.88	$ 79.38	$ 96.49

Sources: *American State Debts*, pp. 441 and 525; "State and Local Debt Limitations," p. 226; *State Government Finances in 1959* (1960), pp. 49-50.

capita debt is larger in Group II than Group I, and in Group III than Group II. A surprising fact is, however, the wide spread in per capita state debt *within* each of the three groups (see Table 8-12). Group I contains several states with a per capita debt *higher* than the average of Group II; similarly, Group III contains states with a *lower* per capita debt than the average of Group II.

Besides limiting their own borrowing, states also impose constitutional or statutory limitations on the borrowing of their local governments. The most common limitation sets a ceiling on debt as a percentage of the property tax base of the local government. In 1961, thirty-four states imposed this by constitutional provision, but in six the limitation was mild, applying only to a single type of local government or to debts incurred for a particular purpose.[12]

[12] Advisory Commission on Intergovernmental Relations (ACIR), *State Constitutional and Statutory Restrictions on Local Government Debt* (1961), p. 28.

TABLE 8-12. Distribution of States by Per Capita State Debt and Limitations on Borrowing Authority, 1959

Per Capita Debt	Number of States		
	Group I	Group II	Group III
Under $30	7	5	—
30–59	5	4	1
60–89	2	4	1
90–119	4	4	1
120–149	1	4	1
150–179	1	—	—
180–209	—	—	1
210–239	—	—	—
240–269	1[a]	—	1
270–299	—	—	—
300–329	—	—	—
330–359	—	—	—
360–389	—	—	1
390 and over	—	—	1[b]
Total	21	21	8

Source: Same as Table 8-11.

[a] Hawaii, $263. This state is classified in Group I. Its legislature, however, has the power to borrow $60 million, and this sum may be raised to 15 percent of the assessed valuation of real property upon approval of two-thirds of the legislature.

[b] Delaware, $453.

Comprehensive information concerning similar limitations on local debt expressed by *statutory* provisions is difficult to summarize.[13]

A second common state device for limiting local debt is to require that the issuance of bonds be approved by *referendum*. In 1961 this was a constitutional requirement in twenty-three states,[14] and a statutory requirement in twenty-seven.

State limitations on local government borrowing are designed (a) to protect the solvency of local governments (as well as that of the states), and (b) to protect bondholders. The ACIR rephrases the purposes as follows: "To empower local governments to make use of borrowing, prudently and in a responsible and locally responsive

[13] The results of a survey made in 1961 by the Council of State Governments at the request of the ACIR, is to be found in *Ibid.*, Appendix A.

[14] In eight other states this constitutional limitation exists in a limited way. *Ibid.*, p. 32.

manner, as one means for financing their requirements."[15]

The limitation that sets a ceiling on local borrowing in terms of the property tax base has often been criticized. Some critics declare that it is technically deficient. It focuses on the property tax base of the individual local government, even though that same base may be shared by several *overlapping* local governments. Summation of the ratios of debt to assessed value of property for all the governmental units in a geographic area might produce an aggregate ratio that would seem alarming to voters. If consolidation of the units in order to achieve a simpler and more efficient governmental structure were under consideration, some officials would oppose this step simply because of their fear that, in the process, the aggregate borrowing power of the area would be curtailed.

Conversely, the creation of new governmental units has been induced and stimulated by a desire to gain new borrowing power. Fragmentation of governmental functions through proliferation of special districts and authorities destroys the unity of governmental budgets and deprives citizens of understandable information concerning government finances. A basic premise of responsible state and local government is thereby impaired.

Limitations tied to the property tax base are less relevant now than in the past. Twenty or thirty years ago the property tax supplied 95 percent of the tax revenue of local governments; in 1963 it supplied 87.6 percent. The debt-carrying capacity of local governments is, therefore, not measured adequately by their property tax base. This is the more so because state-imposed limits usually relate to *assessed* value, which, in most cases, is less than full value. The result is that the impact of debt limitations depends mostly on local assessment practices. In an area where assessed value is less than full value, assessors can lift the debt ceiling by lifting the assessed value, or lower it by dropping the assessed value. The ACIR feels that this situation exposes assessors to undesirable pressures wholly unrelated to their duties. Decisions to borrow should be made by elective bodies; they should not be subject to the irrelevant decisions of assessors. Moreover, the impact of a debt-to-property limitation *within a state* will not be uniform among localities unless

[15] *Ibid.*, p. 39.

assessment is uniform. In most states uniformity of assessment by local governments has not been achieved.

Another and major defect of this debt limitation is that usually it applies only to full faith and credit debt, secured by the general revenues of the government, and not to nonguaranteed debt, secured only by the revenues of the enterprise or activity for which this debt is contracted. As will be shown later, the volume of this latter type of debt has been growing much more rapidly than that of the former.

Nonetheless, there is evidence that the limitations have restrained the volume of local government borrowing (see Table 8-13). The ACIR found that in 1957 "local debt for general gov-

TABLE 8-13. Local Government Debt[a] of "Free" and "Restrained" States, 1957

Type of Debt	States without Specific Constitutional Limitation on Local Debts[b] ("Free")	States with Specific Constitutional Limitations on Local Debt ("Restrained")
(1) Long-term general debt of local governments per $1,000 of personal income	$82.28	$71.06
(2) Full faith and credit debt of local governments per $1,000 of personal income	$63.16	$51.22
(3) (2) as a percentage of (1)	77%	72%

Source: *State Constitutional and Statutory Restrictions*, pp. 91–92.
[a] Debt for local utilities is excluded.
[b] The 14 "free" states are: Connecticut, Delaware, Kansas, Maryland, Massachusetts, Minnesota, Mississippi, Nebraska, Nevada, New Hampshire, New Jersey, Rhode Island, Tennessee, and Vermont. There are 34 "restrained" states.

ernment purposes amounted to $82.28 per $1,000 of personal income in the median 'free' State, as against $71.06 per $1,000 in the median State of those with constitutional debt restraints."[16] The difference cannot be accounted for by relative population growth or by urban-rural distribution of population, because in these respects the two groups of states were very similar. Table 8-13 shows

[16] *Ibid.*, p. 52.

also that local governments of the "free" states borrow more—77 percent compared to 72 percent—through use of full faith and credit debt than do the "restrained" states. Evidently debt limitations have pushed local governments toward use of nonguaranteed debt. They also bias borrowing in favor of functions for which user charges are feasible, even though such borrowing (via the revenue bond) carries a higher rate of interest than full faith and credit debt.

The Nonguaranteed Bond

The most important device used to avoid debt limitations has been the revenue bond. Strictly defined, revenue bonds are those for which interest and principle are payable exclusively from the earnings of a specific enterprise. In such case they are not serviced from the general revenues of a local (state) government; they are not, therefore, subject to the constitutional or statutory limitations imposed on the issuance of full faith and credit bonds.

In their original use, revenue bonds were mostly issued to finance revenue-producing enterprises—public utilities, toll facilities, and so on. This was, and is, an appropriate use. When the borrowing of a commercial enterprise, publicly owned and operated, is backed by the full faith and credit of a state or local government, a lower interest rate is obtained. The governmental guarantee is a protection to investors against default, and the enterprise has to earn less to meet interest charges than if the guarantee were not given. The contention that this differential is a subsidy may be met by the contention that a *public* enterprise is entitled to use of public credit. So long as no *tax* support is needed, the enterprise may, perhaps, be regarded as self-supporting.

This original use of revenue bonds was greatly enlarged during the 1930's when the Public Works Administration (PWA) was attempting to stimulate state and local construction of public works. State and local limitations on borrowing stood in the way. The legal division of PWA decided that nonguaranteed bonds were a device that would circumvent the limitations, and it offered to help state and local governments in drafting bills authorizing the issuance of such bonds. The help was widely accepted. In 1931 only fifteen states permitted local governments to use nonguaranteed bonds; by 1936 the number had risen to forty; and now nonguaranteed bonds are used in every state. Even more surprising than the growth in the volume of such bonds was the expansion in the types of projects financed by them. In addition to the usual public utilities, local governments constructed swimming pools, golf courses, college dormitories, and so on.

Current methods of borrowing by nonguaranteed debt are: (1) use of revenue bonds by state agencies or by a local government; (2) creation of a public authority with power to issue revenue bonds for a specific public purpose; (3) lease-purchase agreements, usually combined with creation of a public authority; and (4) delegation of state functions to local subdivisions that have more freedom to borrow, with reimbursement by the state.

Since World War II the nonguaranteed bond has been widely utilized both by state and local governments. As Table 8-14 and Chart 8-1 show, in 1949 full faith and credit debt comprised 87.6 percent of all state and local long-term debt, while in 1963 it had

TABLE 8-14. Long-Term Debt of State and Local Governments, 1949, 1962, and 1963[a]

(Money amounts in billions of dollars)

Year	Total Long-Term Debt	Full Faith and Credit	Non-guaranteed	Full Faith and Credit as Percentage of Total	Non-guaranteed as Percentage of Total
State and local					
1949	$20.2	$17.7	$ 2.5	87.6	12.4
1962	77.3	48.1	29.2	62.2	37.8
1963	83.2	50.7	32.5	60.9	39.1
State					
1949	4.0	3.4	0.6	85.0	15.0
1962	21.6	10.3	11.3	47.7	52.3
1963	22.8	10.7	12.1	46.9	53.1
Local					
1949	16.2	14.3	1.9	88.3	11.7
1962	55.7	37.8	17.9	67.9	32.1
1963	60.4	40.0	20.4	66.2	33.8

Source: For further details on these and other years, see Appendix Table A-23.
[a] End of fiscal year.

CHART 8-1. Percentage of State and Local Debt in Full Faith and Credit and Nonguaranteed Form, 1949 and 1963

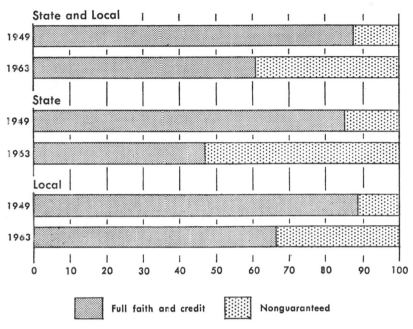

Source: Appendix Table A-23.

fallen to 60.9 percent. While the relative use of full faith and credit debt diminished at both the state and local levels, the decline was greater at the state level where, in 1963, full faith and credit debt comprised only 46.9 percent of the total. Similarly, the figures show that the postwar growth of nonguaranteed debt was greater at the state level.[17]

The annual *Compendium of State Government Finances* supplies debt figures for *individual states*. Table 8-15 indicates that in 1941 more than half of the net long-term debt of thirty-four states was in the form of full faith and credit bonds; by 1963 the number had fallen to twenty-two. Again, in 1941, six states had no long-

[17] A. James Heins, *op. cit.*, pp. 22-24, gives information concerning the purposes for which *outstanding* state nonguaranteed debt in 1958 had been issued. Of the total, 70 percent was for bridges and roads, 13 percent for education, and 9 percent for power and water.

TABLE 8-15. State Governments with More or Less than Half of Net Long-Term Debt in Full Faith and Credit Form, 1941 and 1963

Percentage in Full Faith and Credit	Number of States	
	1941	1963
50% or more	34	22
Under 50%	8	19
None	6	9
	48	50

Source: Appendix Table A-24.

term debt in full faith and credit form; by 1963 the number had risen to nine. This statement should not be taken to mean that the six states in 1941, or the nine states in 1963, had no net long-term debt. All of them (except Florida in 1941) did have some nonguaranteed debt (see Appendix Table A-25).

Self-Financing Projects

When a project is *self-financing,* the price—or toll, or fee—charged for the service includes the cost of servicing the debt, and this cost will be higher than if guaranteed bonds were used. Avoidance of a guarantee may serve to protect the credit of the governmental unit.

Non-Self-Financing Projects

When a project is *not* self-financing, use of nonguaranteed bonds cannot avoid placing an indirect or direct burden on the revenues of state or local government. Since the project will not generate revenues from charges on users, it must receive annual amounts provided by appropriations from the general funds of the state or local government. An example will clarify the principles.

Many local governments have constructed school buildings through lease-financing. A school building authority, created by state law with power to issue nonguaranteed bonds, will undertake to construct school buildings for local governments. The governments rent the buildings for, say, thirty years, promising to make annual payments that service the bonds. The source of the payments is the general revenue of the local unit. In such case, the bonds help finance the essential governmental function of education; they place a financial burden on local revenues. Yet they do not, in law, pledge the credit of the state or the local government. They are payable, and are serviced, from the revenues of the authority, that is, the rentals from its leases. "At common law, rent to fall due beyond the current rent period is not a present debt."[18] The only liability of the lessee is the annual rent as it comes due each year. In practice, leases of this sort are nonterminable, and rental payments must be continued yearly. But the law overlooks these facts.

Industrial Aid Bonds

Nonguaranteed bonds have been used to aid private industry. Twenty-two states, by law, have authorized their local governments to issue revenue bonds in order to acquire land, buildings, and equipment that is leased to private firms. The firms pay a rental to cover servicing of the debt.

The practice is objectionable on several grounds: it exploits the interest exemption of state and local bonds from federal income tax for purposes that are proprietary and private rather than public; it enables recipient firms to derive a cost advantage over other private firms; it induces firms to shift their location, interstate, when market forces by themselves are not favorable. Ratchford has argued that the doctrine of tax immunity and the practice of industrial aid bonds contain a "fundamental inconsistency." These bonds are *not* subject to debt limitations and they are *not,* therefore, the obligations of the issuing governmental unit; yet in order to secure tax immunity, they *are* governmental obligations. The Supreme Court might, Ratchford believes, deny tax immunity to industrial aid bonds on three grounds: (1) such bonds, as nonguaranteed bonds, are not the obligations of a state or local government; (2) the resources secured through the bonds are utilized for a proprietary rather than a public function; (3) states are improperly using their

---

[18] Jon Magnusson, "Lease-Financing by Municipal Corporations as a Way Around Debt Limitations," *George Washington Law Review* (March 1957), p. 377.

sovereign immunity from federal income taxation to benefit private parties.[19]

Disadvantages

The interest rate on nonguaranteed bonds has been 0.5-0.6 percent higher than that on full faith and credit bonds. An increase of 0.5 percent in the interest rate of a 30-year level-payment serial bond raises aggregate interest cost by 19 percent. In practice, nonguaranteed bonds are issued for a longer time period than most general obligations bonds because of a desire to provide "a safe margin for coverage of costs and debt charges."[20] Extension of maturity tends to increase the rate of interest that must be paid. Moreover, nonguaranteed bonds, like earmarked revenues, require that a slice of revenue be set aside for particular purposes. For both of these reasons the bonds limit the future budgetary freedom of borrowing governments more than do full faith and credit bonds. Another fault is that they bias the use of resources by state and local governments toward purposes for which the device is readily applicable.

The most serious present danger arises because nonguaranteed bonds are used extensively for purposes that are not self-financing and which, therefore, burden the budgets of state and local governments. If these purposes are public, and if they should be financed by borrowing, issuance of full faith and credit debt is superior in all respects to the issuance of revenue bonds. By concealing or obscuring what state and local governments are doing, the use of nonguaranteed bonds stimulates imprudent practices. And if even a modest volume of these bonds should default, all state and local credit would be adversely affected.

The rapid growth of nonguaranteed debt has its ironical features. In some measure, the technique of nonguarantee aims at avoiding constitutional or statutory limitations on borrowing. Thus an effort to protect state and local governments against the dan-

---

[19] B. U. Ratchford, "Revenue Bonds and Tax Immunity," *National Tax Journal* (March 1954), pp. 46-49.

[20] *State Constitutional and Statutory Restrictions*, p. 55.

gers of borrowing has induced growth of a type of debt which is more dangerous than the debt which was restricted.[21]

Reform of Borrowing Limitations

The ACIR has recommended a complete revision of "the present maze of constitutional and statutory restrictions upon local government borrowing."[22] Authority to issue bonds "should be legally vested in the governing bodies of local governments, subject to a permissive referendum only, on petition, and with participation in any such referendum available to all eligible local voters and the results determined—except under unusual circumstances—by a simple majority vote on the question." Limitations that tie local debt or debt service to the local base for property taxation should be repealed. The Commission implies that the states might find a substitute control "by reference to the net interest cost of prospective bond issues in relation to the currently prevailing interest rate on high quality municipal securities." In any case, state provisions concerning local indebtedness should "take cognizance of all forms of local borrowing and debt."

In 1941 Professor Ratchford took a cautious attitude toward change. The legislatures of some states for many decades had borrowed "with discretion," despite the absence of limitations.[23] The legislatures of some other states were, in his view, less to be trusted. At present a bolder position seems indicated. While limitations on

[21] State and local governments hold considerable amounts of their own securities, especially in trust funds for employee retirement. The practice is non-economic and is, besides, subject to abuse. When a state or local investment fund buys the securities of its own political unit, it is passing up the opportunity to secure higher yields on other equally creditworthy securities. In short, purchase of tax-exempt securities by a tax-exempt organization is irrational. Actual subversion of the purposes of a state or local fund is more serious. This happens when state and local bonds are taken by direct sale at interest rates below what the market would have required. Heins argues that debt restrictions stimulate employment of these practices (*op cit.*, pp. 78-81).

[22] *State Constitutional and Statutory Restrictions,* p. 4.

[23] Connecticut, Delaware, Massachusetts, and Vermont are mentioned; *American State Debts,* p. 592. The first three had low per capita state debts in 1941, but by 1963 they had high debts.

the state legislative power to borrow have, it appears, had some effect in restraining borrowing, they have had a bad effect on the form of debt. Borrowing by nonguaranteed debt has been stimulated, and, except for limited purposes, this is an imprudent instrumentality. State constitutions should be overhauled to limit the use of non-guaranteed debt to specified self-financing purposes, and to repeal constitutional and statutory limitations on legislative borrowing power.

CHAPTER IX

Earmarked Revenues and Capital Budgets

"If to do were as easy as to know what were good to do, chapels had been churches, and poor men's cottages princes' palaces."

The Merchant of Venice, Act I, scene 2.

THE FISCAL DECISIONS made by the executive officers and legislative bodies of state and local governments are concerned with satisfying the public desires that fall within their jurisdiction. The task of spending, taxing, and borrowing to meet these demands is one of efficient allocation of resources, and a budgetary process has evolved which is designed to provide the necessary funds and to establish priorities of need.

This state-local job differs from the similar budgetary process at the federal level in two major respects: it is concerned only minimally (a) with problems of economic stabilization, and (b) with alterations in the distribution of income and wealth. Stabilization is a national objective, for which responsibility must rest chiefly with Congress and the federal executive. While state-local budgeting may perhaps be arranged to assist federal action, such efforts are supplementary. That alterations in the distribution of income are a federal responsibility may be less obvious and, in practice, has not been accepted by state governments. Nonetheless, the possibility of interstate movement of people and resources limits the force of state initiative.

Behind the state-local budgetary process lie policy decisions. These are rooted in the past; year-by-year alterations can only affect details. Provision of most state and local services must continue, subject to modest enlargement and contraction. But new social objectives do emerge which may, in time, be translated into governmental policies, and then into governmental provision.

The problems of governmental decision-making that lie in the field of political science are outside the scope of this analysis. After a summary statement concerning the budgetary process, the chapter will be devoted to two budgetary topics—earmarking and capital budgets—both of which are now, and have long been, topics for sharp debate.

The Budgetary Process

State and local budgeting aims at an accurate determination of governmental needs and an efficient appraisal of how these needs can be met. Competing needs must be weighed, and revenues must be raised and allotted to them. After formulation and enactment, budget programs must be executed according to plan.

The time-period of a budget depends on the timing of legislative sessions. In more than half the states, sessions are biennial and therefore budgets must be planned for a two-year period. Local budgets are for a one-year period. A fiscal year may, but usually does not, coincide with the calendar year. The most common opening and closing dates are July 1 and June 30, respectively.

A standard textbook rule is that a budget should be comprehensive—*all* expenditures and receipts should be reported in it. Only in this way can proper allocations be made. In practice comprehensiveness is seldom achieved, and for understandable reasons. Some types of spending seem to require different and special treatment. For example, government *enterprises* are excluded from the budgetary process in an effort to secure nonpolitical and efficient business-type operation. What of *capital expenditures,* which are irregular and often provided by borrowing? And what of *special funds,* with earmarked tax revenues? Have they features which justify their exclusion from the budgetary process?

The first step in governmental budgeting is *preparation* of the budget. This should be the job of the executive and, in forty-four states and a growing number of cities, this is the case. An *executive* budget is constructed and presented. But the force of executive recommendations may be strong or weak. It is weak when important agencies, or departments, or activities are exempt from executive control. In some states, departments headed by elective officers are exempt on the ground that they receive a direct mandate from the electorate. Activities financed by earmarked revenues, and those of business-type enterprises, are usually free from executive control since they depend on assigned or earned revenues, and do not compete in the budgetary process with other programs. Budgets of the judiciary and the legislature are exempt in conformity with the theory of separation of governmental powers. Similarly, the budgets of institutions of higher learning—the "fourth branch" of government—are frequently quite free from executive control.

Most—perhaps all—states require the state government, and local governments as well, to present a "balanced" budget. This does *not* mean that current expenditures and revenues must equate, but merely that any excess of expenditures is covered by borrowing. Authorized receipts from loans serve to balance the budget. The balance is often tricky. Estimates of revenue have frequently been higher, and those of expenditure lower, than a candid appraisal would provide. At the local level, "fudging" of this sort may be curbed by requiring that local estimates be reviewed by a state authority; it is less easy to curb at the state level.

The form in which the budget should be presented to the legislature has been much debated. A *line-item* type shows estimates of the sums needed to provide specific objects—salaries for so many clerks, sums for purchase of office supplies, and so on. It leans heavily on prior expenditures, and it does *not* indicate what the clerks are to do or for what the supplies will be used. When a government is small, this method is useful both to the executive and the legislature. But when the government is large, a line-item budget becomes bulky and incomprehensible; it conceals any view of functions or programs. Executives, legislatures, and citizens should be concerned with what government is trying to do, and with reckoning the cost of a program in comparison with what it provides. Budgets should therefore be framed on a *functional* basis, with subdivisions that indicate what functions will be performed.

After the budget has been framed, the next step is its *transmittal* to the legislative body. The primary job of the legislative branch is to examine, modify, and approve the budget. In a state where the budgetary powers of the executive are large, agencies are expected to support the budget as presented. But sometimes this is not the situation. Instead, elected officials will make requests to the legislature which do not coincide with what the budget offers.

The most common legislative organization at the state level for review of the budget provides for an appropriations and revenue committee in each house. As at the federal level, the drawback to this procedure is that separate consideration of expenditure and revenue results, and that repetitive presentation, appraisal, and recommendation occur. Modifications exist in some states—*one* appropriations and *one* revenue committee, or a combined appropriations and revenue committee. The efficiency of legislative examination depends heavily on proper staffing, since members of the legislature cannot themselves find time to analyze budgetary programs in detail. In a few states the power of the legislature to alter the budget—especially the power to add items—is restricted. In New York, for example, the legislature may eliminate or reduce items; it may add items only if they are "stated separately and distinctly from the original items and if they refer to a single object or purpose."[1] Moreover, legislative alteration of a budget has been curbed by giving governors the right of *item veto,* and this is more effective when the governor has the power not only to veto, but also to reduce, items.

Execution of the budget is the step in the budgetary process which follows legislative approval. Expenditure must not only go to the proper purposes; it must also be properly timed. Usually a schedule is set up by which a flow of money will be made available to be spent. This ensures a pattern of spending which fits appropriations, and the executive may be empowered to modify the pattern in the light of changed conditions. The legislature in providing appropriations recognizes that some flexibility must be allowed in execution of the budget, usually by permitting the transfer of items within broad categories. Flexibility at different phases of the business cycle has received little explicit recognition in state budgets. New York, however, has enacted a simple and logical scheme. Two

---

[1] New York Constitution, Art. III, Sec. 52(4).

tax reserves were set up in 1946, one for local assistance, and the other for the remainder of the state budget. An operating surplus is transferred to, or a deficit is withdrawn from, these reserves. By this device state spending in recession can be maintained or expanded, and, at the same time, the budget kept in balance as the law requires.

In postwar years, as governmental activities have grown, application of new managerial techniques to the budgetary process has been a dramatic development. Program and performance budgets, accrual accounting, integrated purchasing—these and others have been applied by some state and local governments. The old objective of checking irregularities, which inspired the early advocates of formal budgeting, has been supplemented by the objective of making the budget a positive tool in the appraisal of competing uses for government money. The specific techniques actually employed are, however, very diverse and cannot be examined here.

Earmarked Revenues

Earmarking may be defined as a restriction imposed on the use to which a governmental revenue may be put. The legislative body is required by statute or by constitutional provision to channel certain revenues to specified purposes. Quite commonly earmarking is accomplished by providing *special* funds, and these are not in the budget. But sometimes revenue that flows into the general fund may have its use restricted.

Earmarking is much more extensively used at the state level than at the federal or local levels of government. *Local* budgets earmark the revenue from special assessments and use it to pay the cost of improvements, such as construction of a boulevard; revenue from fees collected for hunting and fishing licenses is earmarked and used to support related governmental activities; revenue or contributions collected for employee retirement funds are earmarked for benefit payments. More important, and more questionable on logical grounds, is the financing of local education almost everywhere by earmarked revenues, especially property tax collections. Although there are but a few purposes for which revenues are earmarked at the *federal* level, the dollar amount is large. Table 9-1

TABLE 9-1. Governmental Insurance Trust Revenue by Purpose and by Level of Government, 1963

(*In billions of dollars*)

Purpose	Federal	State	Local	Total
Unemployment compensation	$ 0.1	$3.2	—	$ 3.3
Employee retirement	0.9	2.1	$0.6	3.7
Old age, survivors, and disability	14.2	—	—	14.2
Railroad retirement	0.6	—	—	0.6
Other	0.6	0.6	—	1.2
Total	$16.4	$5.9	$0.6	$23.0

Source: U. S. Census Bureau, *Governmental Finances in 1963* (1964), p. 28. Years are fiscal unless otherwise noted. Due to rounding, columns may not total precisely.

shows that, in 1963, federal insurance trust revenue was $16.4 billion. As will be argued subsequently, earmarking for these purposes is sound practice. Earmarking by *state* governments will be examined more fully because of its practical importance and remarkable diversity.

Rationale

Many writers in the field of public finance have been critical of earmarking, and certainly the actual practice offers scope for legitimate criticism. But a rationale can be offered, resting upon a linkage of benefits received by particular users of a governmental service and the taxes collected from them. A level of government will spend appropriately for some purpose, for example, provision of highways, and this expenditure will render particular and measurable benefits to highway users. Taxes may reasonably be imposed, and limited to highway users, in an amount which will roughly equate benefits and payments for each user. This is an example of *indirect pricing*. The government should not collect *less* in annual revenues than the cost of these services because, in such case, it would have to meet the deficiency by general taxes, levied according to ability or sacrifice. The government should not collect and use *more* because this would finance collective benefits through taxes raised from particular groups of taxpayers.[2] On what ground

---

[2] The argument is sometimes made, erroneously, that persons who are forced to pay particular levies should receive particular governmental services in return;

could collection of *more* be justified? If this seemed to be a better method than any other by which to finance expenditures that yielded collective benefits. On what ground could collection of *less* be justified? If a legislature estimated that the collective benefits from the excess expenditure justified the levy of general taxes equal to the deficiency.

The abstract concepts of this rationale are, to be sure, not always readily applicable to clear-cut government functions or to administratively feasible taxes. Moreover, many types of state and local expenditure may seem to yield *some* benefits which are particular rather than collective. The loose statement has been made, for instance, that local expenditure for police, fire protection, streets, and so forth, benefits property and that therefore the property tax is a benefit levy. This is an unacceptable description. Property tax is assessed on the value of property as a general tax, without consideration of the value of the benefits accruing from local government expenditures. Most of these benefits accrue collectively to all residents of the community, regardless of how much or how little property they own or use.

Sometimes, however, the concepts are applied accurately, but to trivial situations. In Montana the constitution requires that the proceeds of a property tax on livestock be used to pay bounties for destruction of predatory animals. While this linkage between cost and benefit may be accurate, petty earmarking of this sort impairs efficient budgeting. The same fault is to be found with the earmarking of many regulatory fees and license charges.

Quite frequently, pragmatic—if illogical—reasons lie behind the earmarking. Pressure groups have sought to ensure that a type of government expenditure will be provided by revenues outside of the appropriation process. They wish to avoid the annual legislative scrutiny, evaluation, and vote of money. Assignment of all, or some

---

that, for example, there should be a linkage between the collections of liquor and tobacco taxes and expenditure of the collections for the benefit of consumers of liquor and tobacco. This inverts the relationship. Government does not try to discover what benefits are received by users of liquor and tobacco. Its decision to tax them grows chiefly out of the sumptuary purpose of limiting and controlling consumption. Taxation raises the price of the taxed product. In itself, this may not be an effective curb on consumption. But it is the only power of a sumptuary tax, and if government is not satisfied, other steps are available.

part, of the revenue from a well-established tax fulfills their aim. The more socially significant the expenditure, or the more powerful the pressure group, the more persuasive will be the appeal to the legislature. The incidence of the allocated tax upon individuals may be wholly unrelated to the benefits which individuals receive. Indeed, a tax based upon ability or sacrifice has no linkage with any particular governmental expenditure. The amount paid by an individual as income, sales, or property tax is unrelated to the benefits he receives either from aggregate or particular government expenditures.

Another pragmatic reason for earmarking has been the association of a needed and widely approved expenditure with new and unpalatable methods of finance. When the city of New York, in 1934, introduced its retail sales tax, the proceeds were earmarked for welfare expenditures; when New Hampshire, in 1963, introduced a state lottery, it earmarked the expected receipts for education. After the new revenue measure has been enacted, inertia— and the obstacles in the way of statutory or constitutional alteration —leads to the continuance of artificial earmarking.

Defects

Even when earmarking meets the test of direct linkage of cost and benefit, it has the fault that it removes certain governmental revenues and expenditures from regular and periodic legislative control. For activities that are similar to those provided by government enterprise, this has recognized advantages. Government enterprises will ordinarily be run more efficiently if they are somewhat outside the budgetary process and if the legislature, when it wishes to act with respect to them, must do so by altering existing legislation. A parallel infringement of the budgetary process may be sensible when pricing for the service is indirect. But earmarking does impair the unity of the governmental budget. The total impact of government finance can be judged only when the spending and receipts of all special funds (or at least the algebraic sum of their surpluses and deficits) are added to those of the legislative budget.

Another practical and related defect is that numerous earmarking formulas, some quite intricate, complicate administration. While this may seem to be a legislative aberration, subject to legislative remedy, it often arises because of attempts to make precise and exclusive tie-ins between particular services and tax collections.

When earmarking does not meet the test of direct linkage of cost and benefit—when finance of a *general* or collective function of government is segregated from other functions—its faults are more serious. In such case the legislature is abdicating an essential duty. It should, through the budgetary process, determine the appropriate expenditure for each collective function, and also how the annual revenues are to be provided. Except when particular expenditures and revenues are naturally linked, failure to make such decisions will allow the levels of particular expenditures and revenues to become too large or too small in relation to current needs. For example, the annual revenue from a state meals tax, earmarked for payment of old age assistance, may be larger or smaller than is needed to meet established standards. Earmarking delays recognition of the situation, and, even more, it delays rectification. Excessive segmentation—multiplication of special funds—builds rigidities into the aggregate revenue system. In recent years, the state government of Michigan, which constitutionally earmarks over 60 percent of its tax revenues, has faced chronic fiscal crises chiefly because of the inflexibility of its revenue system. Deficits in the general fund could not be met by special fund revenues.

Present Status

Earmarking is provided for either by constitutional or statutory provision. Current material showing the status of earmarking can be gleaned only by laborious scrutiny of state budget reports, diverse in accounting practices and tax classifications. The latest compilation was by the Tax Foundation for 1954.[3] At this time only two states, New Jersey and Delaware, earmarked none of their tax revenue. Twenty-four states earmarked over half, and three states (Alabama, Louisiana, and Texas) more than 80 percent (see Table 9-2). In 1960 thirty-five states had some constitutional earmarking. For thirty-one of these states the percentages of tax revenues so earmarked are shown in Table 9-3. The state with the highest percentage was Michigan (60.1 percent). Fifteen states had no constitutional

[3] *Earmarked State Taxes,* Project Note No. 38 (November 1955).

TABLE 9-2. Distribution of States by Percentage of All Earmarked Tax Revenue, 1954

Percentage	Number of States
80.0–89.9%	3
70.0–79.9	7
60.0–69.9	6
50.0–59.9	8
40.0–49.9	14
30.0–39.9	4
20.0–29.9	2
10.0–19.9	1
0.0– 9.9	1
None	4[a]
Total	50

Source: Tax Foundation, *Earmarked State Taxes*, p. 4.
[a] New Jersey and Delaware, as well as the territories of Hawaii and Alaska.

earmarking, although eleven of them (assuming no change had occurred since 1954) earmarked by statute.

HIGHWAY USER TAXES. These taxes are more commonly earmarked than any other. Twenty-eight states in 1960 did so by constitutional provision—indeed, fifteen of the thirty-five states listed in Table 9-3 earmarked *only* highway user taxes.[4] For many years federal policy encouraged the states to earmark all motor fuel tax revenue for highway purposes. "Diversion" to other purposes was frowned upon. When the depression of the 1930's pushed a number of states into using some of this revenue for relief and education, Congress responded in 1934 by passing the Hayden-Cartwright Act which penalized such diversion by cutting federal grants for highway construction. Federal revenue from the *federal* motor fuel tax, first imposed in 1931, was not earmarked for twenty-five years. The Highway Act of 1956, however, reversed this policy. Thereafter, a large slice of the revenue from the motor fuel tax, and the manufacturers' excises on automobiles, trucks, parts, tires, and so on—over $3 billion a year—was assigned to the Highway Trust Fund.

Earmarking of a large portion of highway user revenues for the

[4] These fifteen states are: Arizona, California, Idaho, Iowa, Kentucky, Maine, Massachusetts, Nevada, New Hampshire, North Dakota, Ohio, Pennsylvania, South Dakota, Washington, and West Virginia. *Ibid.*, pp. 12-13.

TABLE 9-3. Distribution of States by Percentage of Constitutionally Earmarked Tax Revenue, 1960

Percentage	Number of States
60.0–69.9%	1
50.0–59.9	2
40.0–49.9	3
30.0–39.9	11
20.0–29.9	6
10.0–19.9	2
0.0– 9.9	6
None	15
Not available	4[a]
Total	50

Source: Citizens Research Council of Michigan, "Constitutional Earmarking of State Tax Revenue," Research Paper No. 7 (January 1962), pp. 7–8.

[a] Alabama, Oregon, Mississippi, and Georgia.

purposes of highway construction and maintenance is now given widespread approval. These taxes provide indirect pricing of the benefits of highway use. To be sure, some *collective* benefits accrue (although technical controversy has not been able to resolve how much), and therefore some part of the cost of highways may be placed on revenues from other sources. Moreover, it is clear that, over time, assignment of revenues by type of highway has been inaccurate, notably by favoring nonurban roads. Part of the explanation is that allocation formulas get out of date, and yet are inflexible against alteration. Another part of the explanation is the overrepresentation of rural areas in state legislatures and in Congress. Moreover, the amount of motor fuel tax and of other user charges paid by an individual can only be a rough measure of the benefits received by this individual. These are important flaws in the application of indirect pricing, and they admit of no sure remedy.

At present the old controversy concerning "diversion" is quiescent. Most state governments are spending more for highways than they collect from highway users, and, when this is so, "diversion" makes no sense. But in a few densely populated states—New Jersey is the best example—an excess of highway user revenue may be an appropriate way to finance nonhighway expenditures. The motor fuel tax, in such cases, is as good a source of general revenue as many other taxes currently in use.

DEBT SERVICE. State governments have very often assigned specific taxes, or some segments of them, to service specific security issues. This practice complicates the debt structure and builds up a confusing system of prior and subordinate liens on state revenues for different issues. The correct technique is to declare by statute (or even constitutional provision) that debt obligations are to be secured by a preferred and equal claim on the general fund. The state credit would thereby be enhanced and the cost of borrowing reduced. Borrowing would have an immediate and direct impact on general fund revenues; it might, therefore, encourage responsible borrowing decisions.

MISCELLANEOUS EARMARKED REVENUES. The justification of earmarking for such purposes as retirement funds, unemployment insurance, and workmen's compensation is rooted in their origins. At the outset all of these schemes leaned heavily on the analogy of private insurance. Contributors made payments which earned them the right to benefits; they were assured of more certain subsequent receipts without danger of legislative cuts. General taxpayers were assured that since benefits were linked to contributions, benefits would not be liberalized for "political" reasons. The applicability of these generalizations has since been eroded, especially in the federal systems, so that the "social" aspects of social insurance are more apparent. But the linkage of contributions and benefits does seem to have induced responsible legislative behavior, and therefore earmarking remains justifiable.

EDUCATION. All state governments provide some aid to education and, in 1957-58, twenty-five of them did so in part with earmarked state taxes. In fourteen of these states, more than half of state aid to education was in this form (Table 9-4). A few states secured a large portion from permanent endowments. The twenty-five states *not* listed in Table 9-4 relied *wholly* on appropriations; twenty-two of the states relied *partially* on appropriations.

State governments have been very eclectic with respect to the *type* of tax earmarked for education, since no major type is unutilized. Indeed, in many states part of the revenue from several taxes is pledged. The broad-based and productive taxes on retail sales and income are most utilized. The following eight states, in 1961,

TABLE 9-4. Earmarked State Taxes as a Percentage of State Grants to School Districts, School Year 1957–58[a]

State	Percentage Earmarked	State	Percentage Earmarked
1. Alabama	99.7%	14. New Jersey	52.6%
2. Michigan	98.5	15. Wisconsin	27.4
3. Kansas	95.6	16. Nebraska	21.7
4. Minnesota	93.6	17. Montana	19.8
5. Tennessee	87.3	18. Florida	18.4
6. Massachusetts	87.1	19. Missouri	17.9
7. North Dakota	83.2	20. Alaska	14.2
8. Louisiana	82.7	21. New Hampshire	8.2
9. Wyoming	78.4	22. Washington	6.9
10. Utah	77.9	23. Indiana	5.4
11. New Mexico	74.3	24. Virginia	1.7
12. West Virginia	65.3	25. Idaho	0.2
13. Texas	53.3		

Source: U. S. Office of Education, *Public School Finance Programs of the United States* (1960), p. 28.
[a] Permanent endowments supplied the following percentages of state grants: Nebraska 64.6 percent, Montana 29.6 percent, New Mexico 25.7 percent, Wyoming 17.1 percent, North Dakota 16.8 percent. Seventeen other states had smaller percentages.

pledged half or more[5] of their sales and use tax collections for public schools:

New Mexico	100.0%
Pennsylvania	100.0
South Carolina	100.0
Alabama	96.8
West Virginia	87.0
Tennessee	86.8
North Dakota	58.3
Michigan	50.0

In Alabama, Massachusetts, Minnesota, Montana, New Mexico, and Wisconsin, part of income tax collections were pledged.

In all of this there is no linkage of cost and benefit. The benefits that flow from governmental expenditure for primary and secondary education are mainly collective, and the costs should, therefore, be provided through general taxes. In this sense the practice of many states is correct. But earmarking all or part of these revenues is questionable since there is no provision for recurrent legislative appraisal of what the state government spends in aid to education.

[5] Seven other states pledged smaller portions. Tax Foundation, *Retail Sales and Individual Income Taxes in State Tax Structures* (1962), p. 28.

Another drawback is that the annual amounts available from ear-marked taxes vary according to changes in economic conditions.

PUBLIC WELFARE. Earmarking revenues for public welfare was a phenomenon of the 1930's. Many states, in order to finance the great expansion of welfare payments, introduced sales taxes and pledged all or part of the receipts. The same period witnessed the repeal of prohibition and, as states secured new revenues from taxa-tion or sale of alcoholic beverages, some chose to assign them to welfare expenditure.

In recent years, as other demands on state budgets grew in rela-tive importance, state reliance on earmarked taxes to finance wel-fare has lessened. But in 1960-61 six states (Colorado, Kansas, Louisiana, North Dakota, Oklahoma, and Texas) financed all their public assistance programs through earmarked taxes, while seven did so in part (Alabama, Arizona, Ohio, Oregon, Rhode Island, South Carolina, and Tennessee).[6] General sales and use taxes still are the dominant types earmarked (see Table 9-5), with tobacco excises and taxation of alcoholic beverages next in importance.

TABLE 9-5. Earmarking by States of General Sales and Use Tax Collections for Welfare, 1961[a]

State	Percentage Earmarked
Oklahoma	99.0
Colorado	69.5
Louisiana	64.2
North Dakota	41.7
Arizona	15.0
Tennessee	3.3
Alabama	2.0

Source: Tax Foundation, *Retail Sales and Individual Income Taxes in State Tax Structures*, p. 28.
[a] Connecticut and Kansas also earmark some indeterminate amounts.

LOCAL GENERAL PURPOSES. The practice of earmarking for this catch-all category developed over many decades as state governments removed some types of property from the local property tax base. A revenue-equivalent was usually promised. A number of state-col-lected locally-shared taxes emerged, and, in approximately twenty-

[6] *Social Security Bulletin* (September 1962), p. 14.

eight states, the practice continues. It is, however, of declining importance. Moreover, since in many states the local governments are allowed to spend their allocations as they choose, no specific earmarking occurs.

Conclusion

The proliferation of earmarking is a major illustration of the distrust shown by voters in the wisdom and integrity of state legislatures. A group of citizens, deeply interested in state performance of a particular activity, will try to free it from legislative control by providing the activity with earmarked funds. Legislatures often acquiesce, debarring themselves from periodic exercise of judgment concerning segments of the state budget. This practice also hampers the chief executive of a state. He should frame a budget with full knowledge of how all state governmental resources are utilized and with freedom to recommend changes. Earmarking limits his powers. When the limitation has a logical rationale—a linkage of benefits and costs—the advantages outweigh the disadvantages. Some students of public finance would, however, limit the autonomy even of legitimate earmarking by requiring (a) legislative appropriation of the *maximum* amount to be used in a budgetary period, and (b) reversion of surpluses to the general fund. These two restrictions seem misdirected; they would interfere with the efficient operation of an activity.

What is required is effective compromise between independent operation and periodic legislative scrutiny. Just as governmental enterprises need to be free from legislative heckling, so do those activities for which earmarking is legitimate. And yet *some* periodic legislative scrutiny is necessary in order to weigh performance of the activity.

Capital Budgets

At the state-local levels some kinds of expenditures raise special difficulties, notably those that are large and irregularly timed. Most commonly, these finance construction of a new facility yielding services over a considerable span of years. On the other hand, state and local governments have to make, year after year and with modest variation, expenditures for current services.

Simply as a matter of procedure, it makes sense to separate out in the budget those items that create special difficulties in planning and execution. School buildings, streets, sewage facilities, and so on, demand long-range planning, and their annual provision must be regularized in order to minimize the problems of financial support. Priorities have to be arranged in advance. In short, state and local governments find it sensible to bundle together certain items into a *capital budget* in order to facilitate financial planning and decisions. Nonetheless, the capital budget is properly a section of the total comprehensive budget. The total budget is a device for handling one-year segments of longer range operating and capital programs; comprehensiveness is a vital feature.

A capital budget[7] in this sense should be distinguished from the budgets of government enterprises. A government *enterprise* spends annually for capital and for current items, but none of its expenditures is appropriated by a vote of the legislature. All of its budget should, ordinarily, be removed from the budgetary process (although the general budget should show any subsidy granted or revenue received from an enterprise). Similarly, trust funds as a whole are outside the budgetary process.

"Pay-As-You-Go" Versus "Pay-As-You-Use"

What is the character of the items to be placed in a capital budget? Their distinctive feature is a yield of returns that stretches into the future. Such budget items, it is argued, should be financed by borrowing. Ordinary items that are consumed currently should be financed "pay-as-you-go" by annual taxes, but items that are used over a considerable time period should be financed "pay-as-you-use." The term of the borrowing should coincide with the life of the capital item, and the current budget should merely carry charges equal to interest and depreciation, paying off the principal of the debt as the benefits from the initial outlay are secured. Only through loan finance for public durable goods will intergenerational equity be provided. A project that yields services over many years should be paid for by people according to their use, so that an aged

---

[7] A descriptive account of state organizations for central capital budgeting—including the preparation, legislative review, and execution of capital budgets—is provided in A. M. Hillhouse and S. K. Howard, *State Capital Budgeting* (1963).

person pays less of the cost of a new project than a younger one. This principle, so Professor Musgrave states, is particularly important in municipal finance "where the composition of the resident group is subject to more or less frequent change."[8] An elderly person who became resident in a locality which, soon thereafter, made large expenditures on durable items that were financed on a "pay-as-you-go" basis, would be treated inequitably. And so would a young person who became a resident in this locality just after a spate of capital expenditures had ended. In order to secure inter-generation equity, loan finance should be used for *all* public durable goods, the loan running for the life of a good and being paid off according to use by annual taxes. Equity requires that benefits received and payments made should coincide.

Another justification of loan finance relates to items of expenditure which are irregular in time and large in amount. Assume a small district is in need of a new school. If the whole cost were provided by raising tax rates for one or two years, the effects would be unnecessarily disturbing. Another alternative would be to establish reserves which could be drawn on to meet such episodic expenditures; and still another would be to borrow to construct the school, raising annual taxes only enough to cover interest and depreciation.

The irregularity argument for loan finance is invalid for all but very small governmental units. The expenditure of a large, or even a moderate-size unit on each particular *type* of public works will be irregular, but the yearly aggregate expenditure is, or can be made, approximately constant. In such a situation financing by "pay-as-you-go" saves a government the large amounts of interest and depreciation that would accrue over time if the policy were "pay-as-you-use."

To be concrete, assume that a government has a stream of capital projects yearly amounting to $1 million, and that its other expenditures are $4 million. If finance were "pay-as-you-go," and if the budget were balanced, the tax levy would be $5 million. But suppose the government shifts to a two-budget system, providing $1 million yearly by borrowing at 4½ percent with amortization on a ten-year basis. Table 9-6 and Chart 9-1 indicate the financial effects of the shift. Tax collections—always assuming a balanced budget

[8] R. A. Musgrave, *The Theory of Public Finance* (1959), p. 563.

TABLE 9-6. Illustrative Effect of Capital Budgeting on Total Annual Spending and Taxing

Year	Expenditures				Tax Collections			
	Current	Capital Projects		Total	"Pay-as-You-Go"	"Pay-as-You-Use"	Decrease	Increase
		Interest	Amortization					
1	$4,000,000	$ 45,000	$ 100,000	$4,145,000	$ 5,000,000	$ 4,145,000	$ 855,000	
2	4,000,000	90,000	200,000	4,290,000	5,000,000	4,290,000	710,000	
3	4,000,000	135,000	300,000	4,435,000	5,000,000	4,435,000	565,000	
4	4,000,000	180,000	400,000	4,580,000	5,000,000	4,580,000	420,000	
5	4,000,000	225,000	500,000	4,725,000	5,000,000	4,725,000	275,000	
6	4,000,000	270,000	600,000	4,870,000	5,000,000	4,870,000	130,000	
7	4,000,000	315,000	700,000	5,015,000	5,000,000	5,015,000		15,000
8	4,000,000	360,000	800,000	5,160,000	5,000,000	5,160,000		160,000
9	4,000,000	405,000	900,000	5,305,000	5,000,000	5,305,000		305,000
10	4,000,000	450,000	1,000,000	5,450,000	5,000,000	5,450,000		450,000
11	4,000,000	450,000	1,000,000	5,450,000	5,000,000	5,450,000		450,000
12	a	a	a	a	5,000,000	5,450,000		450,000
13	a	a	a	a	5,000,000	5,450,000		450,000
14	a	a	a	a	5,000,000	5,450,000		450,000
15	a	a	a	a	5,000,000	5,450,000		450,000
	$75,000,000				$75,000,000	$75,225,000	$2,955,000	$3,180,000

a No change.

CHART 9-1. Illustrative Effect of Capital Budgeting on Total Annual Spending and Taxing

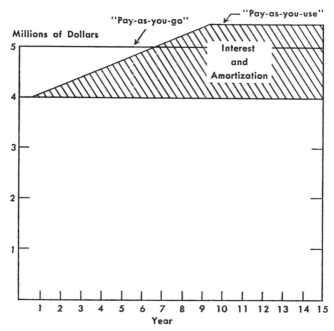

Source: Table 9-6.

—would go down by $1 million in the first year *minus* annual amortization and interest. Thereafter, expenditures would gradually rise as interest and amortization rose. In the seventh year, the total collected in taxes to balance the current budget would be $5,015,000, that is, it would exceed the amount of yearly collections ($5 million) under "pay-as-you-go." In the tenth year, tax collections would be $5,450,000 and at that figure they would remain.

What would be the financial gain and loss by adoption of the capital budget? In the first year, tax collections would decrease by $855,000 ($1 million minus amortization of $100,000 and interest of $45,000). Thereafter, the tax levy would rise steadily until the tenth year in which it would stabilize. By the fifteenth year, the aggregate of tax collections for fifteen years ($75,225,000) would overtake the aggregate amount ($75 million) which would have been collected in fifteen years under "pay-as-you-go." Thereafter, the differential would grow steadily. Under the capital budget system over the fifteen years more than one-fifth of tax collections would go for payment of interest and amortization.

Practical Difficulties

Some practical difficulties of capital budgeting deserve mention. Accurate depreciation of public durable consumer goods is hard to calculate and borrowing has often been abused. Expenditure must be assumed to represent the value of an asset; estimates must be made of the time period of benefits from an outlay. In short, the apparatus of asset accounting should be applied. Depreciation rates for public consumer durables must be either quite subjective or quite routine. In Massachusetts the state law specifies the purposes for which local governments may borrow, and the duration of the loans. The categories of purposes are broad: for example, "stone, block, brick, or other permanent pavement of a similar lasting nature," "extension of water mains and for water departmental equipment," "remodelling or reconstructing public buildings owned by the city or town," and so on. The investment value and the period of depreciation of each project in such categories should not be uniform; yet to determine an appropriate period for each would be difficult. For commercial outlays, public or private, such calculations rest upon market factors which are moderately objective; for noncommercial public outlays, they rest upon "social" appraisals, the nature of which defies analysis. The difficulty does not lie chiefly or wholly in the character of the goods. *Individual* consumer durables are quite frequently financed by formalized borrowing. In this way individuals try to synchronize individual benefit and cost over time. For *public* consumer durables a parallel process must assume a "social" judgment, so that a city council or a state legislature balances social benefits against social costs for the city or state.

Should a capital budget be formulated to include only tangible *assets?* The argument has been made that this procedure rests upon the business concept of *net worth* which is inappropriate for social accounting. Educational training, for instance, brings future benefits; it adds to the productivity of the economy over a period of years. But if such expenditure is accepted as an investment, what should be the time period of borrowing? What should be the depreciation rates?

The purport of these questions is that many unsolved operational issues prevent logical development of full-fledged capital budgets. The merit of capital budgets as a procedural device has been perceived by many state and local governments. But controversy over "pay-as-you-go" versus "pay-as-you-use" remains unresolved. As a practical compromise, a considerable slice of public consumer durables has been loan-financed without formal depreciation through the techniques of asset accounting. But state and local governments have utilized a rough and ready financial equivalent in the form of serial bonds, which mature in installments throughout the life of the issue. They have, moreover, sometimes indicated an intuitive awareness that "social" appraisals, unless restrained, are likely to lead to overborrowing with unfortunate long-run results. The financing of some "capital" items through the ordinary budget has, therefore, been customary. And state and local governments have failed to place "investment in human resources" in capital budgets, not so much because of a "prejudice in favor of expenditures on hardware"[9] as because of a complete inability to measure the effects of such investment on that part of the economy which they can reach by taxes.

Adoption of full-fledged capital budgets, financed "pay-as-you-use," would tend to amplify swings of the business cycle. Contracyclical financing calls for debt creation in recession and debt reduction in boom. A complete capital budget would infringe this rule by coupling debt creation with certain *types* of government spending, regardless of cycle conditions. But if the device of capital budgets persuaded state and local governments to plan stable annual expenditures on a long-run basis, it could readily be adapted to serve contracyclical needs. This would require that, in a normal year, capital items be financed partly "pay-as-you-go" and partly by borrowing. The former portion would be diminished in years of recession and enlarged in years of boom.

[9] *Ibid.*, p. 562.

CHAPTER X

Whither State and Local Finance?

"Read not to contradict and confute, nor to believe and take for
granted, nor to find talk and discourse, but to weigh and consider."
Francis Bacon, *Essays*, 50, "Of Studies."

ANSWERS TO THE QUESTION posed in the title of this chapter may
be sought by extrapolating past financial trends and modifying
them according to expectations of changing conditions.[1] This is
neither an objective nor a certain technique, and readers should,
therefore, be sturdily skeptical. Prior chapters have, moreover, occasionally recalled past predictions. Their frailty, even when made
by experienced observers, should heighten skepticism. The course
of history has often confounded the prophets.

Reallocation of Functions

As the preceding chapters have indicated, the performance of
most civil functions is now a state-local responsibility. The federal
government plays a minor role. Thirty years ago, a semi-revolution
in the allocation of governmental functions erupted—the first in the

[1] I have borrowed the title, as well as certain ideas, from an article by Laszlo
Ecker-Racz in *The Journal of Finance* (May 1964), pp. 370-81. See also the discussion of the article by Jesse Burkhead, *ibid.*, pp. 385-89.

history of the federation. But its force petered out with World War II and, in the postwar years, a new intergovernmental equilibrium seems to have been established. Despite a marked expansion in the overall expenditure on major civil functions, the state-local *share* has been dominant and constant. This generalization hides some ambiguity. Through grants, the federal government does participate in the financing of many civil functions, but in no case has this been a prelude to centralization. Performance of the functions has been left in state-local hands, subject to a modicum of federal conditions.

This practice of cooperative federalism does not correspond to the theory of separation of functions which was in the minds of the Fathers of the Constitution. But the theory was infringed by practice from the beginning, so that nowadays, in the words of Morton Grodzins, "as colors are mixed in the marble cake, so functions are mixed in the American federal system. . . .From abattoirs and accounting through zoning and zoo administration, any governmental activity is almost certain to involve the influence, if not the formal administration, of all three planes of the federal system."[2] Even when the function receives no aid, intergovernmental collaboration is common. But grants have proliferated, and they enable Congress to recognize growth of a national interest in new functions, while leaving administration in state-local hands. State and local governments, responsive to the diversity of civilian needs and demands, secure financial assistance which enables them to achieve a level of performance acceptable to the Congress. No reallocation of functions from the state to the federal level is required.

Expenditure Trends: 1948-63

In the fifteen years 1948–1963, state and local expenditure for general government (less federal grants) rose by $40.4 billion (from $15.9 to $56.3 billion). Some part of the rise was illusory, being attributable to a rise in the prices of what state and local governments bought. The relevant price rise during this period was approximately 72 percent, and deflation of state and local expenditures would reduce the figure for 1963 from $56.3 billion to $32.7 billion. In addition, population had grown by 29.1 percent and

[2] "The Federal System," in *Goals for Americans* (1960), pp. 265-67.

allowance for this increase would reduce the figure to $23.2 billion. If, therefore, the effects of both price and population changes are removed, the increase is not from $15.9 billion to $56.3 billion, that is, by 254 percent, but from $15.9 billion to $23.2 billion, that is, by 46 percent. This figure indicates roughly the quantitative and qualitative growth from 1948 to 1963 in state-local government provision of goods and services.

What kinds of state-local expenditures grew most rapidly? What functions account for the aggregate increase of $40.4 billion? As would be expected, education is the leader, and more than four-tenths ($17.7 of the $40.4 billion) went to it. Table 10-1 and Chart 10-1 show that highways, public welfare, and health and hospitals account for another one-quarter of the increase. These four major functions together were responsible for nearly seven-tenths of the increase.

Refinement of the increases will not be attempted here. Very probably the aggregate price rise of 72 percent in state-local goods was reflected in the prices of goods for each of the major functions, and certainly unusual changes in school population, in the number of the aged, and in the number of motor vehicles help explain the particular functional increases in expenditure. School population rose much faster than did total population from 1948 to 1963 (65 percent compared to 29 percent), and so did enrollment in state and local institutions of higher education; the number of persons aged sixty-five years and over increased by 47 percent; motor vehicle

TABLE 10-1. State-Local General Expenditure (Less Federal Grants) for Civil Functions, 1948 and 1963

(Money amounts in billions of dollars)

Function	1948	1963	Amount of Increase	Percentage of Total
Education	$ 5.0	$22.6	$17.7	43.7
Highways	2.7	8.2	5.4	13.5
Public welfare	1.4	2.7	1.3	3.4
Health and hospitals	1.2	4.5	3.3	8.0
Other	5.6	18.3	12.7	31.4
All functions	$15.9	$56.3	$40.4	100.0

Source: Appendix Table A-5.

CHART 10-1. Increase in State-Local General Expenditure (Less Federal Grants) for Civil Functions, 1948–63

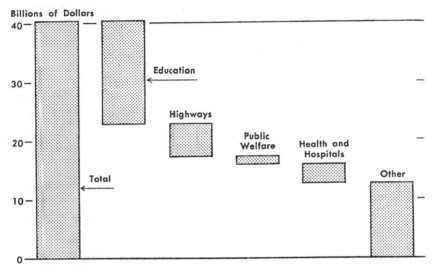

Source: Same as Table 10-1.

registration rose by 103 percent. The old and the young are heavy consumers of state-local expenditure on education, public welfare, and health and hospitals. Nonetheless, some real increase took place—qualitative and quantitative—per relevant unit for all of the functions.

Expenditure Projections

Several investigators have estimated that in the next decade the rate of expansion of state-local expenditures will continue unabated. Population growth—especially in the percentage of young and old—will not decelerate. Standards for governmental services will keep pace with the rising general standards of living in an affluent society. Indeed, their pace may surpass the average because more governmental services will be rendered in city areas which, in comparison with rural, have higher levels of cost. In many states the relatively low level of state-local expenditure is partly attributable to low urbanization; more urbanization will mean higher expenditure. And new social needs are visible which may be expected to burgeon into substantial governmental expenditure. Examples are urban renewal, metropolitan transport, and remedies for air and water pollution.

Revenue Trends: 1948-63

The record of state-local performance in raising revenue during the years 1948–63 was remarkably good (see Table 10-2 and Chart 10-2). Nobody in the immediate postwar years ventured to predict that tax yields would rise by $31.0 billion—by 233 percent (from $13.3 billion to $44.3 billion). By far the largest absolute contributor to the increase was the property tax. Its receipts responded with unexpected elasticity to new construction, higher property values, and higher tax rates. The next largest amount was provided by taxes on sales and gross receipts—the retail sales tax and selective excises. Nine states enacted a retail sales tax during the years 1948–63; many states raised their rates and a few broadened their bases. All of these moves reinforced the revenue productivity of the rapid rise in consumption. Taxes on individual income contributed $2.8 billion of the increase. Only four states enacted such a tax 1948–63. The important forces behind the

TABLE 10-2. State-Local General Revenue Collected from Own Sources, 1948 and 1963

(Money amounts in billions of dollars)

Source	1948	1963	Amount of Increase	Percentage of Total
Taxes	$13.3	$44.3	$31.0	79.7
Property	6.1	20.1	14.0	36.0
Sales and gross receipts	4.4	14.5	10.1	26.0
Individual income	0.5	3.3	2.8	7.2
Corporation income	0.6	1.5	0.9	2.3
Other	1.7	4.9	3.2	8.2
Charges and miscellaneous	2.0	9.9	7.9	20.3
Total Revenue	$15.3	$54.2	$38.9	100.0

Sources: U. S. Census Bureau, *Historical Statistics of the United States: Colonial Times to 1957* (1960); *Governmental Finances in 1963* (1964). Intergovernmental revenues grew by $6.8 billion (from $1.9 to $8.7 billion) from 1948 to 1963.

CHART 10-2. Increase in State-Local General Revenues Collected from Own Sources, 1948–63

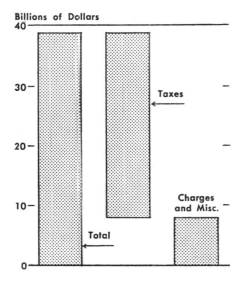

Source: Table 10-2.

remarkable growth in receipts were the rising base, improved administration (especially by withholding), and small increases in the level of rates. The revenue elasticity of this tax is high, but it has failed to gain enactment in seventeen states which, together, account for 40 percent of the nation's population. "Charges and miscellaneous" added $7.9 billion, a very marked relative increase.

Revenue Projections

Growth in the tax base in the years ahead will automatically increase state-local revenues. Most estimators reckon, however, that this increase will not match the increase in expenditures. State and local governments may therefore have to add to the weight of their taxes by higher rates and broadened bases. Will such action create taxpayer resentment and perhaps retard the growth of spending? Surely the answer will depend strongly on what happens to federal taxes. If their level should not be eased, citizen resistance to higher rates of state-local taxes might, perhaps, be significant. The resistance would, of course, be uneven because, in many areas, the present weight of state-local taxes is not heavy. Calculations by the Advisory Commission on Intergovernmental Relations indicate that, in 1960, actual tax collections in thirty states were less than what would be collected through a representative (or average) tax system. In the other twenty states actual collections exceeded the potential collections of a representative system (see Table 10-3); here, the leeway for tax rate increases is less.

The assumption that the level of federal taxes will be retained may be replaced by other assumptions. A very few years ago, some informed people expected (and advocated) a large increase in federal

TABLE 10-3. Actual Tax Collections and Estimated Yield of Representative Tax System, Per Capita, 1960

State	Actual	Representative	Difference	State	Actual	Representative	Difference
Hawaii	$237	$153	$84	Michigan	$220	$201	$19
New York	288	212	76	Maryland	199	187	12
Vermont	223	171	52	Mississippi	130	115	15
Maine	199	158	41	Minnesota	219	209	10
Massachusetts	234	194	40	Louisiana	188	178	10
Oregon	234	208	26	Arizona	209	201	8
California	278	254	24	South Carolina	129	122	7
Alaska	162	140	22	Georgia	142	139	3
Rhode Island	197	176	21	West Virginia	151	150	1
Wisconsin	216	196	20	Colorado	231	231	0
Utah	201	205	− 4	North Dakota	199	219	−20
New Jersey	207	212	− 5	Nevada	274	295	−21
Washington	202	207	− 5	Iowa	209	231	−22
North Carolina	139	145	− 6	Idaho	194	218	−24
Pennsylvania	176	184	− 8	Indiana	180	205	−25
Tennessee	135	144	− 9	Virginia	138	163	−25
Kansas	218	228	−10	Delaware	198	227	−29
New Hampshire	187	197	−10	Illinois	206	235	−29
Oklahoma	177	189	−12	Kentucky	119	149	−30
Alabama	121	134	−13	New Mexico	174	207	−33
Arkansas	126	139	−13	Montana	224	261	−37
Connecticut	213	226	−13	Missouri	152	200	−48
South Dakota	199	217	−18	Nebraska	174	241	−67
Ohio	189	208	−19	Texas	162	243	−81
Florida	184	204	−20	Wyoming	238	325	−87

Source: Advisory Commission on Intergovernmental Relations, *Measures of State and Local Fiscal Capacity and Tax Effort* (1962), pp. 126–27.

expenditure for defense; at present more optimistic expectations are common. If federal taxes were reduced, the ameliorative effects on state-local finances would be important.

What forms might the reduction take? Most obvious would be a simple and unconditional reduction. In such cases the states could move in as their particular situation indicated. What particular federal taxes should be cut? If the test were what taxes the states could handle with efficiency, the choice would fall on such federal excises as taxes on liquor, tobacco, and gasoline.

Reduction might take the form of a tax credit against the federal income tax by which taxpayers could deduct from their federal liability some limited part of the amounts they paid for state income or retail sales tax. For example, Jones, a resident of Wisconsin with a federal liability of $100, who paid $10 as a Wisconsin income (or sales) tax, might be allowed to deduct this latter sum from his federal liability. Obviously Wisconsin could act to increase its tax collection from Jones by $10 without increasing his *total* taxes. Several schemes for credits have been proposed, and no doubt can exist that the device could be used to ease state-local finances.[3] Use of tax credits might be coupled with efforts, in the form of federal conditions, to ameliorate interstate tax conflicts.

A difficulty or fault of either form of federal tax reduction is that the gains would accrue more to richer than to poorer states. The reason is simply that rich states have the productive bases for taxes. For this reason, a plan of tax reduction might reasonably be combined with a plan for equalizing federal grants, or even for a new unconditional grant allocated on the basis of overall state fiscal need. The likelihood that expansion of grants will take place in the years ahead is strong, and the grounds for endorsement of such a step have been examined in Chapter III.

State-Local Debt

In the years since World War II borrowing by state and local governments has grown even more rapidly than ordinary spending and taxing. This increase has been almost entirely for capital pur-

---

[3] See James A. Maxwell, *Tax Credits and Intergovernmental Fiscal Relations* (Brookings Institution, 1962).

poses because state and local governments are narrowly limited in their legal powers to borrow to finance deficits on current operations. The market for state and local bonds has remained receptive and interest rates have been low. And yet several aspects of the state-local debt structure are worrisome. One weighty but unattractive reason for the low yield is the exemption of interest from federal income taxes. This privilege or subsidy is firmly rooted against change, even though change is needed. By offering a legal method of tax avoidance, the exemption impairs the logic of a progressive tax on income and reduces federal revenues. A subsidy geared to the volume of borrowing by a governmental unit is objectionably stimulative of borrowing.

Combined with self-imposed constitutional and statutory limitations on debt, the subsidy has tempted state and local governments into dangerous forms of debt, especially by the issuance of nonguaranteed bonds. Almost nonexistent at the state level before the war, these now make up over half the total outstanding. Through industrial aid bonds, some state and local governments are exploiting the interest exemption for projects which are private rather than public. And the enormous use of nonguaranteed bonds for purposes which are not self-financing is utterly imprudent.

State-Local Intergovernmental Finances

The pattern here is very diverse, and some of the diversity is a natural and desirable product. State governments display different tax preferences, and, so long as they avoid perverse use, this is not objectionable. But perversion has not, in practice, been avoided. It is a perversion when state governments reach outside their boundaries to enlarge their tax base, as, for example, when the value of sales in the state of destination is given heavy weight in allocating the net income base of a corporation, when the income earned in a state by individuals who reside in a different state is included in the tax base of both states, when buyers who purchase out-of-state are charged a use tax by the home state and a sales tax by the other state. When different tax definitions are used by the states, the fact that each definition would be acceptable, if generalized, is not enough. The actual *operation* of the rules of taxation, like rules of the road, should be uniform. If the states cannot, by themselves, achieve this goal, multiplication of inequities will, in time, justify and bring about federal intervention.

State governments have also critical and unfulfilled responsibilities to their local units. Property tax is the one natural and normal source of major tax receipts for these units. But effective utilization of the tax requires state help, and the nexus of the help will consist of framing and enforcing rules of behavior. Here also perverse use —competitive undervaluation and inaccuracies of assessment of individual properties—must be controlled, if not eliminated. Recently local units in some states have levied nonproperty taxes, and in several large cities these have been fiscally productive. Nonetheless, the spread prompts forebodings that the distribution of employment and purchasing power may be distorted, that compliance and administrative costs will prove excessive, and that the structure of federalism will be damaged. Alternatives, both fiscal and nonfiscal, are available. The fiscal program should include reform of the property tax, extension of local user charges, and expansion of state grants. The nonfiscal program should free the cities from the details of legal bondage, and consolidate and rationalize the structure of local governments.

Conclusion

A federalist in the 1960's is plagued with anxiety concerning the problems of American federalism. History will inform him that the course of federalism has seldom run smooth, and that, periodically, for almost one hundred and eighty years similar worries have been endemic. This information will, perhaps, be a consolation, but it is unlikely to be a sedative. Are not the flaws now displayed by American federalism different in nature from those that worried Madison? Are they not less susceptible to remedy? Is not the economy more interdependent and therefore more sensitive? Are not social and welfare problems more national? If the answers are affirmative, does this mean that the states as governmental units are obsolete? The preceding pages support no such conclusion; rather do they present evidence of an opposite tenor.

Yet it would be rash to allow beliefs—not to say dogmas—rooted in past experience to retard search for the ways by which American federalism can be strengthened. Confident complacency would be misplaced because evidence of new flaws is in full view. What, for instance, should the states do concerning the serious economic and social problems of metropolitan areas? Even if federal help is necessary for adequate remedy, state governments should not default on their manifest responsibilities. Must not the states invent ways to cooperate effectively among themselves? Must they not yield sovereignty to the other states as an alternative to loss to the federal level? Should not the states somehow devise rules of tax behavior which will be uniform across the nation?

James Madison, surely a classic federalist, once observed:

If . . . the people should in future become more partial to the federal than to the state governments, the change can only result from such manifest and irresistible proofs of a better administration, as will overcome all their antecedent propensities. And in that case the people ought not surely to be precluded from giving most of their confidence where they may discover it to be most due.[4]

[4] E. G. Bourne (ed.), *The Federalist* (1901), Vol. I, No. XLVI, p. 322.

APPENDIXES

APPENDIX A

Tables

TABLE A-1. General Expenditure for Civil Functions by All Levels of Government, Selected Years, 1902–63

(in millions of dollars)

Level of Government	1902	1927	1938	1948	1963
Intergovernmental Payments Charged to Level of Government Making Final Disbursement					
Federal	230	1,421	5,045	8,713	23,266
State and local	1,013	7,210	8,757	17,684	64,816
Total	1,243	8,631	13,802	26,397	88,082
Intergovernmental Payments Charged to Originating Level of Government					
Federal	237	1,544	5,807	10,484	31,773
State and local	1,006	7,087	7,995	15,913	56,309
Total	1,243	8,631	13,802	26,397	88,082

Sources: U. S. Census Bureau, *Historical Statistics of the United States: Colonial Times to 1957* (1960), pp. 722–30 (cited hereinafter as *Historical Statistics*); and *Governmental Finances in 1963* (1964), p. 25. Years are fiscal unless otherwise noted in all tables. Detail may not add to totals because of rounding.

TABLE A-2. Tax Collections by Type of Tax and Level of Government, Selected Years, 1902–63

(In millions of dollars)

Level of Government	Income	Consumption	Property	Other	Total Tax Collections
Federal					
1902	—	487	—	26	513
1927	2,138	1,088	—	138	3,364
1938	2,610	2,021	—	713	5,344
1948	28,983	7,650	—	1,243	37,876
1963	69,167	14,215	—	3,415	86,797
State					
1902	—	28	82	46	156
1927	162	445	370	631	1,608
1938	383	1,674	244	831	3,132
1948	1,084	4,042	276	1,340	6,742
1963	4,461	14,653	688	2,315	22,117
Local					
1902	—	—	624	80	704
1927	—	25	4,360	94	4,479
1938	—	120	4,196	157	4,473
1948	51	400	5,850	298	6,599
1963	313	1,682	19,401	768	22,164
All Levels					
1902	—	515	706	152	1,373
1927	2,300	1,558	4,730	862	9,451
1938	2,993	3,815	4,440	1,701	12,949
1948	30,118	12,092	6,126	2,882	51,218
1963	73,941	28,671	20,089	8,377	131,078

Sources: *Historical Statistics; Governmental Finances in 1963*, p. 22.

TABLE A-3. General Expenditure for Civil Functions by All Levels of Government as Percentage of Gross National Product, Selected Years, 1902–63

(Money amounts in billions of dollars)

Year	GNP	Expenditure as Percentage of GNP		
		Federal	State-Local	Total
1902	$ 21.6	1.1	4.7	5.8
1927	96.3	1.5	7.5	9.0
1938	85.2	5.9	10.3	16.2
1948	259.4	3.4	6.8	10.2
1963	583.9	4.0	11.1	15.1

Source: Appendix Table A-1. Intergovernmental payments are charged to the level of government making final disbursement.

TABLE A-4. General Expenditure for Selected Civil Functions by All Levels of Government, Selected Years, 1902–63

(In millions of dollars)

Function	1902	1927	1938	1948	1963
Education	258	2,243	2,653	7,721	24,763
Highways	175	1,819	2,150	3,071	11,301
Public welfare	41	161	1,233	2,144	5,599
Hospitals	45	347	496	1,398	5,149
Health	18	84	182	536	1,540
General control	175	526	725	1,325	1,577
Police	50	290	378	724	2,491
Other	481	3,161	5,985	9,478	35,664
Total	1,243	8,631	13,802	26,397	88,082

Sources: Historical Statistics; Governmental Finances in 1963, p. 25.

TABLE A-5. General Expenditure for Selected Civil Functions by State-Local Governments, Selected Years, 1902–63

(In millions of dollars)

Function	1902	1927	1938	1948	1963
	Intergovernmental Payments Charged to Level of Government Making Final Disbursement				
Education	255	2,235	2,491	5,379	24,012
Highways	175	1,809	1,650	3,036	11,136
Public welfare	37	151	1,069	2,099	5,481
Health	17	76	151	292	710
Hospitals	43	279	400	937	3,971
Other	486	2,660	2,996	5,941	19,506
Total	1,013	7,210	8,757	17,684	64,816
	Intergovernmental Payments Charged to Originating Level				
Education	254	2,225	2,379	4,961	22,628
Highways	175	1,726	1,386	2,718	8,155
Public welfare	36	150	851	1,375	2,729
Health	17	76	151	292	593
Hospitals	43	279	400	937	3,904
Other	481	2,631	2,828	5,630	18,300
Total	1,006	7,087	7,995	15,913	56,309

Source: Same as Table A-4.

TABLE A-6. Percentage of General Expenditure for Civil Functions by State and Local Governments, Selected Years, 1902–63

Function	1902	1927	1938	1948	1963
	Intergovernmental Payments Charged to Level of Government Making Final Disbursement				
Education	98.8	99.6	93.9	69.7	97.0
Highways	100.0	99.4	76.7	98.9	98.5
Public welfare	90.2	93.8	86.7	97.9	97.9
Health	94.4	90.5	83.0	54.5	46.1
Hospitals	95.6	80.4	80.6	67.0	77.1
Other	68.8	66.9	42.3	51.5	49.1
	Intergovernmental Payments Charged to Originating Level				
Education	98.4	99.1	89.7	64.3	91.4
Highways	100.0	94.9	64.5	88.5	72.2
Public welfare	87.8	93.2	69.0	64.1	48.7
Health	94.4	90.5	83.0	54.5	38.5
Hospitals	95.6	80.4	80.6	67.0	75.8
Other	68.1	66.2	45.5	57.0	46.1

Source: Tables A-4 and A-5.

TABLE A-7. State-Local Per Capita General Expenditure With and Without Federal Grants, All States, 1963

State	Expenditure Including Federal Grants	Amount of Federal Grants	Expenditure Less Federal Grants		
			Net Expenditure	Rank	Expenditure Relative
United States	$343.64	$ 44.39	$299.25	—	100
Alaska	670.10	176.56	493.54	(1)	165
California	464.98	47.05	417.93	(2)	139
Hawaii	460.30	49.41	410.89	(3)	137
Nevada	491.97	84.40	407.57	(4)	136
New York	432.84	34.62	398.22	(5)	133
Washington	430.98	53.60	377.38	(6)	126
Wyoming	506.68	145.10	361.58	(7)	121
Wisconsin	385.78	34.06	351.72	(8)	118
Oregon	403.96	60.61	343.35	(9)	114
Colorado	401.44	63.28	338.16	(10)	113
Minnesota	374.72	43.20	331.52	(11)	111
Michigan	366.86	36.91	329.95	(12)	110
Delaware	386.09	58.41	327.68	(13)	109
Connecticut	364.19	37.09	327.10	(14)	109
North Dakota	382.69	60.85	321.84	(15)	107
Massachusetts	359.15	39.67	319.48	(16)	106
Utah	380.95	67.84	313.11	(17)	104
Arizona	372.79	59.73	313.06	(18)	104
Montana	399.97	90.31	309.66	(19)	103
Kansas	345.72	39.40	306.32	(20)	102
Iowa	341.16	36.82	304.34	(21)	101
New Mexico	381.37	79.40	301.97	(22)	100
Maryland	332.47	36.68	295.79	(23)	99
Florida	322.50	33.00	289.50	(24)	97
Vermont	366.57	78.93	287.64	(25)	96
Illinois	323.71	38.23	285.48	(26)	95
South Dakota	348.75	64.07	284.68	(27)	95
New Jersey	310.64	27.92	282.72	(28)	94
Louisiana	356.80	74.58	282.22	(29)	94
New Hampshire	322.58	45.76	276.82	(30)	92
Pennsylvania	308.16	37.14	271.02	(31)	90
Idaho	342.12	72.78	269.34	(32)	90
Oklahoma	345.48	76.27	269.21	(33)	90
Rhode Island	315.66	47.51	268.15	(34)	89
Indiana	298.51	30.67	267.84	(35)	89
Nebraska	312.92	48.54	264.38	(36)	88
Ohio	299.98	37.21	262.77	(37)	88
Maine	302.47	51.49	250.98	(38)	83
Missouri	294.69	49.95	244.74	(39)	82
Kentucky	294.54	55.64	238.90	(40)	80
Texas	282.46	43.80	238.66	(41)	80
Virginia	275.89	42.59	233.30	(42)	78
Georgia	276.31	50.48	225.83	(43)	75
Tennessee	255.85	56.68	199.17	(44)	67
North Carolina	232.33	35.45	196.88	(45)	66
West Virginia	250.72	54.58	196.14	(46)	65
Mississippi	252.66	59.19	193.47	(47)	64
Alabama	248.07	55.03	193.04	(48)	64
Arkansas	242.82	65.96	176.86	(49)	59
South Carolina	210.44	37.10	173.34	(50)	58

Sources: *Governmental Finances in 1963*, p. 45; *Social Security Bulletin* (June 1964), p. 21.

TABLE A-8. State Ranks in (a) Per Capita Income, 1962, and (b) Per Capita Governmental Expenditure (Less Federal Grants), 1963

State	Rank		Difference Between (a) and (b)	
	(a) Per Capita Income	(b) Per Capita Governmental Expenditure	Minus	Plus
Nevada	(1)	(4)	3	
Delaware	(2)	(13)	11	
Connecticut	(3)	(14)	11	
New York	(4)	(5)	1	
California	(5)	(2)		3
New Jersey	(6)	(28)	22	
Illinois	(7)	(26)	19	
Massachusetts	(8)	(16)	8	
Maryland	(9)	(23)	14	
Alaska	(10)	(1)		9
Washington	(11)	(6)		5
Michigan	(12)	(12)	—	—
Hawaii	(13)	(3)		10
Ohio	(14)	(37)	23	
Missouri	(15)	(39)	24	
Rhode Island	(16)	(34)	18	
Colorado	(17)	(10)		7
Pennsylvania	(18)	(31)	13	
Indiana	(19)	(35)	16	
Oregon	(20)	(9)		11
Wisconsin	(21)	(8)		13
North Dakota	(22)	(15)		7
Nebraska	(23)	(36)	13	
Minnesota	(24)	(11)		13
Montana	(25)	(19)		6
New Hampshire	(26)	(30)	4	
Iowa	(27)	(21)		6
Kansas	(28)	(20)		8
Wyoming	(29)	(7)		22
Arizona	(30)	(18)		12
Utah	(31)	(17)		14
South Dakota	(32)	(27)		5
Florida	(33)	(24)		9
Virginia	(34)	(42)	8	
Texas	(35)	(41)	6	
Vermont	(36)	(25)		11
Idaho	(37)	(32)		5
Maine	(38)	(38)	—	—
Oklahoma	(39)	(33)		6
New Mexico	(40)	(22)		18
West Virginia	(41)	(46)	5	
Georgia	(42)	(43)	1	
North Carolina	(43)	(45)	2	
Kentucky	(44)	(40)		4
Louisiana	(45)	(29)		16
Tennessee	(46)	(44)		2
Alabama	(47)	(48)	1	
South Carolina	(48)	(50)	2	
Arkansas	(49)	(49)	—	—
Mississippi	(50)	(47)		3

Source: Table A-7.

TABLE A-9. Distribution of States by Percentage of Total State-Local Expenditure (Less Federal Grants) for Selected Functions, 1963

Education		Financial Administration	
Percent	Number of States	Percent	Number of States
30.0–34.9%	4	1.0–1.4%	0
35.0–39.9	7	1.5–1.9	20
40.0–44.9	18	2.0–2.4	22
45.0–49.9	15	2.5–2.9	6
50.0–54.9	5	3.0–3.4	2
55.0–59.9	1		—
	—		50
	50		
Mean	43.8%		2.1%
Standard deviation	5.65		0.40
Coefficient of variation (×100)	12.9%		19.0%

General Control		Police Protection	
Percent	Number of States	Percent	Number of States
1.0–1.4%	9	1.0–1.9%	1
1.5–1.9	25	2.0–2.9	13
2.0–2.4	13	3.0–3.9	24
2.5–2.9	2	4.0–4.9	9
3.0–3.4	1	5.0–5.9	3
	—		—
	50		50
Mean	1.9%		3.5%
Standard deviation	0.42		0.87
Coefficient of variation (×100)	23.0%		24.9%

Health and Hospitals		Highways	
Percent	Number of States	Percent	Number of States
2.0–3.9%	2	5.0–9.9%	2
4.0–5.9	13	10.0–14.9	19
6.0–7.9	23	15.0–19.9	17
8.0–9.9	9	20.0–24.9	10
10.0–11.9	3	25.0–29.9	2
	—		—
	50		50
Mean	6.9%		16.6%
Standard deviation	1.83		4.67
Coefficient of variation (×100)	26.4%		28.1%

TABLE A-9. (Continued)

Public Welfare[a]		Interest on General Debt	
Percent	Number of States	Percent	Number of States
2.0–3.9%	22	0.0–0.9%	1
4.0–5.9	21	1.0–1.9	5
6.0–7.9	5	2.0–2.9	11
8.0–9.9	2	3.0–3.9	15
	‾‾	4.0–4.9	12
	50	5.0–5.9	4
		6.0–6.9	2
			‾‾
			50

Mean	3.74%		3.5%
Standard deviation	2.56		1.31
Coefficient of variation (×100)	28.3%		37.0%

Sanitation (Other than Sewerage)		Fire Protection	
Percent	Number of States	Percent	Number of States
0.0–0.4%	5	0.5–1.4%	21
0.5–0.9	22	1.5–2.4	20
1.0–1.4	16	2.5–3.4	7
1.5–1.9	6	3.5–4.4	2
2.0–2.4	1		‾‾
	‾‾		50
	50		

Mean	0.97%		1.8%
Standard deviation	1.83		0.825
Coefficient of variation (×100)	44.0%		45.8%

Sewerage	
Percent	Number of States
0.5–1.4%	13
1.5–2.4	15
2.5–3.4	11
3.5–4.4	9
4.5–5.4	2
	‾‾
	50

Mean	2.4%
Standard deviation	1.17
Coefficient of variation (×100)	47.9%

Sources: Governmental Finances in 1963, pp. 45–47; Social Security Bulletin (June 1964), p. 21.
[a] Only the federal grants for public assistance are subtracted from state welfare expenditures.

TABLE A-10. General Revenue of State-Local Governments Collected from Own Sources per $1,000 of Personal Income, All States, 1963

State	General Revenue per $1,000 of Income	Effort Relative
United States	$117.61	100
New Mexico	154.77	132
North Dakota	153.68	131
Louisiana	153.14	130
Wyoming	145.09	123
Minnesota	142.31	121
Wisconsin	141.08	120
South Dakota	140.94	120
Arizona	140.58	120
Mississippi	138.58	119
Alaska	137.68	118
Washington	135.42	115
Montana	134.90	115
Kansas	134.88	115
Hawaii	134.03	114
Colorado	133.75	114
Vermont	131.41	112
Idaho	130.52	111
New York	130.07	111
Iowa	129.85	110
California	129.32	110
Oklahoma	128.03	109
Oregon	125.87	107
Utah	125.74	107
Michigan	124.81	106
Florida	122.56	104
Nevada	119.58	102
Maine	118.22	101
Texas	117.86	100
West Virginia	116.20	99
Arkansas	115.70	98
Georgia	115.38	98
South Carolina	114.07	97
North Carolina	113.73	97
Kentucky	111.56	95
Alabama	111.47	95
Nebraska	110.75	94
Massachusetts	110.00	94
Rhode Island	108.94	93
Tennessee	108.94	93
Indiana	107.52	91
New Hampshire	107.31	91
Maryland	102.36	87
Ohio	102.21	87
Pennsylvania	101.54	86
New Jersey	99.99	85
Connecticut	99.63	85
Illinois	99.33	85
Virginia	99.05	84
Delaware	97.80	83
Missouri	93.84	80

Source: *Governmental Finances in 1963*, p. 50.

TABLE A-11. Percentage of State Tax Revenue Collected from Selected Taxes, All States, 1963

State	Sales and Gross Receipts[a]	General Sales and Gross Receipts	Individual Income
Illinois	84.4	48.7	—
Indiana	83.3	48.7	—
Washington	82.1	54.8	—
Nevada	79.2	28.6	—
West Virginia	77.8	44.3	9.8
Maine	75.8	30.8	—
Florida	75.3	32.3	—
Ohio	74.9	29.9	—
South Dakota	74.1	27.9	—
Mississippi	73.9	37.3	3.6
Georgia	73.3	38.8	11.1
Alabama	73.2	32.2	9.5
Rhode Island	72.5	27.4	—
Tennessee	71.8	34.4	1.9
Arkansas	71.5	35.2	7.4
South Carolina	71.0	30.5	12.3
Michigan	70.8	43.7	—
Hawaii	68.9	50.8	23.7
Connecticut	68.4	30.2	—
Pennsylvania	66.3	31.4	—
Kentucky	64.4	30.4	14.0
Arizona	63.4	39.6	6.5
Missouri	63.4	32.7	15.9
Kansas	63.4	35.3	11.8
New Hampshire	62.7	—	3.7
Iowa	60.0	30.3	15.7
North Dakota	59.7	25.6	9.0
Texas	59.3	17.2	—
Utah	58.7	33.7	15.3
Oklahoma	57.9	19.5	5.9
California	57.8	31.8	12.6
New Mexico	56.1	28.7	9.5
North Carolina	55.8	24.7	17.6
New Jersey	55.8	—	1.6
Nebraska	55.1	—	—
Wyoming	54.9	27.5	—
Maryland	54.8	22.4	25.7
Colorado	50.5	25.0	20.0
Louisiana	47.9	19.0	3.6
Montana	46.1	—	18.8
Vermont	45.2	—	26.0
Virginia	41.8	—	31.3
Idaho	34.6	—	28.3
Wisconsin	33.4	9.2	36.4
Massachusetts	33.4	—	32.0
Minnesota	32.7	—	32.6
Alaska	31.2	—	33.2
New York	27.8	—	40.6
Delaware	25.0	—	37.4
Oregon	22.6	—	44.3

Source: Derived from U. S. Census Bureau, *Compendium of State Government Finances in 1963* (1964), pp. 10–12.
[a] Includes revenue from taxes on selective sales as well as on general sales and gross receipts.

TABLE A-12. Personal Income Per Capita, 1962, and Federal Grants Per Capita, 1963, All States

State	Income	Federal Grants	State Rank Per Capita Income	State Rank Per Capita Grants
United States	$2,366	$44.39		
Nevada	3,278	84.40	(1)	(4)
Delaware	3,102	58.41	(2)	(18)
Connecticut	3,089	37.09	(3)	(41)
New York	2,930	34.62	(4)	(46)
California	2,898	47.05	(5)	(30)
New Jersey	2,887	27.92	(6)	(50)
Illinois	2,844	38.23	(7)	(37)
Massachusetts	2,769	39.67	(8)	(35)
Maryland	2,683	36.68	(9)	(44)
Alaska	2,667	176.56	(10)	(1)
Washington	2,485	53.60	(11)	(23)
Michigan	2,416	36.91	(12)	(42)
Hawaii	2,403	49.41	(13)	(27)
Ohio	2,392	37.21	(14)	(38)
Missouri	2,384	49.95	(15)	(26)
Rhode Island	2,372	47.51	(16)	(29)
Colorado	2,370	63.28	(17)	(13)
Pennsylvania	2,363	37.14	(18)	(39)
Indiana	2,350	30.67	(19)	(49)
Oregon	2,333	60.61	(20)	(15)
Wisconsin	2,283	34.06	(21)	(47)
North Dakota	2,273	60.85	(22)	(14)
Nebraska	2,270	48.54	(23)	(28)
Minnesota	2,236	43.20	(24)	(33)
Montana	2,207	90.31	(25)	(3)
New Hampshire	2,206	45.76	(26)	(31)
Iowa	2,189	36.82	(27)	(43)
Kansas	2,188	39.40	(28)	(36)
Wyoming	2,164	145.10	(29)	(2)
Arizona	2,097	59.73	(30)	(16)
Utah	2,084	67.84	(31)	(10)
South Dakota	2,065	64.07	(32)	(12)
Florida	2,044	33.00	(33)	(48)
Virginia	2,018	42.59	(34)	(34)
Texas	2,013	43.80	(35)	(32)
Vermont	2,005	78.93	(36)	(6)
Idaho	1,941	72.78	(37)	(9)
Maine	1,917	51.49	(38)	(24)
Oklahoma	1,905	76.27	(39)	(7)
New Mexico	1,824	79.40	(40)	(5)
West Virginia	1,810	54.58	(41)	(22)
Georgia	1,759	50.48	(42)	(25)
North Carolina	1,732	35.45	(43)	(45)
Kentucky	1,712	55.64	(44)	(20)
Louisiana	1,705	74.58	(45)	(8)
Tennessee	1,702	56.68	(46)	(19)
Alabama	1,567	55.03	(47)	(21)
South Carolina	1,545	37.10	(48)	(40)
Arkansas	1,504	65.96	(49)	(11)
Mississippi	1,285	59.19	(50)	(17)

Source: *Social Security Bulletin* (June 1964), p. 21. The per capita income data are figured on the basis of the calendar year, the grants on the basis of the fiscal year.

TABLE A-13. Estimated Per Capita Incidence of Federal Taxes, All States, 1962

State	Tax Incidence	Ratio of Tax Incidence to Average Incidence
United States	$ 516	1.00
Delaware	$1,072	2.08
Connecticut	801	1.55
New York	750	1.45
Nevada	662	1.28
New Jersey	648	1.26
California	642	1.24
Illinois	637	1.23
Massachusetts	636	1.23
Maryland	574	1.11
Pennsylvania	569	1.10
Rhode Island	566	1.10
Ohio	548	1.06
Michigan	530	1.03
Colorado	514	.99
Washington	513	.99
Wyoming	503	.97
New Hampshire	501	.97
Oregon	498	.97
Missouri	491	.95
Hawaii	489	.95
Wisconsin	486	.94
Indiana	458	.89
Florida	455	.88
Minnesota	446	.86
Alaska	444	.86
Nebraska	428	.83
Arizona	421	.82
Maine	418	.81
Montana	415	.80
Kansas	413	.80
Texas	410	.79
Vermont	405	.78
Virginia	395	.77
Iowa	390	.76
Utah	381	.74
Oklahoma	376	.73
Idaho	358	.69
New Mexico	355	.69
Louisiana	349	.68
West Virginia	346	.67
Kentucky	316	.61
Georgia	315	.61
Tennessee	311	.60
North Dakota	309	.60
South Dakota	301	.58
North Carolina	296	.57
Alabama	277	.54
South Carolina	255	.49
Arkansas	236	.46
Mississippi	196	.37

Source: Tax Foundation, *Facts and Figures on Government Finance* (1963), p. 112.

TABLE A-14. Per Capita Redistribution of Income Attributable to Federal Grant Formulas and Federal Tax Incidence, All States, 1962

State	Cause of Redistribution		Total Redistribution
	Grant Formulas	Tax Incidence	
Alaska	+$143.73	+$ 6.14	+$149.87
Wyoming	+ 99.95	+ 1.32	+ 101.27
Montana	+ 45.94	+ 8.77	+ 54.71
New Mexico	+ 35.94	+ 13.59	+ 49.53
West Virginia	+ 33.59	+ 14.47	+ 48.06
Arkansas	+ 21.61	+ 23.68	+ 45.29
Vermont	+ 34.80	+ 9.65	+ 44.45
Louisiana	+ 29.93	+ 14.03	+ 43.96
Oklahoma	+ 31.47	+ 11.84	+ 43.31
Mississippi	+ 15.29	+ 27.63	+ 42.92
Idaho	+ 28.09	+ 13.59	+ 41.68
South Dakota	+ 20.21	+ 18.42	+ 38.63
North Dakota	+ 17.67	+ 17.54	+ 35.21
Utah	+ 22.69	+ 11.40	+ 34.09
Alabama	+ 10.92	+ 20.17	+ 31.09
Tennessee	+ 12.35	+ 17.54	+ 29.89
Kentucky	+ 12.04	+ 17.10	+ 29.14
Nevada	+ 37.02	− 12.28	+ 24.74
Georgia	+ 6.28	+ 17.10	+ 23.38
Arizona	+ 14.96	+ 7.89	+ 22.85
Hawaii	+ 16.37	+ 2.19	+ 18.56
Colorado	+ 17.38	+ 0.44	+ 17.82
Oregon	+ 16.23	+ 1.32	+ 17.55
Maine	+ 7.63	+ 8.33	+ 15.96
South Carolina	− 6.91	+ 22.36	+ 15.45
Nebraska	+ 4.44	+ 7.45	+ 11.89
North Carolina	− 8.61	+ 18.86	+ 10.25
Washington	+ 9.12	+ 0.44	+ 9.56
Texas	− 0.83	+ 9.21	+ 8.38
Missouri	+ 6.05	+ 2.19	+ 8.24
Virginia	− 1.99	+ 10.09	+ 8.10
Minnesota	− 0.84	+ 6.14	+ 5.30
Kansas	− 4.54	+ 8.77	+ 4.23
Iowa	− 7.05	+ 10.52	+ 3.47
New Hampshire	+ 1.62	+ 1.32	+ 2.94
Rhode Island	+ 3.31	− 4.39	− 1.08
Florida	− 12.06	+ 18.86	− 6.80
California	+ 2.72	− 10.52	− 7.80
Indiana	− 13.31	+ 21.80	− 8.49
Michigan	− 7.20	− 1.32	− 8.52
Ohio	− 7.13	− 2.63	− 9.76
Pennsylvania	− 6.77	− 4.39	− 11.16
Maryland	− 7.78	− 4.28	− 12.06
Massachusetts	− 4.33	− 10.09	− 14.42
Illinois	− 5.93	− 10.09	− 16.02
Wisconsin	− 24.43	+ 2.45	− 21.98
Connecticut	− 7.31	− 26.12	− 33.43
New Jersey	− 16.35	− 11.40	− 27.75
New York	− 9.61	− 19.73	− 29.34
Delaware	+ 13.46	− 47.36	− 33.90

Sources: Grants from *Annual Report of the Secretary of the Treasury*, Fiscal Year 1963, p. 669. Shared revenues and undistributed amounts are excluded. Tax incidence from *Facts and Figures on Government Finance* (1963), p. 112.

TABLE A-15. State Intergovernmental Expenditure, by Function, Selected Years, 1902–63

Function	1902	1927	1938	1948	1963
			In millions of dollars		
Education	45	292	656	1,554	6,993
Highways	2	197	317	507	1,416
Public welfare	—	6	346	648	1,919
Other	5	101	197	574	1,557
All functions	52	596	1,516	3,283	11,885
			Percentage distribution		
Education	87	49	43	47	59
Highways	4	33	21	15	12
Public welfare	—	1	22	20	16
Other	10	17	14	18	13
All functions	100	100	100	100	100

Sources: U. S. Census Bureau, *1957 Census of Governments*, Vol. IV, No. 2, "State Payments to Local Governments," p. 100; *Governmental Finances in 1963*, p. 24.

TABLE A-16. State Intergovernmental Expenditure as Percentage of Local Expenditure on Selected Functions, Selected Years, 1902–63

(In percent)

Function	1902	1927	1938	1948	1963
Public welfare	—	5.4	56.2	57.0	69.4
Education	18.9	14.5	32.7	37.2	36.6
Highways	1.2	15.2	38.0	33.2	38.2
Other	1.0	3.4	7.6	9.0	9.3
All functions	5.4	9.4	24.5	24.6	28.1

Source: Same as Appendix Table A-15.

TABLE A-17. Individual Income Tax and General Sales Tax Collections Per Capita, All States, 1963

State	Individual Income Tax		General Sales Tax	
	Rank	Amount	Rank	Amount
Delaware	(1)	$76.98	—	—
New York	(2)	57.53	—	—
Oregon	(3)	54.73	—	—
Wisconsin	(4)	53.87	(37)	$13.65
Alaska	(5)	52.44	—	—
Hawaii	(6)	45.49	(2)	97.48
Minnesota	(7)	41.31	—	—
Massachusetts	(8)	35.70	—	—
Vermont	(9)	34.52	—	—
Maryland	(10)	33.76	(30)	29.43
Idaho	(11)	30.30	—	—
Virginia	(12)	29.77	—	—
Colorado	(13)	23.69	(29)	29.54
North Carolina	(14)	21.83	(28)	30.66
Montana	(15)	19.71	—	—
Utah	(16)	19.07	(11)	41.89
California	(17)	18.30	(8)	46.24
Iowa	(18)	16.38	(24)	31.70
Kentucky	(19)	15.24	(20)	33.08
Missouri	(20)	15.20	(26)	31.28
New Mexico	(21)	13.96	(10)	42.09
South Carolina	(22)	13.14	(23)	32.42
Kansas	(23)	12.71	(14)	37.90
Georgia	(24)	11.92	(12)	41.54
North Dakota	(25)	9.70	(32)	27.77
West Virginia	(26)	9.68	(4)	56.22
Alabama	(27)	9.30	(25)	31.52
Arizona	(28)	8.69	(7)	52.73
Oklahoma	(29)	7.65	(34)	25.26
Arkansas	(30)	7.56	(17)	35.91
Louisiana	(31)	5.42	(31)	28.35
Mississippi	(32)	3.49	(16)	36.14
New Hampshire	(33)	2.78	—	—
Tennessee	(34)	1.83	(21)	32.83
New Jersey	(35)	1.15	—	—
Washington			(1)	98.93
Michigan			(3)	61.59
Illinois			(5)	53.53
Nevada			(6)	52.96
Indiana			(9)	45.80
Connecticut			(13)	38.21
Wyoming			(15)	36.80
Pennsylvania			(18)	34.82
Florida			(19)	33.85
Rhode Island			(22)	32.69
Maine			(27)	30.69
Ohio			(33)	27.27
South Dakota			(35)	24.65
Texas			(36)	17.48
Nebraska			—	

Source: *State* Government Finances in 1963, p. 47;

TABLE A-18. Operating Revenue and Expenditure[a] of Local Utilities, 1953–63

Year	Water		Electric Power		Transit		Gas Supply	
	Revenue	Expenditure	Revenue	Expenditure	Revenue	Expenditure	Revenue	Expenditure
In millions of dollars								
1953	939	631	713	453	500	529	85	56
1954	971	663	787	502	554	525	90	66
1955	1,092	727	870	538	544	519	104	77
1956	1,162	749	887	558	542	527	127	95
1957	1,246	912	965	738	542	552	138	114
1958	1,237	836	1,110	733	522	550	175	134
1959	1,388	886	1,178	799	565	609	190	149
1960	1,529	1,038	1,307	801	581	656	196	164
1961	1,621	1,116	1,450	966	588	636	197	155
1962	1,741	1,177	1,529	984	635	671	241	194
1963	1,865	1,273	1,728	1,111	639	723	242	202
Expenditure as a Percentage of Revenue								
1953	67.2		63.5		105.8		65.9	
1954	68.3		63.8		94.7		73.3	
1955	66.6		61.8		95.4		74.0	
1956	64.4		62.9		97.2		74.8	
1957	73.2		76.5		101.8		82.6	
1958	67.6		66.0		105.4		76.6	
1959	63.8		67.8		107.8		78.4	
1960	67.9		61.3		112.9		83.7	
1961	68.8		66.6		108.2		78.7	
1962	67.6		64.3		105.7		80.5	
1963	68.3		64.3		113.1		83.5	

Sources: *Governmental Finances*, 1953–63.
[a] Expenditure includes "interest on utility debt."

TABLE A-19. Local Government User Charges by Major Categories of Governmental Services, 1953–63

Service	1953	1954	1955	1956	1957	1958	1959	1960	1961	1962	1963
					In millions of dollars						
Nonhighway											
transportation	129	134	167	202	226	220	215	244	269	299	335
Air	42	48	58	74	87	n.a.	122	140	160	193	216
Other[a]	87	86	109	128	139	n.a.	93	104	109	106	119
Hospitals	230	260	309	371	427	581	639	650	651	790	815
Housing	225	250	269	275	268	280	295	336	381	361	446
Sanitation	154	198	222	246	280	226[b]	357	422	469	527	633
Natural resources, parks, and recreation	91	102	114	134	125	72[c]	169	182	169	207	238
Education	357	400	460	578	655	691	829	946	950	1,104	1,240
Highways	96	110	138	157	165	165	176	186	177	—[d]	—[d]
Other	343	357	339	325	348	523	408	570	680	786	932
Total	1,625	1,811	2,018	2,288	2,494	2,758	3,088	3,536	3,745	4,073	4,639
User charges as percentage of general revenue	12.9	13.3	13.7	14.1	14.0	14.3	14.9	15.4	15.0	15.3	16.3
					User Charges as Percentage of Expenditure						
Nonhighway											
transportation	56.0	46.2	61.9	57.9	47.0	43.4	49.3	51.6	44.8	56.7	59.7
Air	n.a.	45.3	53.7	44.8	39.7	n.a.	42.9	44.3	41.5	57.4	65.4
Other[a]	n.a.	46.7	67.2	69.6	53.1	n.a.	61.2	66.2	50.7	55.5	51.5
Hospitals	27.1	29.8	34.0	39.1	39.3	43.7	46.6	44.4	40.6	46.9	41.5
Housing	35.8	41.0	54.1	63.2	58.5	46.7	48.2	39.5	40.7	32.9	36.1
Sanitation	17.0	17.9	15.4	18.5	19.9	24.6[b]	22.2	24.4	26.4	27.1	28.9
Natural resources, parks, and recreation	16.6	16.4	16.3	17.2	15.6	28.9[e]	17.0	16.3	13.2	16.1	16.2
Education	4.7	4.6	4.6	5.2	5.6	5.4	6.0	6.2	5.8	6.2	6.5
Highways	4.3	4.8	5.4	6.1	5.7	5.2	5.5	5.5	5.0	—[d]	—[d]

n.a. = not available.

Source: Same as Appendix Table A-18.

[a] From 1959 to 1961 only water transportation is included in this category. For these years, data on transportation modes other than air and water are included in the general "Other" category.

[b] Includes sewage and sewage disposal only.

[c] Includes "Natural Resources" only. Parks and recreation data are included under "Other" for 1958.

[d] Not given for 1962 and 1963 (included in "Other").

TABLE A-20. State Government User Charges by Major Categories of Governmental Services, 1953–63

Service	1953	1954	1955	1956	1957	1958	1959	1960	1961	1962	1963
	In millions of dollars										
Nonhighway											
transportation	22	24	24	28	33	34	38	46	48	53	56
Air	2	2	2	2	3	n.a.	5	7	8	10	13
Water transport											
and terminals	20	22	22	26	30	n.a.	33	39	40	43	43
Education	410	425	479	540	613	698	774	850	966	1,098	1,260
Housing	—	—	—	—	—	—	—	3	4	3	8
Hospitals	111	126	143	155	173	188	209	233	258	292	333
Natural resources	81	88	91	99	103	112	126	102	106	111	118
Highways	103	115	136	180	227	277	329	382	401	436	461
Other	78	85	79	88	90	92	101	167	177	205	226
Total	805	863	952	1,090	1,239	1,401	1,575	1,783	1,959	2,198	2,462
User charges as percentage of general revenue	6.7	6.9	7.2	7.2	7.5	8.2	8.7	8.6	8.9	9.3	9.6
	User Charges as Percentage of Expenditure										
Nonhighway											
transportation	47.8	50.0	60.0	50.0	55.0	42.5	33.6	43.4	42.1	42.1	49.5
Air	n.a.	28.6	33.3	33.3	50.0	n.a.	20.8	26.9	22.2	28.5	41.9
Water transport											
and terminals	n.a.	53.7	64.7	52.0	55.6	n.a.	37.1	48.8	51.3	47.2	52.4
Education[a]	27.6	28.0	28.5	28.1	27.5	24.3	23.9	26.5	30.5	25.7	26.6
Housing	—	—	—	—	—	—	—	37.5	57.1	37.5	66.7
Hospitals	10.9	11.6	13.1	13.5	12.9	12.4	13.1	14.4	14.7	16.0	16.6
Natural resources	15.3	15.6	15.2	14.8	13.1	12.8	12.9	12.1	11.7	11.4	10.8
Highways	3.2	3.5	3.5	4.1	4.6	5.0	5.1	6.3	6.4	6.6	6.2

n.a. =not available.
Source: Same as Appendix Table A-18.
[a] Excludes payments to local schools.

TABLE A-21. Per Capita Long–Term State and Local Debt Outstanding and Per Capita Personal Income, by States, 1963

States	Personal Income		Long-Term Debt Outstanding	
	Rank	Amount	Rank	Amount
Nevada	(1)	$3,372	(27)	$360.54
Delaware	(2)	3,250	(2)	796.20
Connecticut	(3)	3,162	(5)	629.22
New York	(4)	3,000	(3)	773.12
California	(5)	2,980	(9)	525.93
Illinois	(6)	2,945	(19)	419.55
New Jersey	(7)	2,900	(13)	444.09
Massachusetts	(8)	2,850	(8)	532.09
Alaska	(9)	2,819	(4)	694.34
Maryland	(10)	2,778	(6)	611.73
Michigan	(11)	2,528	(18)	420.52
Oregon	(12)	2,515	(14)	430.50
Missouri	(13)	2,508	(39)	272.33
Washington	(14)	2,505	(1)	878.96
Ohio	(15)	2,483	(28)	352.78
Hawaii	(16)	2,476	(7)	537.89
Indiana	(17)	2,475	(38)	273.07
Pennsylvania	(18)	2,444	(11)	464.48
Wyoming	(19)	2,427	(30)	322.22
Rhode Island	(20)	2,398	(26)	366.39
Colorado	(21)	2,386	(25)	376.16
Wisconsin	(22)	2,380	(35)	299.14
Minnesota	(23)	2,332	(20)	407.52
New Hampshire	(24)	2,303	(37)	285.28
Nebraska	(25)	2,293	(16)	422.56
Iowa	(26)	2,274	(49)	182.68
Montana	(27)	2,239	(36)	292.09
Kansas	(28)	2,231	(22)	400.61
Utah	(29)	2,129	(33)	307.30
Arizona	(30)	2,115	(21)	401.42
Florida	(31)	2,111	(17)	421.27
Vermont	(32)	2,092	(41)	266.35
Virginia	(33)	2,066	(34)	299.89
Texas	(34)	2,046	(15)	429.39
North Dakota	(35)	2,030	(44)	244.96
Maine	(36)	2,008	(42)	259.20
Oklahoma	(37)	1,953	(24)	387.27
Idaho	(38)	1,934	(45)	215.31
South Dakota	(39)	1,932	(50)	97.25
New Mexico	(40)	1,887	(31)	316.53
West Virginia	(41)	1,872	(43)	250.08
Georgia	(42)	1,865	(29)	324.36
North Carolina	(43)	1,813	(47)	207.45
Kentucky	(44)	1,789	(23)	388.94
Tennessee	(45)	1,776	(12)	444.95
Louisiana	(46)	1,768	(10)	496.10
Alabama	(47)	1,656	(32)	307.63
Arkansas	(48)	1,598	(48)	198.45
South Carolina	(49)	1,584	(46)	207.61
Mississippi	(50)	1,379	(40)	267.95

Source: Governmental Finances in 1963, pp. 48 and 52.

TABLE A-22. States Classified by Limitations on Borrowing Authority, 1958

State	Group[a] I	Group[a] II	Group[a] III[b]
Alabama	x		
Alaska		x	
Arizona	x		
Arkansas		x	
California		x	
Colorado	x		
Connecticut			x
Delaware			x
Florida	x		
Georgia	x		
Hawaii	x		
Idaho		x	
Illinois		x	
Indiana	x		
Iowa		x	
Kansas		x	
Kentucky		x	
Louisiana	x		
Maine		x	
Maryland			x
Massachusetts			x
Michigan	x		
Minnesota	x		
Mississippi			x
Missouri		x	
Montana		x	
Nebraska	x		
Nevada	x		
New Hampshire			x
New Jersey		x	
New Mexico		x	
New York		x	
North Carolina		x	
North Dakota	x		
Ohio	x		
Oklahoma		x	
Oregon	x		
Pennsylvania	x		
Rhode Island		x	
South Carolina		x	
South Dakota	x		
Tennessee			x
Texas	x		
Utah	x		
Vermont			x
Virginia		x	
Washington		x	
West Virginia	x		
Wisconsin	x		
Wyoming		x	
Total (Number of States)	21	21	8

Source: O. F. Gwinn, *State Government Debt Financing, 1946–59* (1962), pp. 14–18.
[a] See p. 194 above for characteristics of each group.
[b] In addition to the eight states listed in Group III, the legislature in thirteen other states has general borrowing power, subject to quantitative limit. When, as in Oregon and Rhode Island, the maximum amount which can so be borrowed is $50,000, the legislative power is very modest. But when, as in Idaho or Maine or North Dakota, the maximum amount is $2,000,000, the legislative power is substantial.

TABLE A-23. Long-Term Debt of State and Local Governments Outstanding at End of Selected Fiscal Years, 1949–63

Year	State and Local Debt			State Debt			Local Debt		
	Total	Full Faith and Credit	Nonguaranteed	Total	Full Faith and Credit	Nonguaranteed	Total	Full Faith and Credit	Nonguaranteed
In billions of dollars									
1949	20.2	17.7	2.5	4.0	3.4	0.6	16.2	14.3	1.9
1956	47.1	32.1	15.0	12.6	6.2	6.4	34.4	25.9	8.5
1957	50.9	32.6	18.3	13.5	6.5	7.0	37.3	26.1	11.2
1958	55.7	35.8	19.9	15.0	7.3	7.7	40.4	28.3	12.1
1959	61.1	39.2	21.9	16.4	8.2	8.2	44.7	31.0	13.7
1960	66.8	41.6	25.2	18.1	8.9	9.2	48.7	32.7	16.0
1962	77.3	48.1	29.2	21.6	10.3	11.3	55.7	37.8	17.9
1963	83.2	50.7	32.5	22.8	10.7	12.1	60.4	40.0	20.4
Percentage Distribution of Debt in Full Faith and Credit and in Nonguaranteed Form									
1949	100.0	87.6	12.4	100.0	85.0	15.0	100.0	88.3	11.7
1960	100.0	62.2	37.8	100.0	49.2	50.8	100.0	67.1	32.9
1962	100.0	62.2	37.8	100.0	47.7	52.3	100.0	67.9	32.1
1963	100.0	60.9	39.1	100.0	46.9	53.1	100.0	66.2	33.8
Relative Change in Debt (Base Year 1949=100)									
1949	100	100	100	100	100	100	100	100	100
1960	331	235	1,008	453	262	1,533	301	229	842
1962	383	272	1,168	540	303	1,883	344	264	942
1963	411	287	1,300	570	315	2,017	373	280	1,074

Source: Governmental Finances, 1949, 1956-60, 1962, and 1963.

TABLE A-24. Distribution of States by Percentage of State Government Net Long-Term Debt in Full Faith and Credit Form, 1941 and 1963

Percentage of State Net Long-Term Debt in Full Faith and Credit Form	Number of States	
	1941	1963
90.0% and over	18	6
80.0–89.9	7	3
70.0–79.9	4	1
60.0–69.9	2	4
50.0–59.9	3	8
40.0–49.9	2	1
30.0–39.9	1	3
20.0–29.9	4	4
10.0–19.9	—	6
0.0–9.9	1	5
	42	41
No full faith and credit net debt	6[a]	9[a]
	48	50

Sources: U. S. Census Bureau, *Financial Statistics of States, 1941*, Vol. 3, "Statistical Compendium" (1943), p. 64 *State Government Finances in 1963*, p. 38.
[a] In 1941 the six were: Florida, Indiana, Kentucky, Ohio, Nebraska, and Wisconsin. In 1963 the nine were: Arizona, Colorado, Florida, Georgia, Nebraska, South Dakota, Utah, Wisconsin, and Wyoming.

TABLE A-25. Net Long-Term Nonguaranteed State Government Debt Per Capita, of States Without Full Faith and Credit Debt, 1941 and 1963

1941		1963	
		Arizona	$13.27
		Colorado	35.66
Florida	—[a]	Florida	78.06
		Georgia	109.54
Indiana	$2.39		
Kentucky	3.72		
Nebraska	1.03	Nebraska	13.59
Ohio	1.82		
		South Dakota	13.47
		Utah	20.11
Wisconsin	1.74	Wisconsin	29.21
		Wyoming	38.01

Source: Same as Table A-24.
[a] Florida had no net long-term debt.

APPENDIX B

Bibliography

EXCELLENT SOURCES of statistical data on state and local public finance are prepared by the Bureau of the Census in the U.S. Department of Commerce. The important yearly publications are: *Compendium of State Government Finances, Compendium of City Government Finances,* and *Governmental Finances.*

For historical material the most convenient sources are *Historical Statistics of the United States: Colonial Times to 1957,* and *Census of Governments,* 1942, 1952, 1957, and 1962.

Descriptions of state functional organization, as well as statistical material, are to be found in *The Book of the States,* issued yearly by the Council of State Governments. The Municipal Yearbook offers similar materials concerning local governments. The Commerce Clearing House of Chicago issues a looseleaf *State Tax Guide* showing rates and major state tax laws. The Tax Institute of Princeton prepares semiannually a *Bookshelf* or periodical bibliography.

In 1959 the Advisory Commission on Intergovernmental Relations was established with twenty-six members drawn from Congress, the executive branch of the federal government, governors, state legislatures, mayors, elected county officials, and private persons. Its aim is to advance cooperation among levels of government and to improve the effectiveness of the federal system. It has prepared and issued numerous and valuable reports dealing with specific intergovernmental problems.

Periodicals

Most useful here for the general reader are:
Municipal Finance. Quarterly.
National Municipal Review. Monthly.

National Tax Journal. Quarterly.
Proceedings of the National Tax Association. Annual.
Tax Administrator's News. Monthly.
Tax Policy. Monthly.

Special Studies

Advisory Commission on Intergovernmental Relations. *Measures of State and Local Fiscal Capacity and Tax Effort* (1962).
————. *The Role of Equalization in Federal Grants* (1964).
————. *The Role of the States in Strengthening the Property Tax.* 2 vols. (1963).
————. *State Constitutional and Statutory Restrictions on Local Government Debt* (1961).
————. *Tax Overlapping in the United States, 1964* (1964).
Benson, George C .S., ed. *Essays in Federalism* (Claremont Men's College, 1961).
Bird, Frederick L. *The General Property Tax: Findings of the 1957 Census of Governments* (Public Administration Service, 1960).
Burkhead, Jesse. *State and Local Taxes for Public Education* (Syracuse University Press, 1963).
Commission on Intergovernmental Relations. *A Report to the President* (1955).
Due, John F. *Sales Taxation* (University of Illinois Press, 1957).
————. *State Sales Tax Administration* (Public Administration Service, 1963).
Heins, A. James. *Constitutional Restrictions Against State Debt* (University of Wisconsin Press, 1963).
Hillhouse, A. M. and S. K. Howard. *State Capital Budgeting* (Council of State Governments, 1963).
Jensen, Jens P. *Property Taxation in the United States* (University of Chicago Press, 1931).
Maxwell, James A. *The Fiscal Impact of Federalism in the United States* (Harvard University Press, 1946).
Netzer, Dick. *The Property Tax* (Brookings Institution, 1965).
Oster, C. V. *State Retail Sales Taxation* (Ohio State University Bureau of Business Research, 1957).
Ott, David J. and Allan H. Meltzer. *Federal Tax Treatment of State and Local Securities* (Brookings Institution, 1963).
Penniman, Clara and Walter W. Heller. *State Income Tax Administration* (Public Administration Service, 1959).
Ratchford, B. U. *American State Debts* (Duke University, 1941).

Robinson, Roland I. *The Postwar Market for State and Local Government Securities* (Princeton University Press for the National Bureau of Economic Research, 1960).

Sigafoos, Robert A. *The Municipal Income Tax: Its History and Problems* (Public Administration Service, 1955).

Studenski, Paul and Herman E. Krooss. *Financial History of the United States* (McGraw, 1952).

Tax Foundation. *Earmarked State Taxes*. Project Note No. 38 (November 1955).

————. *Retail Sales and Individual Income Taxes in State Tax Structures* (1962).

U.S. Congress. House of Representatives. Special Subcommittee . . . of the House Judiciary Committee. *State Taxation of Interstate Commerce*. H. Rept. 1480, 88 Cong. 2 sess. (1964).

Index

DATE DUE

FACULTY			
RESERVED Econ! 34			
RESERVED Econ. 134			
JAN 31 71	Econ. 134		
MAY 26 71			
RESERVED Econ 134			
DEC 18 73			
RESERVED Econ 134			
MAY 25 '77			
GAYLORD			PRINTED IN U.S.A.